D0936954

The Baroque Age in England

Judith Hook

The Baroque Age in England

with 66 black and white illustrations

THAMES AND HUDSON
London

To Margaret Chamberlain

© 1976 THAMES AND HUDSON LTD,
LONDON

Printed in Great Britain by
Latimer Trend & Company Ltd,
Plymouth

Contents

Acknowledgments

I HAVE never been trained as an art historian, but only as an historian. I would therefore like to acknowledge the enormous debt to those art, architectural and musical historians as well as to those numerous literary critics on whom this book depends. Their excellent works are listed in the bibliography and it is my sincere hope that this book will serve as an introduction to their more specialized studies. I have, in addition, incurred more personal obligations. I would therefore like to take this opportunity to thank David Mannings of the Department of the History of Art in the University of Aberdeen, who has a particular interest in English Baroque art and who has consistently encouraged me in this undertaking. Dr Harry Dickinson of the University of Edinburgh and Dr Doreen Milne of the University of Aberdeen have patiently answered a series of questions and demands for information. Mrs Maureen Carr and Mrs Christine Mcleod typed the manuscript efficiently and cheerfully. My children, Sarah and Caspar, have borne with my enthusiasm for English Baroque art but without the services of their wonderful mother's help, Miss Agnes Hardie, I doubt if this book would have been completed. But my main thanks must be reserved for my husband who has contributed so much more than the quotation from Nathaniel Hawthorne on p. 105. Indeed his participation has been so considerable that it would be difficult to say where his work ceases and mine begins. Without his help, patience and kindness during the past two years I would have been lost indeed.

NOTE

In quoting from original sources, spelling and punctuation have been modernized for the sake of easier comprehension. Some flavour of the original has, however, been retained by employing contemporary capitalization and italicization. Until 1752 England was ten days behind the Continent where most countries had introduced the Gregorian calendar. By this the year was also taken to begin on 1 January rather than the English 25 March. In this book the days of the month are given in the old style but, in order to avoid confusion, the year is taken as beginning on 1 January.

CHAPTER I

Introduction

This was my conversion to the Baroque. Here under that high and insolent dome, under those coffered ceilings; here, as I passed through those arches and broken pediments to the pillared shade beyond and sat, hour by hour, before the fountain, probing its shadows, tracing its lingering echoes, rejoicing in all its clustered feats of daring and invention, I felt a whole new system of nerves alive within me, as though the water that spurted and bubbled among its stones, was indeed a life-giving spring.

E. Waugh, *Brideshead Revisited*

*

HISTORIANS ARE NOTORIOUS for their ability to shirk fundamental issues, and nowhere has this ability been made more manifest than in their reluctance to write histories of culture. Political history, diplomatic history, military history, social and economic history, all of these, and more, are giants in the world of historical study; cultural history remains a pygmy by comparison. Yet cultural history's low status is understandable: not only is there a lack of clear agreement among historians and other specialists about what precisely cultural history should embrace, but, as yet, no clearly defined methodology has emerged for describing any culture fully and accurately while at the same time preserving an impression of it as an intelligible and structured whole. The kinds of self-doubt which assail all historians when they become aware of the extent to which they artificially structure any aspect of the past as they think or talk or write about it, are ones with which the cultural historian has to struggle perpetually.

Yet it is difficult to see how the historical description of any society can be complete which takes no account of that society's characteristic forms of self-expression both conscious and unconscious. And fortunately there have always been major historians who have recognized how a particular society defines itself through such expressive forms: Hume and Voltaire in the eighteenth century, Guizot and Macaulay in the nineteenth, while in the works of Burckhardt and Huizinga cultural history is given classic definition as these scholars range over vast areas of man's creative activity in their effort to identify, through its forms and styles, the total way of life of particular periods in the past. Naturally the discussion of the English Baroque undertaken here does not aspire to the range and universality of *The Civilization of the Renaissance in Italy* or *The Waning of the Middle Ages*, but it is an attempt to relate one particular art style to the age and society which sustained it.

One particular art style, of course, because the forms of cultural expression in that age and society were in no way limited to manifestations of the Baroque. In the period in question in England, as in the rest of Europe – and leaving aside all questions of continuing traditions of popular culture – there was a more restrained artistic tradition which would eventually flower as neo-classical art. Hence, by no stretch of the imagination can the total bulk of

7

artistic production in England in the seventeenth and early eighteenth centuries be squeezed into the admittedly elastic term 'Baroque', unless the word is used, not in a critical sense, but merely as a convenient term to describe a particular historical period, in the way that the word 'Renaissance' is still often used.

Although it is true, then, that even in its heyday English Baroque did not reign unchallenged as an artistic style, none the less the baroque current in the arts in England was for a time a powerful one. To understand why this was so requires us to look beyond the emergence and development of a particular style in the various arts over a particular period of time – or, more accurately, beyond the emergence and development of that style considered in complete isolation from other aspects of individual and social activity. But here, of course, we arrive at once at the central issue of cultural history. Today there are still those – and they include not a few art historians – who argue that any attempt to explain culture in terms of the society that engenders it is futile, or at least unprofitable, and that the study of the history of style and of art as more or less autonomous phenomena is the only correct scholarly procedure. But anyone who has been recently concerned in medieval or renaissance studies would be forced to acknowledge that an increased knowledge of the economic and social structures that supported those civilizations has considerably modified, while enriching, our understanding of their spiritual and cultural activities.

The delicately interwoven pattern which any culture presents to the historian should make him hesitate before trying to unwind a single thread. Similarly no one form of human activity – not even aesthetic activity – can take place entirely independently of a whole range of other forms of activity. The individual artist can be no more of an island than any other man. Working in whatever individual artistic form, he still belongs to a social group and experiences the same pressures and influences as the rest of that group. And whatever posture an artist may adopt, he cannot be wholly indifferent to the values of the society in which he lives since the only guarantee he has of success 'depends on the extent to which he can make a group of people believe in him and respond to his work'.[1]

Those who deny any necessary relationship between culture and society do hold one very strong card in their hand. One easily identifiable element in an advanced culture is individual genius and this the cultural historian can observe and record, but not explain. Unfortunately, it has proved only too easy to extend this habit of observing and recording to other areas of cultural history, and to forget that interpretation and explanation are also of the essence of the historical art. It is, for instance, valuable to collect information which reveals patterns of patronage: which patrons supported which writers, painters, musicians or sculptors in a given period of cultural efflorescence. Our historical knowledge of both artists and patrons can be greatly enriched as a result. But it is only too easy to forget that such information, however full, does not and cannot explain that artistic efflorescence itself. We also need to know, in so far as it is possible to know, what conditions in their backgrounds drew patron and artist together into a shared imaginative experience, and at what level they understood or interpreted each other. Why did a patron choose to patronize artists working in one style rather than another? How far were either these patrons or those artists representative of their society as a whole? Why at any given moment did an artist find a particular style or form imaginatively satisfying? How far and in what way did these styles and forms acquire meaning in the response of a contemporary audience?

Few questions of this type have been asked about the culture of seventeenth-century England and, in particular, about its baroque culture. A reason for this is not far to seek. Our understanding of English cultural development has been partially falsified by a tendency to concentrate only on success. Reading history backwards, as in a way we have to, we are aware that in the broadest possible sense the seventeenth-century Puritan sensibility represented the future. But historical concentration on the nonconformist or Puritan ethos in seventeenth-century culture, while it has created a whole new historical industry, and led to some of the most exciting of modern historical writing, has nevertheless effectively disguised the very strong baroque temper in letters and in art in the England of the later Stuarts. Perhaps because there were no theoreticians of English baroque art but only practitioners, capsule descriptions of cultural change tend to leap from the English Renaissance to English Palladianism, unconsciously revealing that, while we may have abandoned the Whig interpretation of political history, the Whig interpretation of cultural history is still very much with us.

Such an interpretation does no kind of justice to the richness and variety of seventeenth-century English culture. It is currently fashionable to argue that periods of outstanding cultural vitality tend to coincide with periods of high stress within society; the greatest kinds of imaginative insight and achievement may be seen as a response to apparently irreconcilable tensions and conflicts experienced by the artist and his society. Such tensions and conflicts certainly characterized seventeenth-century England. 'Liberty' and absolutism; monarchy and aristocracy; 'commonweal' and the individual; free will and predestination; sensuality and sobriety; in politics, 'court' and 'country' or Tory and Whig; the conflicts between all of these were part of the general experience of all men. And the tensions they generated were themselves a response to a wider sense of doubt and uncertainty produced by the slow transition from the scepticism of the Renaissance, with its growing sense of the crumbling of older ideas of a fixed and ordered external reality, to the rationalism of the eighteenth century with its world-view of an ordered universe delineated by Galileo, Newton and Locke.

The English Baroque, then, was one of the cultural manifestations, one of the many 'manners' of this period of transition before 'Pudding-time', with its rigid rules to govern all aspects of social, political and cultural life, set in. But what is the English Baroque? What is baroque art? In an age much given to precise definitions, it seems absurd that no acceptable formula exists to describe the Baroque. But this is partly an inevitable result of the natural inhibitions of scholars. Charpentrat, one of the most imaginative of modern writers on the subject, was present at an international conference on the Baroque, held at Montauban in 1963. Here is his description of the tentative scholarly attitude towards this central question of definition: 'A group of scholars, gathered, about the year 1700, in a Spanish University, close by the office of the Inquisition, in order to discuss the theory of gravity . . . could not have shown more

9

circumspection nor employed greater subterfuge.' Charpentrat continues: 'Certain works, written today on the art and civilization of the seventeenth century, recall those old scientific treatises, which, although entirely based on the discoveries of Galileo, here and there paid homage to the fixity of the earth, in order to escape ecclesiastical censure.'[2] Since 1963 little progress has been made towards discovering a universally acceptable definition of a civilization whose original characteristics are remarkably difficult to describe, since they grew out of an already existing and strong tradition which was utilized in order to express reaction against it. Nevertheless the experience of the Baroque is as universal as the experience of Romanticism, and the prevailing understanding of the word Romanticism perhaps provides us with a useful guide on the way to approach the term Baroque. Romanticism is currently seen as originating in a certain kind of sensibility, a certain spirit or set of attitudes, just as much as in a distinctive mode of handling language or any other artistic material. Just so the term Baroque is most usefully employed to describe not simply a particular style or form, but the spirit of a culture which can in fact have many modes of expression. This is not to deny the existence of something which we can call a distinctive baroque style, but to insist that this style must be explained in terms of a much wider context.

From Italian origins, but blending successfully with native traditions, the Renaissance had gradually spread all over Europe, along the same cultural path which baroque art was afterwards to follow with even greater success. Although it was one of the last countries to be reached, England was not unaffected by this general pattern of cultural diffusion; but, particularly in the visual arts, the Renaissance came very late and passed very quickly. In fact the confusion in taste and style in England, apparent in the seventeenth century, may be partially explained by the fact that changes which, in Italy, occurred over a period of some three hundred years, here took place in little over a century.

Everywhere in Europe, however, the very success of the Renaissance in achieving its own ideals of harmony and proportion meant that revolt against those ideas in the end became inevitable. Baroque style originated in this revolt, and, in its essence, it was anti-authoritarian. Young aspiring artists, brought up in the Renaissance tradition and gazing on Michelangelo's frescoes in the Sistine Chapel, might well have wept because there were no worlds left to conquer. Their answer was rebellion, rebellion which everywhere took one of two forms: either it became Palladianism which grew into neo-classicism, an essentially aristocratic art, dependent on intellectual rigour and sophistication, which aimed to out-renaissance the Renaissance; or, through Mannerism it became the Baroque, an art-form which, while fundamentally also intellectual, drew on popular elements in culture, was not afraid of emotion, and was self-consciously modernistic.

The aim of the Baroque was expressiveness rather than formal beauty. Obsessed by the contradictory nature of human experience, the baroque artist often reveals himself as thirsting for a single reality behind disparate appearances. He often seems to revel in portraying opposing forces, opposites and extremes, expressed most characteristically in the form of paradox; self-indulgence is opposed to self-denial, science walks hand-in-hand with superstition, charity exists side by side with extremes of violence and crime, and squalor squats in condemnation of splendour. It is notable that sexual love and religious devotion – the two areas in which contradiction forces itself on the imagination most insistently – are the two most common subject matters of baroque art, and that sexual imagery, as in the poems of, for example, Donne and Crashaw, is frequently used to express devotional impulses.

No baroque artist ever conceived of a world utterly lacking in order. Indeed, a fundamental premise of baroque art, just as of renaissance art, was a belief in an absolutely ordered universe. What baroque art was concerned about was the fact that actual experience seemed, more often than not, to conceal or deny such an order; the baroque artist's intention was then to systematize disorder to a point where it became once more order. Disorder and asymmetry were made a part of a whole which when seen as a whole was ordered. This explains the baroque artist's interest in total forms – the palace surrounded by its baroque gardens, town planning, or the opera – which gave full reign to diversity within an integrated overall design.

Nevertheless, the baroque artist tended always to become obsessed by the contradictory nature of actual experience, to an extent where he can sometimes be shown to have turned away from the world of appearance entirely, to seek for truth only within himself and his own imagination. 'The world that I regard is myself', writes Sir Thomas Browne in the *Religio Medici*, 'it is the Microcosm of mine own frame, that I cast mine eye on; for the other, I use it but like my Globe, and turn it round sometimes for my recreation.'[3] And Dryden quotes Guido Reni, with approval, as saying

I wish I had the wings of an angel to have ascended into Paradise, and there to have beheld the forms of these beautiful spirits, from which I might have copied my archangel. But not being able to mount so high, it was in vain for me to search his resemblance here below; so that I was forced to make an introspection into my own mind, and into that idea of beauty which I have formed in my own imagination. I have likewise created there the contrary idea of deformity and ugliness; but I leave the consideration of it, till I paint the devil.[4]

It is, therefore, of the essence of baroque art that it preferred imagined truth to objective truth, 'to display not a thought but a mind thinking',[5] for baroque artists were the first to recognize that an idea which is separated from the act of experiencing can never be the idea that was experienced. Inevitably, therefore, such artists preferred art-forms which expressed the energy of minds actually in the process of seeking the truth, rather than forms, like those of the High Renaissance, which asserted a serene enjoyment of 'The Truth'.

The baroque world, then, was characteristically a world of shifting semblance and flux, portrayed by techniques in the visual arts which emphasized depth, recession and the diagonal penetration of space. Instead of the stable equilibrium, dominated by vertical and horizontal areas, typical of the Renaissance, baroque art realized a freer sense of form. Such form was often spiral in its movement, suggesting that the work of art will only be completed beyond its formal limits. In order to produce unity, renaissance art had relied on the coordination of independent parts in formal harmony; the Baroque, by preference, depended on a single, unifying theme – time, flux, power, force or semblance – or on the subordination by one dominant theme of all others. Light and colour became more important than form and linear design – baroque art positively revels in colour – and, although traditional forms were often perpetuated in the Baroque, they were accompanied by a reaction against them, by deliberate dislocation or deformity or accentuation for the sake of greater expressiveness. Basically, baroque art depended for its effect, not on rules, but on appearance; its logic – and, despite the views of later critics, it does have a logic – is visual rather than, in the manner of the art of the Renaissance, structural.

In the interests of its characteristic expressiveness the Baroque also demanded and demands the active participation of an audience whose existence it always assumes. A baroque painting, for instance, will often contain a figure who stares directly from the canvas at the viewer, as if to catch his eye and so involve him in the action of the painting. Similarly, the Baroque always sought to inspire emotion; in music this led to deliberate attempts to express extreme emotional states, ranging from violent pain to exuberant joy and, in the long run, to the development of opera and oratorio. This emphasis on the importance of the emotions, the conviction that it was the artist's duty to induce emotion, was born in turn of the universal assumption that ultimate reality in the shape of some all-embracing unity was perceptible only in moments of intense passionate experience. Unafraid, therefore, of the emotions, baroque art often played on them by resorting to forms which are frequently castigated as excessively theatrical.

Theatricality, however, was not the only source of the Baroque's emotional impact. Emotional appeal was also achieved by the employment of immediately familiar popular and local idioms. Indeed, these local idioms could often be so prominent that the differences between baroque styles in Europe can be more apparent than the similarities. The English Baroque shares in this use of available, local idioms. In striving to give moving imaginative expression to those mighty themes which preoccupied men in seventeenth-century England just as in the rest of Europe – power, time, change, individual genius and assertion, grandeur – it drew upon and acquired strength from existing traditions in literature, music, the theatre and the visual arts, traditions which were already struggling to give adequate expression to precisely the same themes and preoccupations.

There were, therefore, substantial reasons for the growth towards baroque art in England, although that growth was so gradual that it is difficult to establish a satisfactory chronology for a Baroque Age. In Europe as a whole, the age of the High Baroque can, with the minimum of academic argument, be delimited as falling between 1625 and 1700, but, although certain manifestations of the Baroque in England, notably in poetry, would fall within the same chronological limits, the Baroque in the visual arts and in music can in England better be seen as falling between 1660 and 1730.[6] It would therefore seem appropriate to speak of a Baroque Age in England between 1630 and 1730 for, although when talking of the Baroque it has been normal to see architecture, sculpture and painting as the arts most worthy of attention, this is because those were the art-forms most developed on the Continent. In

England, on the other hand, not only was literature the most highly developed art – if there was an English Renaissance it was a literary one – but political circumstances meant that literature and music were the two arts which were able to continue a largely uninterrupted development throughout the whole seventeenth century.

Of course the validity of even the temporal concept of a Baroque Age in England is not yet universally accepted, although it may be worth noting that the title is now increasingly employed. The trouble is our traditional usage of a different nomenclature and periodization. We speak naturally of the Jacobean or Caroline Age; of the Restoration; of the age of Wren, or Queen Anne, etc.; yet we seem understandably reluctant to speak in terms of an all-embracing civilization at a time of very obvious division and of conspicuous political, social and economic change. Nevertheless such a civilization did exist, producing a cultural efflorescence which reflects an underlying unity of concerns, beliefs and aspirations between the English and their Continental contemporaries.

Many of the tangible remains of that civilization have disappeared. It has often been said that baroque art was 'alien to the English spirit' but no one has so far tried to explain what is meant by this singular phrase. If the Baroque is in some way 'un-English', it seems strange that Blenheim Palace should continue to attract more visitors every year than any other English country house, just as it has done ever since it was built. What is true, unfortunately, is that in terms of permanence the English Baroque has been singularly unlucky. Much of it disappeared almost as soon as it was created: Clarendon House, for instance, was barely paid for before it was pulled down. Half the major houses built between 1680 and 1730 have either been destroyed or remodelled. Again, fires took a terrible toll of wall-paintings, carvings and decoration, as well as of whole buildings throughout the seventeenth and eighteenth centuries; a single fire on 29 January 1673 destroyed the Navy Office and thirty other houses, and Hugh May's Berkeley House, whose survival would have made his work as a baroque architect better known, was completely destroyed by fire in 1733. Political considerations had their own repercussions; the beautiful, baroque, Roman Catholic chapel, created for James II at Whitehall, could not survive the debacle of 1688. Then, with the passage of time, the adoption of strict canons of neo-classical taste in the eighteenth century made men unsympathetic to the preservation of what had come to be regarded as 'chimerical beauties'. With less logic but with more thoroughness, the Victorians continued the process of destruction – May's important interiors at Windsor Castle were a victim of the passion for the Gothic – and, finally, in the Second World War, with almost unerring accuracy, enemy bombers seem to have homed in on the surviving memorials of the English Baroque Age. It is almost as if there has been a universal conspiracy to destroy all evidence that a taste for baroque art ever existed in England.

That such a taste did once exist can be illustrated simply enough by considering the success of baroque artists in England. Certainly Vanbrugh never lacked for commissions throughout his career as an architect; Castle Howard was swiftly followed by the plans for Blenheim, where the foundation stone was laid in 1705; by alterations at Kimbolton; the building of King's Weston;

the alteration of Claremont for the Duke of Newcastle; the building of Eastbury for George Dodington; of Seaton Delaval; and the alterations at Lumley
and Grimsthorpe castles. And it is difficult to believe that the many foreign
artists who came to England, the majority of whom were practitioners of the
grand baroque manner, should have done so, unless there was a very considerable demand for their talents.

English baroque sensibility in fact produced great monuments, good
paintings and music, and some of the greatest works of English literature. That
that same sensibility also produced a lot of second-rate and some downright
bad art concerns the cultural historian less than the critic, for, as the great
historian George Kitson Clark remarked of another artistic phenomenon in
another period of English cultural development,

> If he is to realize the significance of such evidence . . . an historian must
> first accomplish for himself two difficult tasks; he must silence the
> promptings of good taste or at least of contemporary taste. Much . . . will
> seem to him tasteless, often mawkish, sometimes meaningless, normally
> absurd, but this must not lead him to believe that it was unimportant if it
> meant something that was of vital significance to contemporary men and
> women. His other task is to discriminate between what was the mere
> adaptation of fashion or the copying of a useful practice and what was the
> use of a form which had very profound implications for those who had
> originated or were employing it.[7]

Baroque artists in England were in no way merely adapting or copying a
fashion. They came to understand and use the cultural idioms of continental
Europe, but they also made substantial and original contributions to European
culture. As a result, by the end of the Baroque Age, England was emerging as
the pre-eminent cultural centre in Europe, a position of dominance which was
to be maintained for more than a century.[8] At the beginning of Charles II's
reign Louis XIV asked his ambassador at the court of St James's to tell him
about the prominent writers and artists, and received the reply that no such
individuals existed. In cultural terms England did not count. Within one
generation, and still in the lifetime of Louis XIV, England was to challenge
not only France's political and military superiority in Europe, but even her
cultural leadership. How this situation was reached, what was achieved subsequently, and how these achievements came to be superseded, will be the
subject of the following pages.

CHAPTER II

Origins of the English Baroque

Thus these Dreams passed, and these Pomps vanished.
Bulstrode Whitelocke

*

IN ITS ORIGINS, English baroque art was largely court art and a taste for it the deliberate creation of a small circle surrounding and including the Stuart monarchy. Despite the distinguished part which the English played in the revival of letters and in renaissance music, before the seventeenth century the impact of European changes in the visual arts on England was relatively small. It is true that during the reign of Henry VIII, two very considerable foreign artists, Pietro Torrigiani and Hans Holbein, had worked in England, but this initiative was not followed up. Elizabeth I knew that of European artists 'the Italians . . . had the name to be the cunningest and draw best', but she was unwilling to spend large sums in order to attract them to her court. Nor were the English aristocracy any more forward in patronage, and the inevitable consequence was that in the late sixteenth century only two foreign artists of any distinction – Antonio Moro and Federico Zuccaro – entered England and even they painted nothing but portraits during their brief visits.

It was left to Elizabeth's Stuart successors to encourage the collection of renaissance and contemporary mannerist and baroque works of art. Although James I was not, personally, a great connoisseur of the arts he was surrounded by those who were. His wife, Anne of Denmark, had a passionate commitment to all the arts. It was she who was largely responsible for reinstituting the court masque and for encouraging the fruitful collaboration of Ben Jonson and Inigo Jones, who, during the reigns of James and his son Charles I, were to produce together a long series of such court entertainments.

Of James I's courtiers who showed an interest in the arts the most original was probably Lord Arundel; his passion for antiquity had driven him to spend many months in study and excavation in Italy in the early years of James's reign. An indefatigable purchaser of good paintings, Arundel was responsible for the introduction of Mytens, Inigo Jones and Van Dyck to other distinguished patrons in the court circle including Prince Henry, the King's elder and brilliant son, who was well known 'to value none but extraordinary persons', and James's two favourites, Robert Carr, Earl of Somerset, and George Villiers, Duke of Buckingham. As collectors, Buckingham and Arundel were famed for their rivalry; Arundel is reputed to have once offered £7,000 in money or land in exchange for Buckingham's famous Titian, *Ecce Homo*, which the Duke's agent had purchased in Venice for £275. This agent, Balthazar Gerbier, dispatched by Buckingham to Rome and Venice in 1621 in order to buy paintings, by a series of successful transactions built up for the

King's favourite a truly remarkable collection at surprisingly low prices; apart from the Titian, it included works by Guido Reni, Tintoretto's *Woman Taken in Adultery*, works by both Jacopo and Francesco Bassano and a Manfredi. The creation of collections of this nature and on this scale was in the end to be an important influence in the development of English culture, but more immediately significant was Buckingham's influence over the young Prince Charles, whom he early learnt to dominate. As far as the arts were concerned, this dominance had beneficial results, and under Buckingham's fascinating tutelage, the natural enthusiasm of the young prince was soon engaged. As early as 1622 the Venetian ambassador could write home that Charles 'loves old paintings especially those of our province and city'.

As a result of the interest of a few brilliant and influential individuals, the court of James I, therefore, had become receptive to any new artistic developments. James was well aware that among the monarchs of Europe ostentatious patronage and appreciation of the arts were now recognized as the natural and necessary accompaniments to kingly dignity. If James wished – as, indeed, he did wish – to stand as an equal among other monarchs, then he too must attempt to appear as a generous and discriminating patron. Such a stance was particularly essential if he wished to marry his children into any of the principal royal families of Europe where a munificent patronage of the arts had long been a part of the court way of life. Hence a new era in the English arts can ultimately be attributed to James I's perhaps crude desire to emulate other European monarchs, and in particular to persuade the Spanish and French royal families that they would not be socially degraded by marrying into his.

Encouraged by the new court attitudes, foreign artists began to arrive in England: the painters Paul van Somer, Abraham von Blijenberch and Cornelius Johnson, for instance. Their hopes were not disappointed. Despite the poverty of the English crown, and even during the worst years of depression in the royal finances between 1619 and 1623, court patronage was rapidly expanded. This was the first period of Inigo Jones's building projects, and of the foundation of the Mortlake tapestry works modelled on Henry IV of France's successful Gobelins factory; the first set of tapestries, 'Vulcan and Venus', were woven between 16 September 1620 and 5 June 1622, the bottom border bearing the optimistic inscription *Sceptra fovent artes* as an earnest of the King's good intentions. It was in 1619 that Hubert Le Sueur was appointed Sculptor of the Royal Works. And in the following years regular official payments to Daniel Mytens began, culminating in 1624 in the grant of an annual life pension of £50, 'on condition that he do not depart from the realm without a warrant from the King or the Council'.[1] Then came a whole series of building projects of the first importance associated with the Spanish match: the building of the Banqueting House at Whitehall, the first approaches to Rubens about the decoration of the ceiling, and the building of the Catholic chapel at St James's, of which the foundation stone was laid by the Spanish ambassador in May 1623. Although political tact determined that the exterior of this chapel should be as neutral and 'unchurchlike' as possible, thus precluding an ornate, modern baroque façade, this was still a building of great architectural significance, the first place of worship in England to be built entirely in the classical style.

(1) James I, by Paul van Somer. Through the window can be seen the façade of the Whitehall Banqueting Hall (1619–22), designed by Inigo Jones.

ROYAL PATRONAGE OF THE ARTS. (2) *Charles I and Henrietta Maria with the Liberal Arts*, by Gerard van Honthorst. (3) Charles I. Detail from an equestrian portrait by Van Dyck. (4) Henrietta Maria with a pet monkey and a dwarf, by Van Dyck (detail).

(5) *An Allegory of the Restoration*. A ceiling piece for the bedroom of Charles II by Michael Wright. The figure of Justice points to a portrait of Charles I while *putti* bear up the Boscobel oak below the allegorical winged figure.
(6) *Sea triumph of Charles II, 1674*, by Antonio Verrio.

ROYAL PATRONAGE OF THE SCIENCES. (7) The Royal Observatory, Greenwich. The building on the hill above Greenwich was erected by order of Charles II in 1675 to designs by Wren. The Queen's House, by Inigo Jones, can be seen in the distance. (8) Frontispiece to *A History of the Royal Society*, by Thomas Spratt (1667).

ROYAL FOUNDATIONS. (9) The Royal Military Hospital, Chelsea, founded in 1682. (10) The Royal Naval Hospital, Greenwich, founded in 1694. Both buildings are by Wren although Greenwich incorporates work by Webb and others and uses the Queen's House (1616–35) as its centrepiece. (11) The Royal Bethlehem Hospital (Bedlam) (1675–76) by Robert Hooke.

ARISTOCRATIC PATRONS. (12) Thomas Howard, Earl of Arundel, with his collection of antique sculpture, painted by Daniel Mytens. (13) *The Apotheosis of the Duke of Buckingham*, by Rubens. (14) Memorial to the eldest son of the Earl and Countess of Dorset, by the Danish-born sculptor Caius Gabriel Cibber. Withyham Church, Sussex.

PRIVATE PATRONS. Three portraits by Sir Godfrey Kneller. (15) Sir Isaac Newton. (16) John Dryden. (17) Jacob Tonson, founder and secretary of the Kit Kat Club. Tonson commissioned Kneller to make portraits of all the members of the club. (18) Isaac Fuller; a self portrait, painted for the owner of the Mitre Tavern.

THE ARCHITECTS. (19) Sir Christopher Wren (1632–1723), by Edward Pierce. (20) James Gibbs (1682–1754), by Rysbrack. (21) Nicholas Hawksmoor (1661–1736), attributed to Sir Henry Cheere. (22) Sir John Vanbrugh (1664–1726), architect and playwright, by Kneller.

THE FORERUNNER. (23) The Banqueting Hall, Whitehall, by Inigo Jones, finished in 1622. A magnificent setting for receptions, masques and entertainments. The ceiling painting is by Rubens and has as its principal subject the apotheosis of James I.

INIGO JONES. (24) James II's Chapel Royal in St James's Palace, the only major Roman Catholic work of the late seventeenth century. (25) A design for 'The Masque of Queens'. Through his theatre designs Jones introduced the forms of the Italian Baroque while his architecture remained strictly Palladian. (26) The colonnaded west front to Old St Paul's, added 1633–40.

(27) The Double Cube room at Wilton House, Wiltshire. Designed by Inigo Jones with a painted ceiling by Edward Pierce, 'the only man who doth understand perspective of all the painters in London'. Their work at Wilton is the first English example of the baroque manner adapted for domestic use.

ROYAL SPLENDOUR. (28) Wren's projected palace for Charles II at Winchester, seen here in an eighteenth-century reconstruction. (29) Hampton Court. Wren's additions to Cardinal Wolsey's palace, like his designs for Winchester, reflect Charles II's desire to emulate the glories of Versailles.

(30) Hampton Court. A detail of the pediment on the east front, by Cibber, which shows William III as Hercules. (31) The theme is taken up by the window frames in the Fountain Court, with *grisaille* paintings by Laguerre. (32) Wrought iron work by Tijou.

PAINTERS IN THE SERVICE OF THE COURT. (33) Hampton Court. The ceiling of the Queen's Bedchamber, by Sir James Thornhill. (34) The King's Staircase. William III appears once again as Hercules.

(35) Interior of the dome and part of the ceiling of the Painted Hall at Greenwich. Thornhill's paintings glorifying the reign of William III are his most notable achievement.

(36) Chatsworth, Derbyshire. The interior of the Chapel. Paintings by Laguerre and sculpture by Cibber combine to create a total art-form. Such collaborations were an essential element of the Baroque.

These projects, all initiated by James I, came to fulfilment after the accession of his son as King Charles I in 1625. Over the years Charles's love of the arts had continued to grow, and the court he created was fashioned as a mirror of his interests. His father's court had been characterized by lavish but somewhat disorderly ostentation and luxury; the court of Charles, 'temperate, chaste, and serious', while equally rich, was considerably more dignified and better run. It reflected a new refinement of taste, and Charles's own wider aesthetic interests. An important source of the new King's highly developed aesthetic appreciation and understanding, particularly in the visual arts, had been his unsuccessful courtship trip to Spain in 1623. Accompanied by Buckingham, he had travelled overland through Paris to Madrid. In the Spanish royal collection, particularly rich in Venetian art, Charles for the first time encountered some of the great masterpieces of renaissance painting. The political affronts involved in being made to kick his heels in the Spanish court, while the Spanish devised a polite formula for jilting him, were not lost on Charles, but his stay in Madrid was not a complete waste of time. He occupied himself in the purchase of pictures and in sitting to Velasquez for his portrait. On his departure, although he was unable to take away his hoped-for Spanish bride, he did take a kind of substitute in the shape of Titian's *Venus of the Pardo*, the gift of Philip IV.

The Spanish trip definitely encouraged Charles's already strong preference for Italian, and specifically Venetian, masters, but as king he never showed himself exclusive in his tastes. He intended to preside over a court which could hold its own aesthetically with any in Europe, and, towards this end, he would employ whatever talents presented themselves.

In this, of all his royal aims, Charles I was completely and permanently successful, raising the English court to the position of arbiter of good taste in the country, a position which, despite the Interregnum, it retained until well into the eighteenth century. Looking back on the court of Charles I from the vantage point of 1685, William Aglionby recognized that no happier ambience for the encouragement of the arts could have existed, for 'King *Charles* the First . . . was not only the greatest Favourer, but the truest Knower of all those *Arts*; and by his Countenance, the whole Court gave themselves up to those *Refined Pleasures*; there being hardly a man of *Great Quality*, that had not a Collection, either of Pictures or Antiques.'[2]

Aglionby recognized painting as the first interest of Charles I, 'the *Darling* of that Virtuous Monarch',[3] and, as we have seen, it was through painting that the King's taste had been formed. As prince and as king, he assembled the finest collection of paintings ever created in England; it included some magnificent Titians, a painter whom Charles had come to love during his visit to Spain, several works of Correggio, the Bassani and Tintoretto, as well as paintings by Bellini, Giorgione, Veronese, Andrea del Sarto, Bronzino, Dosso Dossi, Giulio Romano, the Palmas and Parmigianino. The King was always an eager buyer and his envoys abroad were all commissioned to buy up works of art. Some paintings were specially commissioned, the most famous being the ceiling of Inigo Jones's Banqueting House at Whitehall with its nine compartments divided by heavy ribs, filled by Rubens' allegories exalting the beneficent rule of James I. Commissioned in 1625 they were completed in

August 1634, and, despite the financial problems of the monarchy, Charles paid Rubens £3,000 for them.

Among the serious-minded, connoisseurship on such a scale seemed entirely frivolous. Worse, the King's artistic interests seemed to be leading directly to Rome; it was learnt that ministers of state on urgent business were kept waiting while the King walked round his picture gallery with the papal agent in England – one of the few men he knew who shared his artistic tastes. Cardinal Francesco Barberini's conviction that he could ensure the King's conversion by sending a constant stream of Correggios, Andrea del Sartos, Leonardos and Veroneses to England, coupled with Urban VIII's encouragement of Bernini to carve his famous bust of Charles I, merely confirmed extant impressions. And it was, to say the least, impolitic of the Queen to put on display in her private chapel at Somerset House the numerous pictures which Cardinal Barberini had sent her, at a time when there were already complaints that the King was being deceived by 'gifts of paintings, antique idols and such like trumperies brought from Rome'.[4]

Painting remained the first, but not the sole love of the King. Despite his spectacular failures as a ruler – their source not badly illustrated by his readiness to ignore his subjects' anti-papal prejudices in pursuit of his own aesthetic interests – Charles remained a most generous patron of all the arts. Nor was he content simply to buy works of dead or living Italian masters, he also set about creating an English artistic tradition. The Mortlake tapestry works, dying for lack of funds, he revived by a generous payment of his father's debts, by an annual disbursal of £3,000, 'for the better maintenance of the said works of tapestries', and, eventually, in 1636 by taking over entire financial responsibility for the concern. From this period of Charles's patronage date the Mortlake series of 'Hero and Leander', the 'Horses', the 'Five Senses', the 'Prodigal Son', 'The Four Seasons', 'Diana and Calisto', 'The History of St Paul', 'Supper at Emmaus' and the 'History of Alexander'. Since several of these sets went to decorate the country houses of Charles I's leading nobility, court tastes in interior decoration were gradually spread around the country.

Meanwhile, at court, Charles I and Inigo Jones were able to train the taste of their generation in new directions which were to survive both the Civil War and Interregnum. Even more important, perhaps, the court nourished a school of native talent on which future artistic developments would depend. In particular, the Caroline court is notable for having fostered the talents of such English painters as John de Critz, Matthew Gooderick and Edward Pierce, and, above all, of Inigo Jones himself whose work was to remain *the* standard of excellence for the next century.

Yet in this embryonic period of the English Baroque it was inevitable that the court should employ a large number of foreign artists and craftsmen. Within months of coming to the throne, Charles had tried to entice the Bolognese painter, Guercino, to settle at the English court, but Guercino refused on the grounds that he would be able to stand neither English heretics nor English weather. Charles had no more success when he attempted to bring the sculptor, Pietro Tacca, to London, but by about 1635 the Florentine Francesco Fanelli was at work in England. Fanelli made bronzes for Charles and Henrietta Maria as well as for his greatest patron, the Duke of Newcastle.

Meanwhile, another Italian, Orazio Gentileschi, was being paid an annual pension of £100 by the crown and was provided with special apartments in the royal household. In return he painted the ceiling of the Queen's House at Greenwich, as well as several easel paintings. Dutch painters also found employment; Gerard van Honthorst visited England in 1628 and painted for the King one of his most important works – *Charles I and Henrietta Maria with the Liberal Arts*; and Van Dyck, whose style, so dependent on Titian and Correggio, naturally appealed to the King's refined tastes, is indelibly associated with the Caroline court.

The employment of these foreign artists turned out eventually to have political as well as cultural significance. The genius which Charles showed elsewhere in offending his subjects by doing what he believed to be right, was at work here as well. The widespread use of foreign artists offended the Painter-Stainers' Company, who between 1627 and 1640 made several attempts to force them to submit to guild regulations. The Company opposed Charles I's artistic policies because they threatened guild interests, and when Charles persisted in protecting his foreign artists he lost not only the support of many English artists, but also support in the City of London where the royal position was already seriously deteriorating. It made little difference that the attitude of the guilds was already essentially out-of-date, nor even that Charles was even more anxious to encourage native talents than he was to entice foreign artists to England. His cultural policy remained offensive to many of his subjects.

Music at the court of Charles I, who maintained some eighty-eight royal musicians, was never neglected. Here the King was working within the context of a well-developed tradition, but even in this area he proved incapable of avoiding giving offence: while church music was encouraged by the Laudian party, who favoured organs and anthems, it was anathema to most Puritans because it emphasized the ceremonial side of Anglican church worship. Secular music, however, was less controversial and equally favoured by the court. As a result it rapidly developed along the lines of change being pursued throughout Europe, so that by the outbreak of the English Civil War in 1642 the baroque style in music was well established in England. Another art-form – the masque – played an important part in the introduction of this new musical style. Although at first the Jacobean masque showed no signs of operatic influence from Europe – typically it was built round the traditional lute song and instrumental dances and consorts – after 1617, when Jonson's *Vision of Delight* first introduced recitative, European influences became steadily more apparent. The Frenchman, Nicholas Lanier, Master of the King's Music, William and Henry Lawes, Simon Ives, Wilson and Coleman all built on this development and their work was an essential preparation for the eventual English acceptance of opera, the dramatic expression of the baroque style.

Charles's patronage of poetry was no less generous and no less significant. Indeed of all the arts it is its poetry that best suggests the tone and quality of the Caroline court. The lyrical poetry of such men as Carew, Suckling, Denham, Davenant and Godolphin is light and elegant, but also witty and sometimes learned. It is a refined, sophisticated, civilized poetry, with an occasional flash of sensuality, which perfectly reflects the attitudes and instincts of the aristocratic social group which produced it. Admittedly Cavalier poetry owes most to two great English masters: Jonson and Donne. But this native literary tradition was modified by the poets' own cosmopolitan and classical interests; Carew, for example, the finest of all the court poets, wrote imitations of Marino, the Italian baroque poet, as well as of other continental writers. The Cavalier poetry of Charles's court could not survive the Civil War, but some of its qualities – like those of the music of the Caroline Age – helped to establish conventions that were to develop quickly after the Restoration. Even more important, however, in creating and developing a taste for the Baroque, was the impact of a world that was itself essentially ephemeral – the world of stage design and theatrical production.

The court of Charles I had an almost insatiable appetite for drama and the masque, as for entertainment of any kind. Charles's queen, Henrietta Maria, seems to have been one of those women who need constant amusement and diversion. She played at games of all kinds, surrounded herself with monkeys, dogs and dwarves, and played a leading part as a dancer and amateur actress in more and more elaborate court entertainments.[5] Creator of the vast majority of these entertainments was Inigo Jones who, between 1605 and 1640, devised the scenery for and the staging of more than thirty masques and pastoral plays. And whereas, in his architecture, Inigo Jones was to create a Palladian tradition in England, through these entertainments he was creating quite alternative tastes. For his theatrical presentations derived increasingly from baroque models and, in particular, from the work of the famed Parigi.

In England, then, as elsewhere in Europe, the Baroque grew out of and alongside the theatre, with its new experiments in illusionism. Scenes suggesting changes in the weather, for example, became a standard feature of the masque after 1625, and although Inigo Jones never reached the peak of the Italian masters with their artificial floods, threatening to engulf the audience, or their recreated gardens with gushing fountains, it remains true that on the stage and in stage settings he experimented with baroque forms which he never translated into stone. At the same time, the technique of illusionism which he was developing in the theatre involved taking up and utilizing common baroque devices already established on the Continent.

Equally characteristic of the Baroque Age, seen in a European context, was the essentially political function of these masques. For although Charles I had a genuine love of the arts, as we have seen, he was also intensely aware of their political value, and, like all contemporary rulers, he knew that to control the way in which people saw their monarch was in some degree to control their response to royal policy. In his reign the arts were expected to apotheosize the monarch and to present for automatic acceptance a series of royal policies. Thus his imperial ambitions are reflected in a whole series of works of art: the equestrian statue by Le Sueur; Van Dyck's portrait of Charles on horseback riding through a classical triumphal arch, a picture which was specifically designed for a particular setting in St James's where the rest of the walls were hung with pictures of Roman emperors by Titian and Giulio Romano; and, most successfully of all, in 1633 in Aurelian Townshend's masque, *Albion' Triumph*, which portrayed Charles as a new Roman emperor.

It was the masque, above all, which served as a vehicle to proclaim royal policies, and Charles I was very specific in the demands which he placed on a masque's creators. On occasion it was even the King who dictated the plot. In Inigo Jones he found a most faithful interpreter of his ideals. This relationship between the King and a creator of entertainments for political purposes can be paralleled all over Europe at this time, where at several prominent courts, a number of distinguished artists were engaged in essentially the same tasks as Inigo Jones was performing for Charles I in London. New techniques discovered in painting, perspective and the use of light were used to create an ideal, imagined world, intended to be the aspiration of every court, where, since the King and courtiers were also the performers of the action, the real and imagined worlds might blur, until the difference between them could no longer be distinguished.

Inigo Jones has long been regarded as the father of Neo-Palladianism in England, but his work in the masque reveals him as the founder of English baroque art as well. It is no accident that the painter most closely associated with his theatrical work, Edward Pierce, said to be 'the only man who doth understand perspective of all the painters in London', in his treatment of the double cube room at Wilton should have been the first artist in England to adopt the grand baroque manner for a domestic interior.

Yet it should be recognized that men like Inigo Jones and Pierce were essentially ahead of contemporary taste in England, and that the real importance of their work lay in the fact that they were educating a new generation. Among his contemporaries, Jones found few Englishmen who appreciated his work in the masque outside the charmed circle of the King, the Queen and their intimate advisers. As his work on the masque became more sophisticated, so it became increasingly unpopular with English audiences. French and Italian visitors at the Caroline court became more and more impressed by his work at a time when his fellow-countrymen were losing patience with what they neither understood nor, apparently, wanted to understand. Charles I wished to use the masque to educate his subjects in their duty to their sovereign, but the political message which every masque was intended to convey only reached those who were already converted. Those who had no sympathy with the court and court policies remained unimpressed.

Thus the full impact of Charles I's artistic policies, even in the area of the masque, where they were fulfilled most splendidly, was essentially an equivocal one. The general acceptance of the masque as an art-form was also to a degree prevented by the public knowledge that, of all art-forms, the masque was the most costly. Public complaints about their cost grew very common, and it is true that, in any one year, a substantial sum was absorbed in these ephemeral theatrical and court entertainments: the staging of *Albion's Triumph*, for instance, cost over £1,000, of *Coelum Britannicum*, £1,200, and of *The Temple of Love*, *Britannia Triumphans*, *Luminalia* and of *Salamacida Spolia*, £1,400 each. The *Hue and Cry after Cupid*, performed in 1608 in honour of Lord Haddington's marriage, cost an astronomical £20,000 of which £1,000 was paid to William Lawes for composing the music; but even this pales into insignificance beside £120,000, reputedly spent by the Inns of Court in 1633 on a performance of *The Triumph of Peace* by the popular playwright, Shirley, with music by Lawes and Simon Ives.

The occasion for this last performance was the renewal of controversy between the crown and the Puritans over the masque. That irrepressible pamphleteer, William Prynne, had chosen to publish his all-embracing condemnation of the stage – *Histriomastix* – at a time when it was public knowledge that the Queen had recently appeared in Wat Montagu's play, *Shepherd's Pastoral*. To add insult to injury Prynne's index included such tendentious items as 'women actors notorious whores' and 'delight and skill in dancing a badge of lewd lascivious women and strumpets'. Nor was majesty endeared by what amounted to an open invitation to assassination; had not Nero been murdered, Prynne enquired, for his addiction to theatre-going?

Given the contemporary political climate some prosecution of Prynne was inevitable, but that he was tried for High Treason is a strong indication of the significance of the masque and his cultural projects in Charles I's policy. That their importance in the King's eyes was understood by contemporaries is indicated in turn by the fact that, even before the proceedings against Prynne had run their gruesome course – he was sentenced to life imprisonment, fined £5,000, disbarred, deprived of his academic degree, and had his ears cut off – there was a rush, on the part of those on whom suspicion might be expected to fall, to dissociate themselves from him. Prynne had been a member of Lincoln's Inn, and, at the King's suggestion, the Inns of Court therefore established their orthodoxy in relation to royal policy and the stage by their production of *The Triumph of Peace*.

But *Histriomastix* was more than just a condemnation of the theatre. It was a comprehensive indictment of the King's entire artistic policy, for Prynne included in his denunciation: bay windows, New Year's gifts, may-games, dancing, organs and pictures in church, i.e. all that in his terms smacked of popery and superstition. Nor did Prynne exist in a vacuum. Ever since the early years of the seventeenth century a series of pamphlets had poured from the presses attacking the crown's patronage of the arts in similar terms, and arguing that expenditure on the arts must lead, inevitably, to the impoverishment and ruin of the state. As early as 1612 Puritan objections to the masque had been so vociferous that James I had been forced to curtail expenditure on *Love Restored* in order to placate them, and by the 1620s opposition to the royal position in relation to the arts was merging with attacks on the crown's religious, political and constitutional policies. This was the first expression of a 'Country' view of the arts; love of them, it was argued, was an outward and visible sign of the King's inner corruption. Thereafter, attacks on royal patronage of the arts, on church policy, on corruption at court and on crypto-popery tended to go hand in hand. In 1637, for instance, a Mr Oldham of Shipton Moyne in Gloucestershire was reported as having preached 'in derogation of the cathedral service and of pictures of the Saviour. He also complained of the want of able counsellors; that the people were contented with the present ill-government. . . . Speaking of the buying and selling of places, he said, "all things are to be sold at Rome".'[6]

It was, perhaps, unfortunate that contemporary attacks on court art, based on religious principle, fitted in so admirably with a well-established and enduring literary tradition. The strong pastoral tradition in English literature, still dominant at the beginning of the seventeenth century, traditionally saw the court, not as the benefactor of the arts, but as their corruptor. Donne, describing London in 1607 as 'a place full of danger and vanity and vice, though the Court be gone',[7] was doing no more than expressing a literary commonplace in doing so.

The crown therefore could not automatically expect support even from those who most benefited from its largesse, the English artists, writers and musicians. Indeed the masque found attackers not just among the Puritans but among the luminaries of the literary world: 'These things', wrote Bacon in 1625, 'are but Toyes, to come amongst such Serious Observations. But yet since Princes will have such Things, it is better, they should be Graced with Elegancy than Daubed with Cost.' Bacon's view was merely a sophisticated expression of a widespread prejudice against the masque which was felt not just in extreme Puritan circles but even among men whom we tend to see as moderates, men like Bulstrode Whitelocke, who, although one of the committee responsible for the staging of *The Triumph of Peace*, remarked of that magnificent production that 'this earthly Pomp and Glory, if not vanity' was 'soon past over and gone, as if it had never been'.[8]

Whitelocke's remark hints at the deep spiritual divisions in English society which would soon bring Charles I's reign to its bitter and bloody end. The argument over the masque makes it clear that English culture in the Caroline Age was profoundly affected by the same divisions. Indeed, in a sense, the English Baroque may be said to have emerged out of them. What is certainly true is that, even in its origins, the English Baroque cannot be understood outside the social and political context of its age.

CHAPTER III

The Political Framework of the English Baroque

Others with towering Piles may please the Sight,
And in their proud aspiring Domes delight;
A nicer touch to the stretched Canvas give,
Or teach the animated Rocks *to live:*
Tis Britain's care to watch o'er Europe's Fate,
And hold in balance each contending state.
Addison

*

THE ENGLISH BAROQUE AGE coincides, not entirely fortuitously, with one of the periods of greatest political change and instability in English history. The period in question was one of very fast adaptation to changing conditions and circumstances, as the English tried to discover a political system which would reflect the fact that power in the country had now to be shared between the crown and the country's most powerful interest groups. At the same time a process of readjustment was going on in the relationships between these powerful groups producing a long-term tendency for one to become most important. The leading aristocratic and landed families, who controlled parliament and local government because they could command huge blocks of votes at will, and who drew as much as half their income from sources other than land, emerged as the primary centre of power in the country.

It was the peculiar achievement of this aristocratic group to make the late seventeenth and early eighteenth centuries a period in which the greatest restrictions were placed on the power of the monarch, often deliberately, but sometimes accidentally. It is true that Charles II was restored to the throne in 1660 with many of the prerogatives which had been enjoyed by his father, and that there was a general expectation that Charles would rule and govern. And, despite the succession of political crises in his reign, Charles was more than successful in fulfilling this general expectation, so whittling away the power of parliament that his brother James succeeded to the English throne with more theoretical power than any former English monarch. Only a man as monumentally stubborn and stupid as James II could have failed in such circumstances, but fail he did, and at the Glorious Revolution of 1688 new restrictions were placed on the English crown.

These changes in the power structure of England had consequences for almost every aspect of the country's life. One was that since power was no longer absolute in any sense, since, indeed, it had become a shared commodity, public opinion emerged as a more and more potent political force. Every successive political crisis that the nation faced revealed that this was so, and the development of the party system after 1688 merely accentuated a tendency which had already been long established. But just as politics were influenced by public opinion, so was the cultural life of the nation, and men who spent money on the arts needed to have one eye over their shoulder to gauge the effect of this expenditure. The court art of Jacobean and Caroline England had been criticized by men who had no first-hand experience of that art, and we have already seen how criticism of Charles I's artistic programme went hand-in-hand with criticism of his political programme.

Public criticism of the arts did not end with the downfall of Charles I, however; public opinion remained of great importance in cultural history until well into the eighteenth century. The advantages of ostentatious building in order to build up political weight had often to be weighed against solid disadvantages. The Earl of Clarendon came to believe that the new London townhouse he built in 1664 contributed more to his downfall than anything else. Popular opinion, expressed in the street ballads of London, outraged by the use of stones from Old St Paul's for the building, held that the palace had been paid for by bribes, the price of the disasters associated with Clarendon's rule as first minister:

> Here lie the consecrated bones
> Of Paul's, late gelded of his stones,
> Here lies the golden Briberies,
> The price of ruin's Families.
> The Cavaliers debenter wall
> Built in th'eccentric Basis,
> Here's Dunkirk Town and Tangier hall,
> The marriage of the Queen and all,
> The Dutchman's *Templum Pacis*.

The references to the Cavalier families who had been ruined by their support of the royal cause, and received no real compensation in 1660, to the marriage of Charles II to the barren and Catholic Catherine of Braganza, which Clarendon was rumoured to have encouraged so that his own grandchild might succeed to the English throne, to the ignominious surrender of Dunkirk to the French, and to the humiliating Dutch peace, in the context of the building of Clarendon's house, exemplify in the most precise way possible how politics and the arts could interact in the seventeenth and eighteenth centuries.

The bourgeois newspaper press played an important role in linking the two worlds. Since all the newspapers had a particular political bias, it was very easy for journalists to make or break a particular artist or a particular patron. Thus Sarah, Duchess of Marlborough, and Wren were publicly pilloried on the subject of Marlborough House in the *Examiner* in 1712 when Wren was accused of having received bribes from his master craftsmen in return for having granted them particular contracts. In the *Post Boy* for 27 December of the same year, a public advertisement, paid for by the master craftsmen concerned, had to be inserted in order to deal with the worst of the charges. In the advertisement the craftsmen asserted with some vigour that not only had they never offered any bribes or gratuities to the Surveyor-General but that 'we did, on the Surveyor's account, submit to less prices than we would otherwise have done.'[1] It is significant, in this context, that the attacks on the building of Marlborough House coincided precisely with the fall of the Marlboroughs from that position of political dominance which they had enjoyed since the beginning of the reign of Queen Anne.

Such detailed connections between political change and cultural development could be made many times over. But one may also point to wider areas in which the seesaw politics of the period did not fail to produce an effect on cultural and artistic life. It is quite obvious, for example, that the events of 1641–42, culminating in the outbreak of Civil War, brought the whole precarious edifice of artistic patronage nourished by Charles I tumbling to the ground. Not that the consequences of this collapse were wholly negative. In the perpetual game of rewriting history, to which all historians are rightly professionally committed, it has recently become fashionable to re-establish the artistic reputation of the Commonwealth leaders and to argue that the England of the Interregnum, between 1649 and 1660, was not quite the cultural desert which royalist propaganda made it out to be. Clearly there is a sense in which the arts continued to flourish in this period. Not surprisingly, Cavalier poetry hardly survived the outbreak of the Civil War; Suckling had fled abroad as early as 1641, and he died in 1642; Godolphin was killed in 1643, and by the late 1640s Davenant and Denham were in exile. But all poetry did not cease to be written. The case of Milton is a complex one. His European reputation as a great baroque poet was already secure before the Civil War; but once the war had begun, and in the early years of the Commonwealth, all his massive intellectual energies went into the promotion of the Puritan cause through his political prose. It was only towards the end of the 1650s, after the defeat of his hopes for the creation of a new society under the rule of the saints, that he turned back to his youthful ambition to honour his nation by writing a great epic poem. Yet even if Milton is set aside, in the work of Andrew Marvell the Interregnum may fairly lay claim to one major English poet.

Despite the views of the Committee for the Advancement of Music, who, in 1657, explained in a petition to Cromwell that,

> by reason of the late dissolution of the Choirs in the Cathedrals where the study and practice of the Science of Music was especially cherished, many of the skilful Professors of the Science have during the late Wars and troubles died in want, and there being now no preferment or Encouragement in the way of Music, no man will breed his child in it, so that it needs must be, that the Science itself must die in this Nation,

music in fact flourished. The baroque style found some of its most ardent admirers among the Puritans. Milton's sonnet to Henry Lawes, whose songs for *Comus* were among the earliest examples of English baroque *continuo* song, suggests that the composer's

> . . . tuneful and well-measured song
> First taught our English music how to span
> Words with just note and accent.

In fact, provided it was not church music, music was as much beloved by parliamentarians as by royalists. Cromwell himself maintained a small body of domestic players and the marriage of his favourite daughter, Frances, in November 1657, was celebrated with music from forty-eight violins and fifty trumpets.

Nor can the visual arts be said to have entirely collapsed during the Interregnum, although those artists who had been most closely connected with the Stuart court found it expedient to leave the country. The Commonwealth leaders had few if any objections to the visual arts in principle and one of their number, General Lambert, was a very accomplished flower painter. In the interests of encouraging industry and assisting co-religionists – the works after all were manned by Protestant refugees from Catholic Europe – the Puritan leaders gladly rescued the Mortlake tapestry works from the bankruptcy into which the Civil War had once again plunged them. Subsequently Cromwell's apartments at Hampton Court were to be lavishly hung with products of the Mortlake works, including some repurchased from the royal collection. Again, throughout the period of the Interregnum, Emmanuel de Critz and Edward Pierce continued serenely at work on the decoration of the new wing at Wilton, an important cultural link between the world of Inigo Jones and that of the Restoration. Nor did all contemporary artists believe that the new forms of government were essentially antithetical to the new baroque styles; or at least we may deduce as much from the fact that in 1651 Gerbier, Lely and George Geldorp solemnly proposed decorating Whitehall with portraits and battle-pieces to illustrate the memorable achievements of parliament.

Nevertheless there is some significance in the fact that this suggestion, which a republican government in Florence two hundred years before would have seized on with enthusiasm, never came to anything. Again Interregnum music seems to have been largely patronized and played by the gentry and wealthier townsmen in their own homes – leading, incidentally, with the emergence of John Playford, to the establishment of the printed music business as a flourishing commercial enterprise. Portraiture was another flourishing art-form; Lely made a great deal of money during the Commonwealth, and, by 1653, he was painting official portraits of Cromwell. Normally, however, during the Interregnum he found that he had to travel around the country to get his commissions, and he had to accept fees which were a quarter of those he was able to command ten years later. The general point about the Interregnum, in fact, seems to be that with the disappearance of almost all sources of public patronage, the arts tended to become more private than public. Baroque art, on the other hand, as we have seen, designed to move or flatter or sway, was essentially public art.

It is interesting to note that in the later years of the Interregnum the restraints imposed upon the arts for ideological reasons were beginning to weaken, and spontaneous social pressures were mounting for their restoration to a more public role. That taste for scenographic display, which, as we have seen, was nurtured during the reigns of the early Stuarts, broke out in two distinct areas. First, at the popular level, the late 1650s saw a revival of the Lord Mayors' Shows, in all their traditional splendour, mounted under the direction of the City Surveyor Edward Jarman and his assistant, the painter John Fordham. Secondly, there was a gradual move towards the restoration of the public theatre. The closure of the theatres had never of course affected private dramatic performances and in 1653 Shirley's masque, *Cupid and Death*, with music by Christopher Gibbons and Matthew Locke, was privately performed. Clearly a taste for the entertainments fostered in the Caroline court did still exist. Equally clear was the pressure for a more public entertainment and in 1656 the ban on the public stage was relaxed sufficiently for there to be a performance of Davenant's English opera, *The Siege of Rhodes*, with elaborate settings by John Webb. The opera escaped the ban on stage performances by describing itself as an 'Entertainment . . . by Declamations and Musick after the Manner of the Ancients'.

We have become accustomed to thinking that a particular structure of patronage will produce a particular kind of art, but it may well be that the relationship is a two-way one and that a particular kind of art will look for and find a form of patronage which will suit it, and will even encourage the creation of the kind of society and political structure which will enable it to flourish. Certainly it does seem probable that a mounting pressure to restore the arts to a more positive role in the life of the nation contributed in some degree to creating an atmosphere in which the Restoration of 1660 became not only one possible solution to a political crisis, but a positive act of commitment to the idea of monarchy.

However important, then, the artistic developments of the Interregnum were, the process of historical revisionism should not be taken too far. All artistic sensibility need not be denied to the Commonwealth leaders and to Cromwell, with his delight in music, in particular; but it remains difficult to believe that that sensibility was very highly developed in a group of men who presided over the dispersal of Charles I's picture collection between 1649 and 1652. The visual arts, in particular, undoubtedly did suffer a decline under the Commonwealth. In the first place, foreign artists did not find England a very congenial place to work in after 1642; and, in the second, as we have seen, many leading artists were closely connected with the court of Charles I, or had strong royalist convictions, and so were forced into exile. It was his royalist sympathies, for example, which drove Isaac Fuller to France in the 1640s where he studied under the French history painter François Perrier, and it is an indication of the changing artistic climate that he felt able to return to England in the late 1650s. Similar reasons also sent Robert Streeter to travel in France and Italy, and the brilliant Anglo-Scottish painter, Michael Wright, spent the Interregnum years in Rome where he became a member of the Academy of St Luke.

Architecture suffered an even greater blight at one of the most important points in the development of that art in England, for the outbreak of the Civil War had followed hard upon the unveiling of Inigo Jones's portico at Old St Paul's which Webb described as 'a piece of architecture not to be paralleled in these last ages of the world'.[2] Inigo Jones and his master mason buried the rebuilding fund money in the Lambeth marshes, and went to join the royal armies, but the parliamentarians recovered the money and confiscated it to spend on the war. This was an episode which symbolizes the public eclipse of architecture as an art until after the events of 1660.

Because of the success which had attended Charles I in his efforts to create a new cultural ambience, many Englishmen who regarded themselves as *virtuosi* in the arts hailed the restoration of Charles II as the dawn of a second golden age. It was widely believed that the restoration would have the effect of reuniting England with the mainstream of European culture with entirely beneficial results. John Evelyn, for instance, an experienced and unprejudiced traveller with a strong visual understanding, believed that England would now come into her own and stand as the cultural equal of all other nations. Under the enlightened patronage of the newly restored court she could, at last, cast off a certain backwardness in the arts. And Evelyn was not entirely wrong. The events of 1660, among other things, restored to the arts a lost prestige and to artists a lost social standing. Symbolically, a special committee of the House of Lords was created, which succeeded in recovering some of Charles I's dispersed art collection, and so formed the nucleus of the modern royal picture collection. The official artistic appointments of the crown were filled once more; Peter Bennier, the only foreign sculptor who had remained in England after 1642, was rewarded for his tenacity by being appointed Sculptor-in-Ordinary to the Crown, and Lely was appointed Principal Painter to the King with a pension of £200 a year.

The Restoration, however, did nothing to make the position of the artist, or of culture in general, any more immune to the consequences of the continuing process of social and political change. Both the individual artist and the country's cultural life remained at the mercy of political swings for the rest of the period under consideration and may, indeed, have become more vulnerable. The wars with the Dutch and the wars with the French, for example, could lead to a swing against Dutch or French cultural influences. Thus we tend to think of the reign of Charles II as being a period when good taste and fashion tended to look to France for their models, and to forget that this passion for things French in the 1660s and 1670s was really exceptional, and existed only during a period of close Anglo-French relations, diplomatic ties and friendship, which did not survive the 1670s. By then, Colbert's economic policies, so damaging to many vital British interests, with the associated development of the French navy and Franco-British colonial rivalry, had produced in England a distinct anti-French mood and Whig propaganda, with its famous slogan 'no wooden shoes', had created an image of France in which undoubted cultural achievements were based on the abject poverty of the French peasant. As far as individual artists were concerned, the fact that so many were foreign Catholics left them always at the mercy of anti-papal hysteria. At the time of the 'Papal Plot' in 1679 and the subsequent Exclusion crisis, many Catholic musicians and at least one Catholic painter, Hendrick Danckerts, who had decorated the interiors of Clarendon House, found it expedient to leave the country.

The Revolution of 1688 also occasioned immediate cultural changes. Up and down the country tangible reminders of James II's reign were obliterated – from the King's magnificent Whitehall chapel, which was dismantled, to the 'noble statue' of James which Ralph Thoresby saw in Newcastle in 1703 being melted down to make church bells.[3] The Glorious Revolution also ended Verrio's career as a court painter, for he was a convinced Jacobite and was unwilling to work for William and Mary; his son served as a captain in James's army in Ireland and was taken prisoner at Drogheda in 1690. The Revolution led also to a passion for Dutch comforts and Dutch fashions, introduced initially by William's ultra-modern Dutch courtiers.

Again, party conflict also had its effect on the arts. The talents of many of England's great literary figures were exercised in the ceaseless pamphlet controversies which are associated with this period of expanding political journalism, as well as in political writing of a less scurrilous nature. Architecture was pressed into the service of the parties as well. What more natural than that the Tories – the High Church party – should have celebrated their return to power in 1710, for the first time since 1688, not merely negatively, by cutting off supplies for the building of Whig Blenheim, but positively, by building 'fifty' new churches to meet the needs of London's expanding population. These new churches, together with the City churches rebuilt after the Fire of London, represented the single largest building operation of the baroque period, offering an opportunity for the emergence of a uniquely English, baroque style. In the constant party warfare, individual artists also suffered; Wren, under the Whigs, found his activities at St Paul's perpetually hamstrung, while Vanbrugh was dismissed from the Comptrollership of the Works in 1713 on the entirely partisan grounds that he had written a letter which was supposed to reflect adversely on the Tory government, that he was a known supporter of the Duke of Marlborough, and that he had continued the works at Blenheim under the Harley-Bolingbroke ministry although he had been expressly forbidden to do so.

For this dismissal the Whigs, too, were eventually to have their revenge, and in the establishment of the Whig supremacy in the early eighteenth century and the consequent shift from baroque to Palladian norms in artistic style we can see how fundamental the effect of political change on English culture could be. The early Whigs were, of course, as ardent patrons of baroque forms as any one. The Whigs' own peculiar preserve – The Kit Cat Club – was also the centre from which Vanbrugh's influence radiated. But the mounting influence of the third Earl of Shaftesbury on the Whig party and Whig philosophy at the beginning of the eighteenth century, led eventually to the conversion to Palladianism.

Shaftesbury, whose views first became public in 1712, was one of the few really important commentators on aesthetics of his age. He was also one of the very few Englishmen who attempted, at this early date, to put forward some coherent view of the relationship between society and culture. Art, for Shaftesbury, was the product of economic, social, climatic and political forces, and took different forms in different historical periods. To each nation, therefore, Shaftesbury attributed its own particular 'Spirit' or 'Genius', what we would call its 'culture', which he saw as manifesting itself in all areas of a nation's life. Where political institutions were sound then art would flourish; similarly, where political institutions were corrupt, corrupt art would be found. The baroque admiration of Will and Power he saw as leading directly to tyranny, and tyranny to superstition, immorality, injustice and bad taste. Tyranny and good art were essentially inimical to each other so that the Romans 'with their Liberty . . . lost not only their Force of Eloquence, but even their Style and Language itself'.[4] Thus Shaftesbury argued that tragedy, which he saw as the highest form of dramatic art, could never flourish where 'the *Spirit of Liberty* is wanting', for the genius of this Poetry consists in the Lively Representation of the Disorders and Misery *of the Great*; to the end that *the People* and those of a lower sort may be taught the better to Content themselves with Privacy, enjoy their Safer State, and prize the Equality and Justice of their *Guardian* LAWS. If this be found agreeable to the just *Tragic Model*, which the Antients have deliver'd to us; 'twill easily be conceived how little such a Model is proportioned to the Capacity or Taste of those, who in a long Series of Degrees, from the lowest Peasant to the high Slave of Royal Blood, are taught to idolize the next in Power above them, and think nothing so adorable as that unlimited Greatness, and Tyrannic Power, which is raised at *their own* Expense, and exercised over themselves.[5]

The converse of this argument was that a society whose moving spirit was a search for liberty and truth was one in which good government, true religion, good morals and good taste were inseparably to be found: 'When the *free* Spirit of a Nation turns it-self this way, Judgments are formed; Critics arise; the public Eye and Ear improve; a right Taste prevails, and in a manner forces its way.' For 'Nothing is so improving, nothing so natural, so *congenial* to the Liberal Arts, as that reigning Liberty and high spirit of a People, which from the Habit of judging in the highest Matters for themselves, makes them freely judge other Subjects, and enter thoroughly into the Characters as well of *Men* and *Manners*, as of the *Products* or *Works* of Men, in Art and Science.'[6]

In this explanation of the relationship between society and culture, Shaftesbury's real problem was that while he believed passionately in the 'English Spirit of Liberty', which he saw as the reincarnation of all the virtues of ancient republican Rome, so he was also convinced that no really good art was being produced in England.

Shaftesbury and several of his fellow Whigs saw in Palladianism the style which best expressed the new English liberty, for they assumed that its rules had been derived from the free spirit of enquiry which had existed in republican Rome. Just as much of the cultural history of renaissance Italy can be traced in terms of a perpetual debate between the classical past and the present, so in eighteenth-century England changes in culture were intimately linked to a similar concern with the civilization of ancient Rome. Every educated man had been trained in the history and language of that civilization, and that training constituted the largest and most significant part of his education. Inevitably, therefore, he tended to draw parallels and to make comparisons between his contemporary world and that of ancient Rome.

The Whigs, in particular, were prone to find their political ideas in the classical past. At the turn of the century, in his commentaries on the War of the Spanish Succession, Addison had begun to draw parallels between the 'deathless acts' of the Romans and the role which the English were playing in defending the liberties of Europe; and, in his drama, *Cato*, he used a Roman republican theme to attack the Duke of Marlborough. Jonathan Richardson the painter went even further, arguing in 1715 that 'no nation under Heaven so nearly resembles the ancient Greeks and Romans than we. There is a haughty courage, an elevation of thought, a greatness of taste, a love of liberty, a simplicity, and honesty among us, and which belongs to us as Englishmen; and it is in these that resemblance consists.'[7]

In such a context it was natural, therefore, that Shaftesbury should be an ardent supporter of neo-classicism, which he saw as a reincarnation of the artistic standards of the ancient world, just as he criticized baroque art because it observed neither the rules nor the proportions of the ancients. Shaftesbury did not, of course, use the word 'baroque' but he did describe a new style of architecture in England – more monumental, more romanized and more decorated – which had emerged with the Restoration of 1660, and he associated this style with the autocratic government of Charles II and James II. The Whig party was built on opposition to such government and against the Tory Wren Shaftesbury, with more political than aesthetic sense, inveighed as 'one single court architect' who had been imposed on the country by force. All Shaftesbury would admit on Wren's behalf was that he 'would long since . . . have proved the Greatest Master in the World',[8] had he but formed his taste correctly on the great monuments of the classical world or modern Italy instead of ruining the skyline of the City of London with his buildings, domes and church spires which retained 'much of what Artists call the Gothic kind'.[9]

It was a curious irony that it was contemporary French civilization which most nearly fulfilled Shaftesbury's artistic ideal. True, England had once had great, if barbaric, poets – Shakespeare, Fletcher, Jonson and Milton – all of whom 'To their eternal Honour . . . have withal been the first of Europeans, who since the Gothic Model of Poetry attempted to throw off the horrid Discord of jingling Rhyme'[10] – but where, Shaftesbury demanded, were the Shakespeares and Miltons of his own day? Why was it that although ' 'Tis evident, our Natural Genius shines above that airy, neighbouring Nation' of France, English culture was sunk in apathy and decay? Had he been less honest, Shaftesbury might have solved his problem by finding things to praise in contemporary English literature and art, but this he could not do for he was tied by his own philosophy and he specifically condemned those who 'are glad to take up what our Language can afford us; and by a sort of *Emulation* with other Nations, are forced to cry up such Writers of our own, as may best serve us for Comparison'.[11]

Eventually Shaftesbury came to explain what he saw as the contemporary decadence of English culture in several ways. Firstly he pointed to the long wars with France which had absorbed English energies and English money; the English were, in fact, in the same position as the 'Ancient Romans in those early Days, when they wanted only repose from Arms to apply themselves to the Improvement of Arts and Sciences'.[12] Secondly, Shaftesbury saw the key in a lack of discriminating patronage on the part of the English, and particularly on the part of the English aristocracy. Unlike the French, the English had not devoted enough time, energy or enthusiasm to the cultivation of '*Politeness*'. Such patronage as had been available in the past had been largely uncritical and perverse because, as we have seen, it was over-influenced by the attitudes of the Stuart court.

For the future, however, Shaftesbury hoped for great things, for, 'When the Spirit of the Nation was grown more *free* . . . we no sooner began to turn ourselves towards *Music*, and enquire what Italy in particular produced, than in an instant we outstripped our Neighbours the French, entered into a Genius far beyond theirs, and raised ourselves an *Ear*, and *Judgment*, not inferior to the best now in the World.'[13] If this could happen to music so, surely, it could happen to all the arts, if only the English would turn to true classical models in order to train their taste, and if only adequate systems of patronage could be created with which to sustain the arts.

Since Shaftesbury believed that good taste could produce good morals and that good morals produced good government, it was for the benefit of England as a whole that he appealed to the English aristocracy to exert themselves to encourage the arts:

> Well it would be indeed, and much to the Honour of our *Nobles* and *Princes* would they freely help in this Affair; and by a judicious Application of their Bounty, facilitate this happy Birth.[14]

Such pleas did not fall on deaf ears. As the grandson of the founding father of Whiggism, Shaftesbury's political credentials were impeccable, and the leading Whig politicians were happy to digest what he said and to make it a part of their political ideology, recognizing in Shaftesbury the greatest exponent of the Whig/Country position on the arts. Moreover, all that Shaftesbury said fitted in peculiarly well with that particular mood of xenophobia which the war with France created.

Even in the 1660s it is possible to discern a marked tendency to regard the work of English artists as automatically superior to even the best work done by foreigners. This tendency found its most interesting expression in the cult surrounding the English decorative painter, Robert Streeter, who was acclaimed by his contemporaries as the 'greatest and most universal painter that England ever bred'. In particular, they admired his illusionistic decoration of Wren's Sheldonian Theatre which he painted in 1668–69, with its allegory of 'Truth descending on the Arts and Sciences', and its painted network of ropes, designed to give the impression of the canvas awning of a Roman theatre open to the sky. In 1669 Pepys visited Streeter's studio and 'found him and Dr Wren, and several virtuosos, looking upon the paintings . . . and, indeed, they look as if they would be very fine, and the rest think better than those of Rubens, in the Banqueting-house at Whitehall'. Certainly, Wren thought highly enough of Streeter to employ him frequently on the newly built City churches, but there were those who were prepared to go even further in their praise and to make the rather surprising prophecy

> That Future ages must confess they owe
> To STREETER more than Michel Angelo.[15]

This artistic judgment, which cannot entirely be explained by the exigencies of the rhyming couplet, must be associated with the contemporary belief in England that native talent must be encourged by all possible means. This belief Lord Halifax expressed when he explained his reasons for preferring Thornhill to Sebastiano Ricci for the decoration of the Prince of Wales's bedchamber (now known as the Queen's Bedchamber) at Hampton Court:

> Mr Thornhill our countryman . . . strove against all oppositions and difficulties and now had got near the very top of the Mountain and his

grace would throw him down and oust all his endeavours, which would prevent and discourage all our countrymen ever after to attempt the like again.

The sense of self-confidence bred in the English by the Glorious Revolution of 1688 only strengthened such nationalistic prejudices, while the bitterness engendered by the French Wars, and particularly by the War of the Spanish Succession, increased the awareness of foreign fashions and encouraged withdrawal from them. In particular it led to the rejection of French culture, which carried with it connotations of absolutism, popery and persecution, and which it was believed was a potential agent of French imperialism, since 'The *French*, naturally active, insinuating, and bold' had 'with their trifles and new modes almost debauched all the sobriety of former times, continually aspiring to enlarge their Tyranny by all the arts of dissimulation and treachery.'[16] Even Italian art was now becoming suspect as the product of 'Slavery and the Inquisition',[17] and in 1693 Dryden felt that he must warn his countrymen against the danger of allowing their nationalist sympathies to interfere with their critical judgment.

Yet Dryden was supporting a lost cause, as he well knew. At the beginning of the eighteenth century, in a remarkable synthesis, Shaftesbury's aesthetic views and aggressive nationalism were brought together in Colen Campbell's famous work on English architecture, the *Vitruvius Britannicus*. The first volume appeared in 1715, immediately after the ending of the war with France and during the high tide of English nationalism. A hymn to the triumphs of Palladio and Inigo Jones, *Vitruvius Britannicus* suggested that it was indiscriminate and uncritical foreign travel that had led 'so many of the British Quality' to 'have so mean an Opinion of what is performed in our own Country; though perhaps in most we equal, and in some Things we surpass, our Neighbours'; it also expressed a pious hope that Inigo Jones's Banqueting House would be completed as the vast palace he had originally planned, for then it would 'far exceed all the Palaces of the Universe, as the Valour of our Troops and Conduct of our Generals have surpassed all others'. Thornhill's decorations at Greenwich Palace were singled out for particular comment simply because Thornhill was *English*, and 'Here Foreigners may view with Amaze, our Countrymen with Pleasure, and all with Admiration, the Beauty, the Force, the Majesty of a *British* pencil.'

In this kind of atmosphere it is scarcely surprising that by the second decade of the eighteenth century foreign artists in England were beginning to find the ambience uncongenial. All the best contracts were going to the English. Alessandro Galilei had come over to England with the highest hopes of finding work in a country whose social climate he had been predisposed to like. Five years later he returned to Italy, a bitterly disillusioned man, having even failed to obtain a hoped-for contract to design one of the fifty new London churches.

Now I see [he wrote] that all of my hopes were always vain, that the English do not behave as we do in Italy. For there whenever a foreigner arrives of even the meanest ability, everyone chases after him, and our native artists who have twenty times his ability are ignored. Here it is quite a different story, because they always want to employ their own countrymen even if they are complete donkeys.[18]

Another reason for Galilei's failure may well have been the fact that he was a baroque architect, while Shaftesbury, Colen Campbell and Lord Burlington had already begun to view Palladianism as that architectural form which best expressed the new English political liberty. The adoption of the Palladian style had become a test of Whig political orthodoxy, just as persistence in building in baroque styles became a statement about a man's Toryism. Long after the baroque style had been largely abandoned some Tory squires continued to employ it in building their country houses as a means of snubbing the orthodox, Palladian Whigs.

Yet, those Tory squires were an exception. Predominant in politics after 1715, predominant socially, the great Whig aristocrats soon imposed their artistic rules on the nation. The Board of Works was totally unmade. After 1715, although Wren was allowed to retain his Surveyorship, the office was made almost nominal, 'by appointing other worthy gentlemen with me in the Commission, which was under such regulations and restrictions, as that although I had the first named with the old title of Surveyor, yet in acting I had no power to override or to give a casting vote'.[19] In 1717 Wren's son was deprived of his office of Chief Clerk and replaced by Colen Campbell. In the following year the Whig revolution was completed; Dartiquenave, whose only qualification for the job was his membership of the Kit Cat Club, became Paymaster in the Board of Works and William Benson replaced Wren as Surveyor-General. Benson's appointment was purely a political one. The son of a man who had made a fortune in the City, he had visited Italy and, on his return, bought a Wiltshire estate on which he built himself a Palladian mansion. Much of his fortune having been spent on this project and on political support for the Whigs, it was felt that a Whig ministry should find him a valuable sinecure and its choice, unfortunately, fell on the Board of Works. Here he was joined by his brother, Benjamin, who replaced Hawksmoor as Clerk of the Works. This ended the great days of the Works, which, as we shall see, coincided with the great age in English baroque architecture. Thereafter the Works became the sole preserve of artistic nonentities who were fortunately possessed of political influence and Palladian patrons.

In 1726 John Molesworth, the Irishman, sent a letter to his protégé Alessandro Galilei, describing the artistic revolution which had been wrought in England as a result of political change and warned him that the Baroque Age was effectively over:

> here the reigning taste is Palladio's style . . . and a man is a heretic that he should talk of Michel Angelo or any other modern architect. You must diligently copy all the noted fabrics of Palladio for those very drafts would introduce you here, and without them you may despair of success.

CHAPTER IV

The Artist in Society

There is nothing more certain, than that a real Genius, and thorough Artist, in whatever kind, can never, without the greatest Unwillingness and Shame, be induced to act below his Character, and for mere Interest be prevailed with to prostitute his Art or Science, by performing contrary to its known Rules.

Shaftesbury

*

THE ENGLAND of the late seventeenth and early eighteenth centuries was a small country, with a total population of a little under six million, bound together in a complicated hierarchical society, which does not lend itself readily to accurate description.[1] That society did not consist of a triangle with the king at the apex, the peasantry and day labourers forming the base, and an aristocracy and rising middle class conveniently placed along the sides, although it is possible that the chief error of both Charles I and James II was to imagine that they lived in such a world. Rather, English society was made up of a series of pyramids, groupings in what the eighteenth century knew as 'Interests', and England was governed by a loose alliance or working agreement between those at the top of each pyramid. England was an agglomeration of different pressure groups and powers, among them the territorial landed gentlemen, headed by the aristocracy; the Church of England, led by its own aristocracy of archbishops and bishops, its power reaching down to every parish in the country making it an integral part of the governmental structure of England; the army and the navy; the nonconformist interests; the legal world, centred on the Inns of Court; the nascent East Indian and West Indian interests; the merchant body of the country; the City of London with its financial interests. All of these were a permanent and important part of the structure of English society in this period.

This complex of social hierarchies existed in a world of continuing social and economic change, of adjustment and dynamic development. It is now recognized that the much-vaunted 'age of stability', supposedly introduced into English social, economic and political life by the settlement which followed the 1688 revolution, was largely illusory, and at best can only be regarded as a brief interlude before the initiation of another era of even greater and more rapid social and economic change which, for convenience, we call the Industrial Revolution. Indeed, a necessary precondition for that *industrial* revolution was the commercial revolution which, during the period we are considering, was transforming England from a mainly agricultural community, in which wool, salt and wines were the mainstays of a regular, traditional trade with Europe, to one in which trade, transformed into a worldwide business based on the bulk transport and exchange of tobacco, tea, coffee, beer and fish, was fast becoming an increasingly important part of the country's wealth. As a result of this process of change, new economic groups were becoming of great importance, but, although fortunes were now made in new ways, the social structure of pre-industrial England remained essentially hierarchical.

Within this hierarchical social world what was the status of artists? Like that of other social groups it was changing. Such change had gradually occurred over the previous two centuries in Europe. But, just as England was slow to adopt new styles in the visual arts, so it was slow to recognize artistic genius by according to the artist that higher social status which he had come to enjoy in countries like France and Italy, and which is closely associated with the Baroque Age.

The rise in the social status of the artist was essentially a minor dimension of the transition from the 'medieval' to the 'modern' world. In the Middle Ages the artist was, technically speaking, a 'craftsman', and practising artists emerged at best from the lower middle classes. The artist was a manual worker, performing a practical function under the organization and control of the guilds, working in the same way as any other craftsman. Since the guilds exercised a close supervision over the artist's work, which was subjected to a very large number of rules and controls, there was no room for what we might call 'artistic temperament', for the assertion of individuality or for any eccentric, wayward genius.

It was a triumph of the Renaissance to formulate the theories which eroded this traditional system and significantly raised the status of the arts. But it took at least two hundred years for theories first put forward in the fifteenth century to be accepted in practice. English artists in the seventeenth century were still, on occasion, having to struggle against the power of the guilds and many artists continued to be recruited from the traditional lower social classes. Change did occur during the Baroque Age, but that change was slow and much dependent upon a new generation of patrons, who genuinely believed in the claims of genius to respect and reward.

In considering the wide question of the changing status of the artist in society, one is handicapped by the fact that the evidence is most abundant for those artists whose reputation was high. Seventeenth-century society was too familiar with the artisan starving in his garret to comment on the artist starving in his. Yet the picture is seriously distorted if one forgets both the unsuccessful, and the majority of artists working in England who made no claims to being more than good craftsmen, and who showed no desire to rise in the world or to acquire fame beyond their own immediate environment.

An additional handicap in establishing the social status of the artist lies in the fact that, to some extent, the artist was a social outsider. This does not mean that society as yet had any clear idea of the eccentric genius or artistic temperament. On the contrary, the artist was expected to conform to conventional morals and mores, and to share contemporary social aspirations. And there is little evidence that the baroque artist revolted against this form of social restraint. Sir John Vanbrugh, it is true, was a larger-than-life figure, but even his social aspirations were more than respectable. Few, in any age, seem to have enjoyed aristocratic company quite so whole-heartedly as Vanbrugh. There were, inevitably, a few artists who were squanderers, bad managers or spendthrifts. Despite his fame, Caius Gabriel Cibber rarely managed to keep his head above water, was constantly in debt and several times imprisoned. When in 1668 he gained his long-coveted admittance as a Liveryman of the Leather-sellers' Company, which gave him the legal right to work within the boundaries of the City of London, he could not even raise the necessary fee of £25 and eventually discharged this debt, at least, by making 'a stone mermaid over the pump' in the courtyard of Leathersellers' Hall. The successful portraitist, John Vanderbank, also lived extravagantly and was normally in debt, but in this he differed little from many of his clients. A few artists acquired a certain notoriety for immorality; Verrio's love-life must, even by the most charitable, be described as erratic, and Isaac (I) Fuller, was certainly famous for his drink-ing. In 1670 he painted a portrait of himself when drunk, which is now in the Bodleian Library, for Daniel Rawlinson, the owner of the Mitre tavern in Fenchurch Street. James Gibbs would appear to have had the reputation of always being late. But it is only in the rare case that we can equate unconven-tionality in conduct with a particular kind of genius. William Talman is an exception; of all practising architects in England, the one who showed the most original, unconventional and inventive mind, brilliant as much for the way in which he ignored rules and assumptions as for anything else, he was always the most ill-tempered of men and no artist has a worse record in terms of quarrelling with his patrons.

But, by and large, the late seventeenth- and early eighteenth-century artist was a conformist and those who made money from their art tended to spend that money in socially acceptable ways. Above all they used their money to buy property; Thornhill, for instance, employed his in repurchasing former family properties, Lely left an estate of £900 a year which included the manor of Wellingham in Lincolnshire, and James Gibbs died possessed of six houses in Marylebone and one in Argyll Steet, London. Even William Talman was, in this area, sufficient of a conformist to purchase a landed estate in 1718. Similarly artists are to be found occupying traditional prestige posts or positions of power in the country; Thomas Archer held an appointment as Groom Porter to Queen Anne, for instance, and both Thornhill and Wren served as members of parliament.

Yet, although the artist was treated as a perfectly ordinary member of society and, on the whole, behaved no differently, he still lacked any very clear or secure position in the English social hierarchy. The baroque artist, in particular, often remained something of an outsider. This was partly the result of the peculiar circumstance that so many practitioners of baroque art in England either belonged to, or were attached to, the growing community of foreigners in England, particularly in London, where not just individual artists, musicians and merchants, but large groups of persecuted Protestants from Europe were settling on a more or less permanent basis. Some of the best work done in England in the late seventeenth and early eighteenth centuries was by refugees from Louis XIV's France: the decorative painters, Pierre Berchet, Nicholas Hende and Louis Chèron, for instance, who decorated Boughton for Lord Montagu, or the Huguenot smith, Jean Tijou. And although foreign skills were clearly welcomed in England, their foreign ex-ponents were never really integrated into English society which remained basically hostile to all outsiders. It is a remarkable fact that the only issue which could unite Whig and Tory in the reign of William III was hatred of the foreigner, among whom politicians frequently numbered the King.

Another factor contributing to the 'apartness' of the artistic community was the tendency for artists, writers, musicians, etc. to group together to form their own small interests. The successful artist, far from being a solitary genius, was in this period normally the vital centre of a large group of other artists and artisans. Thus, if we take Wren as the centre of one such group, we find that he was Robert Hooke's friend and collaborator, a friend of Vanbrugh and Gibbs, the friend and teacher of Hawksmoor, and a frequent collaborator with Cibber, Grinling Gibbons and Tijou. But Hooke himself, besides being Cibber's friend and collaborator, numbered Sir Godfrey Kneller and Isaac Fuller among his friends, while Hawksmoor worked on terms of the closest intimacy with Vanbrugh. Similarly, if we take Grinling Gibbons as our starting point, besides the extended relationships we have noted, we should also recall his close friendship with Peter Lely and Hugh May, and the fact that he habitually worked in close partnership as a sculptor with Arnold Quellin, who in turn worked with the Flemish sculptor John Nost. Kneller, whose house at Witton was decorated by Laguerre, was the centre of yet another important group which also included many literary figures. This is hardly surprising, for Kneller, of whom Dryden wrote that

> Some other hand perhaps may reach a Face
> But none like thee, a finished Figure place:
> None of this Age; for that's enough for thee
> The first of these Inferior Times to be. . . .

was celebrated in verse more frequently than any other English painter before or since. Not only were many artists on intimate social terms with each other; some even lived in close proximity. Among those who took leases on the Harley Marylebone estate in the early eighteenth century, and who were in consequence close neighbours, were James Gibbs, the estate's designer, Rysbrack the sculptor, who often worked for Gibbs, John Wood and John James.

For the fruitfulness of such relationships between artists, we have the authority of Pope, for whom Kneller painted three *grisaille* portraits of Apollo, Venus and Hercules which went to decorate the poet's Twickenham staircase. In a poem written to his friend the painter Jervas, Pope commented on the great importance of these relationships in the development of the creative imaginations of those who enjoyed them:

> Smit with the love of sister-arts we came,
> And met congenial, mingling flame with flame;
> Like friendly colours found our arts unite,
> And each from each contract new strength and light . . .
> How oft our slowly growing works impart
> While images reflect from art to art? . . .
> Together o'er the Alps methinks we fly,
> Fired with ideas of fair Italy . . .
> While fancy brings the vanished piles to view,
> And builds imaginary Rome anew.[2]

55

Apart from such claims of interest and friendship, there are several additional reasons why the creative elite of the Baroque in England is to be found closely grouped together. First there was the tendency for practising artists to be members of the same family, engaged in what amounted to a small family business. It was normal practice for a son to be apprenticed to his father and even for a wife to learn her husband's craft and carry on his business after his death. Such a situation tells us something about the status of the artist, for it is a practice which is very common in societies in which the artist is regarded more as a highly accomplished craftsman than as a peculiarly gifted individual. In this period we find a typical group in the Streeter family; Robert (I) Streeter and Thomas Streeter, both practising artists, were the sons of a painter and Thomas then married the artist daughter of the Flemish painter Rémy van Leemput. Robert (I) Streeter's son was also a painter and succeeded his father as Sergeant-Painter to the Crown in 1679. Isaac (I) Fuller, of whom it was said that he had 'a quicker hand at painting than any other',[3] had two sons, both of whom were well known to their contemporaries, Isaac (II) and Nicholas, who was a very fashionable coach painter and who led a dissolute life and died young. George Holmes (d. 1705), who was employed on the famous series of Lord Mayors' Shows of 1687–1702 and was described as 'a great master of his profession', also had two painter sons to inherit his business: Thomas of whom nothing is known, and John, who decorated the interior of St Mary Redcliffe, Bristol, and died in 1710. From the world of architecture come the examples of William Talman and his son John, who, although trained as an architect, never actually practised, but did become one of the age's most famous collectors and virtuosi, honoured even by contemporary Italians; or Sir Christopher Wren's son, who was trained in the Board of Works until he lost his job during the Palladian revolution.

Such close-knit family networks were, therefore, another factor which tended to create a specific kind of separate artistic community. Yet another binding force between artists was the fact that so many of them were commonly employed in the world of the theatre. The theatre had been restored to England with the Restoration of 1660, but it was a theatre which had been transformed by the importation from France of all the new illusionistic devices and scenic effects of the day, including elaborate scenery and costly machinery. The provision of this scenery and machinery for the baroque stage offered tolerable rewards to artists who were unable to support themselves completely by alternative commissions. In 1700, for instance, the decorative painter Robert Robinson, entered into an agreement to paint several 'sets of scenes and Machines for a new Opera' for £130. This relatively high fee perhaps explains why, at one time or another, we find so many prominent baroque artists connected with the theatre: John Freeman, 'a good history painter in the reign of King Charles II',[4] spent his later years painting scenery at Covent Garden. Isaac (I) Fuller painted scenery for a production of Dryden's *Tyrannic Love* at Drury Lane; Streeter designed all the scenery for the *Siege of Granada* which was acted at Whitehall in 1670; Thornhill's first recorded commission was for the painting of the scenery for Thomas Clayton's opera, *Arsinoe, Queen of Cyprus*, in 1705; Marco Ricci and Giovanni Pellegrini were first employed in England designing stage settings and John Vanbrugh's entire career was intimately linked with the theatre. In fact, Vanbrugh first came to public notice, not as an architect, but as the author of *The Relapse* and *The Provok'd Wife*. Then, after 1705, he became the manager and principal author of the Queen's Theatre in the Haymarket, learning from his theatrical experiences the techniques of surprise and illusion which are so characteristic of his architecture. So many artists were at work in the theatre at this time that there can be little doubt that it was another important factor creating a separate social grouping of artists.

A final factor which underlay the creation of a specific kind of artistic community lay in the nature of the formal demands of baroque art itself, which virtually required a large group of artists able to work together on one project. Close collaboration between artists working in different media is an essential element in baroque art, which, as we have seen, aimed to create a total art-form. In England a good example of what this could mean is to be found in the chapel at Chatsworth (Derbyshire). Here Laguerre and Cibber had to work closely together on their creations, for Cibber's carvings on the altarpiece are extended by Laguerre into his wall-paintings on either side. The sheer scale and monumentality of many baroque undertakings ensured that the individual artist had to be ready to delegate much of its work to trusted assistants. Thus Verrio, for instance, was always surrounded by a whole household of relatives, apprentices, co-artists and hangers-on who did the bulk of the painting work and craftsmanship in all of his commissions. When he was engaged on the decoration of Hugh May's reconstructed North Range at Windsor Castle between 1675 and 1684, his work was carried out by a veritable little army of assistants both male and female: 'Francis d'Angley, his wife, and John Baptiste and Francis their sons; Michel Tourarde, Jacob Coquet, [Gerard] Lanscroon, Bertrand au Mailhey, painters . . . René du Four, his apprentice; Robert Sernitte and his wife, grinder of colours . . . René Cousin, gilder, and Etienne Dimanche, his wife . . . John Carrée his apprentice, John Vanderstaine, stone carver . . . Lawrence Vandermulen and Anthony Verhenck, servants to Grinling Gibbons the carver.'[5] When Verrio was working for Lord Exeter at Burghley, his household – entirely maintained by Exeter – included his wife and two sons and René Cousin the gilder whom he had already employed at Windsor. The painters Alexandre Souville and Richard Feuilliet were employed to help with the figures; Ricard, a friend of Laguerre, did the architecture in the painting, and Queney Cousin was also employed.

An extension of this kind of mobile household was the studio or shop found in London. Caius Gabriel Cibber maintained such an establishment where a number of journeymen worked with and under him. In 1678 these included Salvator Musco, 'an Italian', Henry de Young, 'a Dutchman', James Berger alias Shepherd, who was presumably French, Michael Losnitz and Henrich Brochamp. Grinling Gibbons also kept a shop with a large group of assistants, both English and foreign, who were trained to reproduce models provided by the master and so to supply the constantly expanding market for Gibbons' work. Both Peter Lely and Godfrey Kneller seem to have run studios on much the same basis. The commissions they received were so numerous that they had to delegate much of the work to assistants and students. Lely's pupil-assistants included the Dutchmen, Joseph Buckshorn and Wilhelm

Wissing (1656–87), John Greenhill who 'at first was very laborious'[6] but then fell into bad company, the German, Prosper Henry Lankrink from Antwerp (1628–92) who did backgrounds, ornaments and draperies, John Baptist Gaspars (d. 1692) who 'was employed . . . to paint . . . postures, and was known by the name of Lely's Baptist',[7] and Benedetto Gennari. Kneller's practice was even more extensive than Lely's, and in order to keep up with his commissions he had to organize his studio almost as a small factory; he himself would draw the face of his sitter from life and would then transfer it to the canvas, which would be finished off by his little army of assistants who were all specialists in one area or another: in perukes, draperies, lace, landscapes or in architectural backgrounds.

The existence of such different forms of tight-knit artistic communities helps to explain a degree of isolation from the rest of society experienced by most baroque artists. None the less, other factors in the total social situation do make it possible to trace a gradual improvement in the general social status of the artist and the arts in the period of the English Baroque. Wealth is the least helpful guide, since wealth remained an uncertain gauge of a man's position in the seventeenth and early eighteenth centuries when a minor country squire with a small rent-roll saw himself as superior to the wealthiest financier. Lord Sandwich was typical of his age in declaring that he would rather 'see his daughter with a pedlar's pack upon her back so long as she married a gentleman, rather than that she should marry a citizen'.[8] Wealth could buy status in the form of land and titles, but it did not confer it.

Birth is a far more satisfactory way of determining status. Although no rigid caste system existed in the seventeenth century, there is no doubt that inequalities in social status began with a man's parents. Thus, to take the most obvious example, a man born a gentleman remained a gentleman until his death, and, as a gentleman, enjoyed an automatically privileged status in society. Equally, as a gentleman, he was socially restricted in his choice of occupation; any which involved manual work or day labour was regarded as socially demeaning and therefore unsuitable.

If, then, we wish to place the arts in some kind of social hierarchy, it is helpful to observe whether or not gentlemen felt free to practise them. Interestingly enough, given the English weakness in sculpture which even contemporaries recognized and deplored, the English native-sculptors were drawn from the manual working class; John Bushnell was the son of a plumber, Edward Pierce of a decorative painter, Nicholas Stone and William Stanton (1639–1705) of masons. It seems likely that, despite the contemporary view of sculpture as the most noble of the visual arts, in England the link between masonry and sculpture was still too strong for it to be seen as a gentleman's occupation; hence it was only artists of foreign origin who were able to break through the *cordon sanitaire* associated with this essentially manual occupation, and so mix freely with the higher levels of society.

Painting does not seem to have suffered from similar prejudices. Not only were there a number of amateur gentlemen-painters, and indeed one or two gentlewomen amateurs, but there are several instances of gentlemen entering or endeavouring to enter the profession. Robert Hooke, for instance, who came from a gentleman's family on the Isle of Wight, had been apprenticed to

Kneller as a young man, although he had to abandon the profession when he found that the smell of paint gave him headaches; John Greenhill was of 'a good family'[9] of substantial Wiltshire yeoman; Thornhill was born a gentleman of ancient Dorset stock, although his family had fallen on bad days; and his relative and pupil, Thomas Highmore, who was made free of the Painter-Stainers' Company on 6 October 1685, was also described as a gentleman.

Similarly, no prejudice existed against the career of architecture. The native English architect seems rather to have been distinguished in two ways. He was, in the first place, usually of marked intellectual attainment, which may well explain the sternly rational element in English baroque architecture. Wren, of whom Robert Hooke was to say that 'since the time of Archimedes . . . scarce ever has met in one man, in so great perfection, such a mechanical hand, and so philosophical a mind', was a professor of astronomy before he was an architect. Hooke himself was a distinguished scientist, Thomas Archer had studied at Trinity College, Oxford, and James Gibbs was reputed to have attended the Grammar School at Aberdeen and certainly did study for a brief period at the Scots College in Rome. Secondly, the English architect was drawn from the 'middling ranks' of society; Wren came from a solid gentleman's family, Hawksmoor was of Nottinghamshire yeoman stock, Archer was the younger son of a Warwickshire gentleman, Gibbs's father was a wealthy Aberdeen merchant, and Vanbrugh's fathʳr was a sugar baker.

All these men, therefore, were drawn from that distinctive social group for whom, in the seventeenth century, it was imperative that their children be launched on a profitable career. They were given a good education in the hope that this would open up career possibilities within which some kind of upward social mobility would be possible. As it happened, in the course of the seventeenth century, architecture became one such career.

The practice of literature and music remained, of course, compatible with gentlemanly status, so in the course of the seventeenth century we can say that most of the arts became possible gentlemanly pursuits. Equally, in the same century, success in the arts became a sure way by which to mount the social ladder and the successful artist, whatever his origins, could be accepted socially among the highest.

As on the continent of Europe, where Bernini numbered among his friends Queen Christina of Sweden, royalty itself condescended to treat the successful artist almost as an equal. It is clear that Inigo Jones was only able to interpret in artistic terms the deeply held beliefs of James I and Charles I because he was on terms of intimate friendship with them both, a friendship which transcended all social distinctions. A similar quality existed in the relationship of Verrio with Charles II and James II. Charles would often come to watch the painter at work, and when Verrio, as Royal Gardener, actually came to reside within St James's Park, he sometimes entertained James II and his court in his own house. Although Wren served all of the later Stuarts faithfully, his relationship with them never seems to have been quite as intimate as that enjoyed by Jones, Verrio and even Van Dyck, but it is recorded that he had 'many Opportunities of a free Conversation' with Queen Mary, 'not only on the subject of Architecture, but other Branches of *Mathematics* and *Useful Learning*'.[10]

Since the beginning of the seventeenth century, in imitation of Continental modes, the crown had contributed to formalizing the rising status of the artist by conferring the honour of knighthood on the successful. Painters were the first to be so recognized; Rubens and Van Dyck were both knighted by Charles I, Lely by Charles II, Kneller by William III in 1692 'with the additional present of a gold medal and chain, weighing 300 lb',[11] Thornhill was knighted by George I in 1720, while in 1715 Kneller became the first painter in Britain to be created a baronet. By the second half of the seventeenth century architects were also being so honoured: Roger Pratt, Wren and Vanbrugh all received knighthoods.

Given this seal of royal approval it was inevitable that successful artists should mix freely among the socially elevated. Vanbrugh was the friend and frequent guest of many of the English aristocracy, and particularly of the Dukes of Manchester and Newcastle, the Earl of Carlisle and Lord Cobham, the owner of Stowe House (Bucks.). With the Marlboroughs he was initially on such confidential terms that he was used as the go-between in the negotiations for the marriage of their granddaugher, Lady Henrietta Godolphin, with the Duke of Newcastle. Vanbrugh himself married a gentlewoman, the daughter of a Colonel Yarburgh of Snaith Hall, and when his son was born Carlisle stood godfather to him. Thomas Archer counted among his friends the Duke of Shrewsbury, Lord Bingley and the Earl of Strafford. Men of a slightly lower status themselves, like John Evelyn, were therefore more than proud to number artists among their closest friends. In the aristocratic world of London it became fashionable to visit artists in their studios; the diaries of Pepys, Hooke and Evelyn make it clear that all three became inveterate droppers-in on members of the artistic community, with which they happily associated.

Many of these friendships and social groupings were formalized in the numerous social, political and educational clubs of the age, whose very variety and number proclaim the contemporary obsession with belonging. A question of status was clearly involved; all of these clubs were exclusive rather than inclusive, their general attitude being aptly expressed in a rule of the embryonic Royal Society drawn up on 12 December 1660, 'that no person shall be admitted into this Society without scrutiny, excepting only such as are of the degree of Baron or above'. In-groups flourished in this increasingly aristocratic world, but practitioners of the baroque arts were to be found not just in the Royal Society, of which Hooke and Wren were founding fellows, of which James Gibbs subsequently became a fellow, and to which Thornhill was elected in 1728, but in the most exclusive clubs and discussion groups in the country where they mingled freely with their aristocratic patrons. Thus Verrio, for instance, was a member of the 'Honourable Order of Bedlam', a frankly convivial society founded by his patron, Lord Exeter. More interesting is Vanbrugh's membership of the most exclusive club of them all – the Kit Cat – for there is considerable evidence to suggest that it was this club which served as a creative centre of the arts in England. The Kit Cat was probably started at the time of the Glorious Revolution as a non-political dining club by the famous publisher Jacob Tonson, who became its secretary; and by 1703, when it had become the preserve of the Whig party, it included among its members Vanbrugh, Congreve, Steele, Addison and all the great

Whig magnates. It was at the Kit Cat that Vanbrugh obtained some of his most important commissions, and it was the Kit Cat, through the agency of Tonson, which provided Kneller with his most memorable commission – that of painting the portraits of all of the members, a series which now forms a major collection in the National Portrait Gallery.

Despite these developments, one handicap which stood in the way of the full integration of practitioners of the arts into society was that the arts were still largely unprofessionalized. Society, as we have seen, had no real understanding of the architect or sculptor, for example, other than as a master craftsman who had risen in the traditional guild system or as a brilliant amateur. It would appear, however, that some recognition was given to painters as professionals, a recognition which took the form of giving painters special privileges and paying them high fees. From time to time, for instance, Roman Catholic painters were specifically exempted from the application of anti-papal laws. Then we find that when painters had to be resident in country houses in order to complete a large project they were normally treated with considerable generosity. So Thornhill was to claim that 'The late Duke of Montagu paid Monsieur Rosso for his Salon £2,000, and kept an extraordinary table for him, his friends and servants, for two years, whilst the work was doing, at an expense computed at £500 per annum. . . .'[12] and that Verrio, while working at Windsor and Hampton Court, was provided not only with free lodgings but with a daily allowance of wine as well. By the time that Verrio went to work for Lord Exeter at Burghley House, he was so used to being spoiled that he demanded and obtained from his patron not only a coach and horses, expensive furniture, choice wines and brandy, but also Parmesan cheese, Mortadella, olives and caviar which had to be specially imported for him. A similar act of generosity in the face of genius was the action of Charles II on behalf of his Sergeant-Painter, Robert Streeter, for when Streeter had to be operated on for the stone, the King 'had so much kindness for him as to send for a surgeon from Paris to perform the operation'.[13]

Yet, although in such privileged treatment we can discern an underlying recognition of the claims of the history painter, at least, to a special status in society, obstacles continued to exist which prevented the extension of such ideas by analogy to other artists. No real distinction, for instance, was yet drawn between one art or another, between an art and a trade or craft, or, for that matter, between science and art. In point of fact, architecture was usually regarded as a science – a branch of applied mathematics.

In all the arts, including painting, there was an absence of professional training outside the outmoded guild and apprenticeship system, with one notable exception. That exception was music, fully integrated into the existing social structure, and with many opportunities for training which were accessible to all classes. The Chapel Royal was a goal for any musician of talent, for the choristers were drawn from cathedral schools from all over the country, and were taught the basic skills of reading, writing and arithmetic, as well as composition and how to play a variety of instruments. Private, professional music teachers were common; music formed a part of the school curriculum – Purcell wrote his *Dido and Aeneas* for performance at a girl's boarding school – and the universities awarded degrees in the subject.

The visual arts present quite a different picture. Aspiring artists were dependent either on study abroad or on entering the studio of some well-established figure, although a minority were still trained within the guild structure. Some painters attempted a species of self-education, copying drawings, paintings and prints of established painters or old masters, and occasionally such primitive methods of self-improvement were successful, even very successful in the case of Inigo Jones. Compared with France, however, with its carefully structured academies, England was very badly placed.

Why the English should have been quite so slow to imitate Continental training methods or to devise new ones of their own, it is difficult to say. The problem was diagnosed early enough and expounded by Wren in a letter to the Treasurer of Christ's Hospital in 1694, in which he remarked that

> our English artists are dull enough at Inventions but when once a foreign pattern is set, they imitate so well that commonly they exceed the original . . . this shows that our Natives want not a Genius but an education in that which is the foundation of all Mechanic Arts, a practice in designing or drawing, to which everybody in Italy, France and the Low Countries pretends to more or less. ·

Yet nothing comparable to the French academy system was introduced into England until 1711 when Kneller founded an academy of painting in his house in Great King Street, London. Here, aspiring students were able to learn to draw and paint under the supervision of a board of directors. Nor were architecture and sculpture ignored: James Gibbs was a member of the academy; Francis Bird (the sculptor), who had worked both in Flanders and in Rome, and had been engaged to complete the sculpture for St Paul's after Cibber's death, was among the first directors and provided a series of casts from which students could learn.

In many ways it was architecture which stood most in need of a new professional attitude for it had suffered most severely as a result of the inevitable separation from Continental traditions in the sixteenth century. After the break from Rome, direct contact with Italy had been replaced by a knowledge of contemporary architecture gleaned at second hand, usually from Dutch or German sources. Houses were designed by their owners within the limits of what the craftsmen they employed could build, and were then embellished with decorations lifted from prints and books. Out of this situation two types of men emerged, both types groping towards a more professional attitude and knowledge. The first type was the man who started out as the house-builder's 'tame' craftsman, what we can call the craftsman-architect. These men had all served an apprenticeship in one of the building trades, had become master craftsmen, and had then moved on to the design of buildings as a natural extension of their trade. Among such men we can number John Prince, who was a master bricklayer, and William Coleman and William Etty who were master joiners.

The major drawback to these craftsmen-architects was that although they could competently design and build a house within a fixed pattern or style, they do not seem to have been capable of original imaginative creation. Their normal method of designing was either to take a pattern from a copybook, or to imitate some building in the neighbourhood which had taken their patron's fancy. Too often the result was unsatisfactory. In the words of James Gibbs,

> Some, for want of better Helps, have unfortunately put into the hands of common workmen, the management of Buildings of considerable expense; which when finished they have had the mortification to find condemned by persons of Taste, to that degree that sometimes they have been pulled down, at least altered at a greater charge than would have procured better advice from an able Artist; or if they have stood they have remained lasting Monuments of the Ignorance or Parsimoniousness of the Owners, or (it may be) of a wrong-judged Profuseness.[14]

The second type of architect to emerge was the gentleman-amateur, a type which up to the mid-seventeenth century can safely be regarded as the norm. As late as 1660, Sir Roger Pratt still considered it was the business of every gentleman to design his own house, and well into the eighteenth century there were a number of landowners who were prepared to do so. Sir John Lowther designed his own Lowther Castle, and his friend, Daniel Finch, second Earl of Nottingham, may well have been the architect of his own distinctive and beautiful baroque mansion of Burley-on-the-Hill (Rutland). Indeed, we may see Lord Burlington as being in the same tradition of amateur-gentleman-architect. Yet, as Pratt understood, there were changing circumstances which were unfavourable to the continued existence of the amateur. Modern ideas about house design, he recognized, demanded a total concept of form and style, and not just the haphazard addition of renaissance decorative features to a basically Gothic design. Pratt also recognized that the growing custom of employing contract labour implied the existence of an architect with a very clear idea of both an end-product, and the methods by which that end-product could be achieved.

The most important of the pressures towards the development of a profession of architecture, and the provision of proper training for architects, came almost fortuitously through the growth of the government's Board of Works, under the guidance of Wren, into a veritable school of architecture. Indeed, even before Wren's day, the existence of this Board, a single body charged with the care and alteration of all royal buildings and responsible for the temporary arrangements which might be demanded by state functions, meant that there was already in existence a body of men whose job it was to plan, coordinate and manage building operations outside the traditional structure of guild labour. Such a body must have operated as a positive educative influence. It is certainly true that Hugh May, who was rewarded for his loyalty during the Interregnum by the grant of the Paymastership of the Works in 1660, although trained as a painter, blossomed into a very competent architect, as a result of his close contact with the Works.

What Wren did was to build upon this existing structure, bringing the Board of Works to a peak of perfection as an institution capable of producing and nurturing outstanding artistic talent. By the last quarter of the seventeenth century the Board of Works thus became one of the single most important forces behind artistic change in England.

The Works, which was directly responsible to the Treasury, was both bureaucratic and efficient with an extensive permanent staff. Although a hierarchy of status within the Works did exist it was a department of state which was, in many ways, much less hierarchical than was normal. It was a place in which everyone's function was carefully defined, so that occasions for friction were minimized and efficiency increased. The Surveyor-General, for instance, had duties which were largely administrative: he was responsible for organizing royal progresses and for the removals of the court from one residence to another; for supervising repairs and alterations to crown buildings, and for the handling of all the reports and accounts of the Works. In practice, much of this administrative work was delegated to local surveyors or clerks who were attached to the various royal residences, but the ultimate overall responsibility for the smooth running not only of the Board of Works but of all royal building operations, as well as for the physical surroundings of royalty, always lay with the Surveyor-General.

Yet an effective check on the activities of this omnipotent and omni-competent figure did exist in the person of the co-equal Comptroller of the Works, whose principal responsibility was to ensure the proper financial con-duct of the Works and to maintain its professional standards. An obstreperous Comptroller could make life very difficult indeed for the Surveyor-General. After the Glorious Revolution, when the Tory Wren was under a political cloud, the Whigs endeavoured to place a check on him by having their gentle-man-architect, William Talman, put into the Works as Comptroller. From the point of view of trouble-making they could hardly have made a better choice. Never an easy man to work with, for professional reasons Talman was intensely jealous of Wren, and, as his office fully entitled him to do, he used his position to make constant attacks on the competence of the workmen whom Wren employed. There was scarcely an area where Talman's arrogance and mania for interference did not lead to trouble with the Surveyor-General. Even the vital Portland stone, so necessary for the completion of St Paul's, was not sacrosanct to Talman, and in October 1699 Wren complained that he 'had given his Warrant to one Mitchell, a Quarryman there to raise 500 tons of stone . . . for the use of his Majesty's Gardens at Hampton Court, which proceedings . . . was contrary to rule and method . . . and would be very prejudicial. . . .'[15]

The other major office holders in the Works were the Clerk Engrosser, responsible for auditing the accounts, the Paymaster, who disbursed the actual cash to pay for materials, wages and other approved charges, a Purveyor who purchased materials and disposed of any surplus stocks, the Surveyor's Clerk, Comptroller's Clerk, the Measuring Surveyor, and the Clerk assistant. At a second level in the hierarchy, and directly responsible to the Surveyor-General, were the crown's Master Craftsmen, the executive officers of the royal building operations: the Master Mason, the Master Carpenter, the Master Joiner, Sergeant Plumber and Master Glazier. Like all the officers of the Works, these men were paid both a fixed salary and travelling expenses.

The lower levels of the Works hierarchy were thronged with a multitude of clerks and draughtsmen over whom Sir Christopher Wren had absolute control until 1715, and it was among these men that the Works acted most fruitfully as an educator and trainer. Wren, and his great friend and collaborator, Robert Hooke, realized that what was basically required for architects in England was training in drawing and in design, and it was this they succeeded in providing for their subordinates at the Board of Works, many of whom were 'bred up to the business of the office from childhood'.[16] This minor revolution was admirably described in a memorial from the Board of Works to the Treasury in 1717:

> Whatever the clerks may have been formerly, they are now required to be well skilled in all kinds of admeasurement, in drawing, making plans of all the palaces, and taking elevations, and completely versed in all parts of architecture . . . likewise knowing in the goodness, choice and value of all sorts of materials.[17]

It is difficult to imagine a better means of providing education for budding architects, and the clerks of the Office of Works were therefore in a position analogous to that of contemporary apprentices; poorly paid and overworked, they were yet learning a trade and so had their feet on the first rung of a ladder of upward social mobility.

One of the more successful climbers of this ladder was Nicholas Hawksmoor, whose entire career was solidly grounded in the training he received under Wren at the Board of Works. First attached to Wren as a personal clerk in 1678, he was in an essentially lowly position, and as late as 1685 he was still only earning a wage of 2s a day. But Hawksmoor continued to study and learn, using the discipline of his Works training to control his perpetual dreaming. As a result, some two years later he was beginning to be engaged on supervisory tasks as Wren handed more and more work over to him; soon after he emerged as a skilled architect in his own right, well on the way to financial success. But the process had taken him ten years – hardly a meteoric rise to fame.

So efficient was the organization which Wren, by these means, was able to build up that it was able to respond to even the most strenuous professional demands. When James II came to the throne and demanded that the Board of Works erect a full-scale baroque chapel for him at the palace of Whitehall, it was actually possible to complete the whole building between May 1685 and November 1686. During Wren's time, therefore, the Board of Works earned considerable respect and was a positive influence in determining the professional status of the architect. Throughout his long career, Wren was always acutely conscious of that status, as he was also aware that the practice of architecture was a science which required certain skills, as well as an art which demanded genius, inspiration or talents. Together the science and the art constituted the mystery of his trade, a fact which Wren never tired of impressing on his patrons.

Since so much of Wren's success in establishing a general recognition of the professional status of the architect was closely linked to the changes he affected in the organization and working of the Board of Works, it was particularly unfortunate that, as we have seen, the Palladian revolution should have been spearheaded by an attack on that office. In the series of accusations and counter-accusations between the Palladians and the dispossessed supporters of Wren which occupied the years between 1715 and 1720, it is sometimes difficult to discern the true state of affairs, but there seems little doubt that the chief effect of the Palladian influx into the Works was to make it a far less efficient and much more expensive organization which soon degenerated into total mediocrity.

All this would have mattered much less had Wren not made the Board of Works so vital a centre for training English architects. It is of course true, as we have seen, that even during the period of Wren's dominance, the Works had never been the sole cradle of talent in the country. Many so-called architects still tended to be little more than master craftsmen, or men who picked up their trade as they went along. Of all the great baroque architects, only three were professionally trained in the Works, and the greatest of them all, Sir John Vanbrugh, was a captain in the Marines when he won his astonishing commission to design Castle Howard. As late as 1699, Vanbrugh still lacked the most basic architectural skills and could hardly draw. But this was precisely the area where the professional Works-trained man came into his own as the essential provider of technical assistance rather than artistic direction. Vanbrugh, both at Castle Howard and at Blenheim, was totally dependent on the self-effacing Hawksmoor as his organizer, designer and draughtsman. In a situation where even the most brilliant amateur architect was increasingly dependent on the professional, it was regrettable that the one available source of training should have become so deeply involved in the power struggle of contemporary politics. None the less, the continued existence of even this form of professional training for the architect did in the long run help to elevate the status of both the artist and his art.

A more professional artistic attitude, however, was not in every case an unmixed blessing. Professionalism in music, for example, did have its drawbacks. During the Renaissance in England, a knowledge and enjoyment of music had been part of the equipment for life of any educated man or woman. Music was not only known but was also practised by those whom subsequent centuries would come to disparage as 'amateurs'. In 1622 Henry Peacham could still assume in his *Compleat Gentleman* that those who did not love music were 'by nature ill-disposed and of such *brutish stupidity* that scarce anything else that is good and savoureth of virtue' was 'to be found in them'. Half a century later the whole ambience which had made such an assumption possible had disappeared. From the vantage point of 1676, in his *Musick's Monument*, Thomas Mace could look back on Peacham's day with nostalgia as a time when 'we had Music most excellently choice and most eminently rare', and when music had been essentially a social activity, a binding force among friends.

By 1676 the adoption of Continental fashions in music had certainly transformed the musician into a complete professional but it had also transformed him into an entertainer. Music had become less a shared experience and more a relationship between performer and audience. As the fashion for virtuosi players and singers became more and more all-pervading the divergence between domestic and concert music became more and more complete.

However one may feel about developments of this kind, the central point remains that by the end of the Baroque Age in England a transformation had occurred in the relationship of the artist to society. The artist had become

66

more professional, better off, more independent and, if successful, admired and acclaimed by society. No doubt many of these changes would have occurred whatever artistic manner or style happened to characterize the period. But there was much about baroque art, in its demands both on the artist and his audience, that ensured that such developments should occur within the social framework of the arts.

CHAPTER V

Patrons

. . . hence the Poor are clothed the Hungry fed;
Health to himself, and to his Infants bread
The Labourer bears: What his hard heart denies,
It's charitable Vanity Supplies.
Pope

*

WRITING IN 1667, Thomas Sprat, the historian of the Royal Society, remarked on the fact that no two civilizations ever express themselves in the same way and that each new culture has a different bias and centre of interest from the one that preceded it. 'It is most usually found', he wrote, 'that every People has some study or other in their View, about which their minds are most intent and their Purses readier to open. This is sometimes a profusion in Habit and Diet sometimes *Religious Buildings*; and sometimes the *Civil Ornaments* of their Cities, and Country.'[1] Sprat went on to wonder why this should be so and, in doing so, raised what is the fundamental question for any cultural historian, and a question which underlies all the enquiries pursued in this book: what is the precise relationship between a society and its culture, and why does a particular society express itself in a particular culture?

Sprat himself found the answer to lie very largely in structures of patronage, which, he argued, had in his day determined the predominance of 'civil' over religious art. Now it is certainly true that, like every other artistic movement, the English Baroque was dependent on patronage, perhaps more dependent than any previous or subsequent art-form. And structures of patronage were indeed more elaborate and more far-reaching than they had ever been before, so much so that the English Baroque Age has also been termed 'The Age of Patronage'. Yet, having accepted this general observation that art was very dependent on the patronage structure, we need to go further, examining the nature of the patronage available to the artist in the period, and attempting to answer the kind of questions raised in Chapter I. Did the nature of patronage change during this period? What effect did patronage structures have on the arts? Why did some patrons patronize some artists as opposed to others? Why, above all, was patronage so erratic in its support for the English Baroque?

We should note, first of all, that the very expense of baroque art placed it automatically out of reach of all but the wealthiest. But seventeenth-century England seemed well able to support expensive art. This was, above all, a century of growth and of increased prosperity for the nation as a whole, although this may not have been apparent to the vast bulk of the population living at or below subsistence level. Much of the growth was centred on London, which by 1700 was sixteen times larger than Bristol, the second city in the country. Contemporaries were not slow to remark that the built-up areas of the capital could be seen to be expanding almost daily. In such a situation, one might well have expected London to become a great baroque city like Prague, Rome or Vienna. That it did not in fact become such a city may be partly attributed to the peculiar political system under which Britain was governed, and which we have already partially examined, partly to the contemporary social framework, and largely to the patterns of patronage that existed in seventeenth-century England.

In the creation of English baroque art it would seem that the most important source of patronage was that which emanated from the crown and the immediate royal circle. All the Stuarts, as we have seen, were lovers of the arts, and on the whole, the later Stuarts showed a marked preference for baroque art-forms. When the dynasty passed, so also there passed the age of the English Baroque, for, after the death of Queen Anne, court patronage virtually ceased and artists had to look elsewhere for patronage, often to sources of support which regarded baroque art with hostility.

During the Middle Ages and the Renaissance a typical form of patronage developed all over Europe, based on a royal or noble household, in which the artist became part of his patron's establishment and created works of art to order. Although less extensively practised than on the Continent, the same type of patronage was to be found in England, and almost all royal patronage was based on this household system. In the later seventeenth century, although every aspect of government was becoming rapidly bureaucratized, the English court still remained at heart an overgrown aristocratic household where there existed a whole structure of posts which had traditionally supported and encouraged the arts.

The oldest and most institutionalized part of this patronage structure was the Chapel Royal, which, with the Restoration, resumed its traditional role and as a result its pre-eminence in English music. Support for the other arts came from such traditional offices as that of Sergeant-Painter, now used less for practical services which the crown could command of the painter in question, and more as a means of rewarding men of established talent; this post was held by Robert (I) Streeter from 1663, and by his son from 1679. From 1702 until his death in 1711, Robert (II) Streeter shared the office with Thomas Highmore. By the time Thornhill succeeded to the position in 1720 it had become a virtual sinecure. In the same category of household offices we can place the posts of History Painter in Ordinary, which was given to Thornhill in 1718, of Principal Painter, held jointly by Kneller and Riley from 1688 until 1691 when Riley died and Kneller succeeded to the whole office, and of Master Sculptor. An old household office, which received a considerable increase in prestige in the later seventeenth century, was that of Royal Gardener, for the new concept of art as the recreation of the total environment, together with the examples of contemporary French and Dutch practice, meant that it was felt that this post also should be held by an artist of reputation.

The Stuart queen-consorts, who maintained separate courts and who were all lively and discriminating patrons of the arts, also exercised their patronage through a household system which served to provide support for several struggling artists, men-of-letters and musicians. But it was, above all, the

Catholic chapels of the Stuart queens which contributed to the development of the arts in England. In the reign of Charles II, both his mother, Queen Henrietta Maria, and his wife, Queen Catharine of Braganza, maintained separate establishments for the purpose of Catholic worship, and Catharine retained her own chapel as a widow. The chapel at St James's, formerly that of Henrietta Maria in the reign of Charles I, was decorated by one of her favourite artists, the Fleming, Jacob Huysmans, with an elaborate composition representing St Catherine, St Cecilia and adoring angels. The choice of St Cecilia as a subject was particularly apt, for Catharine of Braganza was musically very gifted. When she first came to England, a frightened and forlorn bride, she brought with her her own group of Portuguese musicians, but Catharine was always very advanced in her musical tastes, and, as the years passed, her affections were transferred to Italian music. She gradually introduced musicians from Italy into her chapel, which, in consequence, for long remained a resort for the fashionable London elite.

The crown and the royal family, including the royal mistresses and bastards, also exercised a personal patronage either by buying works on the open market, or by commission. In such cases the relationship developed between patron and artist was a purely temporary one. In addition to this, in the reigns of the later Stuarts there existed a grey area of patronage exercised by the crown neither through the household nor on a purely personal basis. Within this area, the interests of the monarch could be cultivated to the advantage of the community as a whole. Because Charles II was interested in the new science, for instance, in 1675 he ordered the building of the Royal Observatory at Greenwich for the use of the first Astronomer Royal. Such projects would in time become the preserve of government and the state rather than of the monarch, but in the late seventeenth century the crown's particular and personal inclinations could still have a decisive impact.

None the less, the shift whereby patronage once chiefly the personal concern of the crown was more frequently exercised by the state, and by organs created by the state, is increasingly evident in the same period. These new sources of patronage included traditional parts of the bureaucracy like the office of the Board of Works, which we have already considered in another context. They also included, increasingly so in the later part of the period, the award of governmental posts, not directly connected with the arts, but of a largely honorific nature; in 1704, through the political influence of Lord Carlisle, Vanbrugh was appointed Clarenceux King-at-Arms, an appointment scarcely less ludicrous than that of William Benson to the Surveyorship of the Works, to which Vanbrugh subsequently took such exception. Vanbrugh's fellow baroque architect, Thomas Archer, was similarly provided for with a whole series of rich sinecures, which, as we have seen, included the position of Groom Porter to Queen Anne. Another artist in the same category is the Dublin gentleman-painter, Hugh Howard, a protégé of the Earl of Pembroke and the Duke of Devonshire, who in 1714, through Devonshire's influence, was appointed Keeper and Register of the Papers and Records of State, and promptly gave up painting because he held that it was no occupation for a man of his standing.

The common characteristic of all these men is that their appointment was made by the machinery of the English state rather than by the crown. The monarch's personal preferences in the arts no longer operated. The fact was that no English monarch could imitate Louis XIV and declare 'L'Etat c'est moi', for if the experience of the Commonwealth and Protectorate had taught Englishmen nothing else, it had taught them that the continued existence of the state and the continued existence of the monarchy were separate things. Practical experience of government merely confirmed this fact. In the act of embellishing or improving his kingdom the absolutist monarch did not need to seek constitutional support, and could ride roughshod over vested interests. In England this was impossible. As was the case in so many other areas of government, state patronage of the arts had to be exercised within the limits established by the crown and its executive, in the context of a limited monarchy. Even the simplest urbanization programme in England needed parliamentary support. Acts of Parliament had to be passed 'for *clearing* and *beautifying* of Streets, for the *repairing* of *Highways*, for the *cutting* of *Rivers* . . . and many other such Public Works, to adorn the State'.[2] And because public works normally needed such parliamentary support, they became a shared responsibility, subject to all the pressures and limitations experienced in every area of government, which meant that, all too often, they did not happen at all. What the long-term effects of this situation could be becomes apparent if we examine events in the aftermath of the Great Fire of London.

In the first week of September 1666, fire swept through the City of London, consuming everything in its path. When the time for assessment of the damage came, it was found that almost the whole city had been destroyed; more than 13,000 houses lay in ashes. Coming, as it did, as a sequel to a year of plague, it was inevitable that the Great Fire of London should be seen as a disaster unparalleled in English history, and that it should be popularly regarded as a divine judgment. But not all saw it in this light. Some, at least, saw in the occasion an unprecedented opportunity to profit from the new ideas about urban planning, central to the European baroque tradition, and aimed to rebuild London as a great baroque city.

One of the chief propagandists for the new London was John Evelyn, an experienced Continental traveller, who had been much impressed by the contemporary development of cities such as Paris, where he had delighted in the uniform streets and carefully planned spaces. Ever since his return to England, Evelyn had been distressed by what he regarded as the barbarous irregularity of London's buildings, and had deplored the lack of any distinguished edifices. Only the Banqueting House at Whitehall and the Inigo Jones portal of Old St Paul's met with his approval. Like contemporary theorists on the Continent, Evelyn believed that art and cultural values found their truest expression in urbanization programmes, with the creation of the city as the desirable end-product of all total art.

Evelyn, like a few of his enlightened contemporaries, including the King and Sir Christopher Wren, therefore hoped that the new London which, like the phoenix, would rise from the ashes of the old, would be a carefully planned, regular and spacious city of a monumental character. That these hopes were vain was entirely due to the existing system of political and artistic patronage which meant there could be no one directing intelligence to impose order on the chaos of London. Even the few controls and guide-lines which the King was able to establish required three separate acts of parliament: one to establish tribunals to deal with disputes about rent payments and other obligations arising in respect of buildings destroyed in the fire; a rebuilding act which required that in future all houses should be built of bricks or stone and should be arranged in streets marked out by the City authorities; and a third act which arranged for the raising of money to pay for such part of the rebuilding as was undertaken as a governmental responsibility, parliament proving ready to vote finance for only the most essential public works.

These minor controls and directions were not exerted by the crown but rather through the machinery of the state as a whole, and governmental patronage was exercised through a royal commission. Such commissions were no novelty. They had been used by Charles I in his attempts to do something about the squalor of London, and for the purpose of repairing St Paul's. Only four years before the Great Fire a similar commission had been set up to deal with a number of problems created by the rapid growth of London, including the repair of the streets, the widening of particularly narrow ones, street lighting and general cleanliness. And while that commission was unable to proceed arbitrarily it did have the power to purchase property compulsorily.

This commission had had a membership including the King's Surveyor of Works, and the Lord Mayor and Aldermen of the City of London. The same model was followed in the 1666 commission, and for all the subsequent commissions for major public works in the period. Among the most important were those for the rebuilding of St Paul's and, after 1710, for providing new churches – fifty were proposed – for the newly settled areas of London.

Thus the main characteristic of state patronage at this period is that it was essentially group patronage. Decisions were made by a large committee of men, and, like all decisions made by a committee in any age, they frequently represented a compromise between or a fusion of differing views. On the whole, if we exclude the great aristocratic palaces, in which the English Baroque is often held to have been most vigorously expressed, the most important building projects in this period were almost all the result of similar group patronage.

The major drawback to group patronage we have already noted: a tendency towards a choice of the acceptable compromise. But it is also true that such patronage enabled individuals to recommend or encourage projects which would have been too costly for them to support on their own. As a result we can see that individual group members – often of middling income – tended to favour the same kind of art and architecture as was patronized by the court, and by prominent members of the aristocracy; that a taste for baroque art, in other words, was not restricted to the outstandingly powerful or wealthy, but permeated the entire social structure.

Of all the corporate patrons, the most discriminating were to be found in the universities of Oxford and Cambridge. This is perhaps surprising, for in the past the English universities of the late seventeenth and eighteenth centuries have not been regarded as outposts of enlightenment. Oxford, in particular, it has been pointed out, under the influence of its Chancellor, Archbishop Laud, in the reign of Charles I became the centre of the Arminian

High Church party, and well into the late eighteenth century remained a centre of reaction and obscurantism. It is true that, like Laud himself, the University was often to show itself intolerant and unreceptive to new ideas; it burnt Hobbes's *Leviathan* and expelled Locke. But Oxford was also the home of much that was unorthodox and exciting, and this characteristic showed itself particularly in its patronage of the new architecture and of new architects. Wren's first architectural commission was at Oxford, and Hawksmoor too has left his indelible imprint on the University. In any aerial photograph of Oxford it is Hawksmoor's buildings that spring first to the eye, for he was responsible for the new Queen's College, for the extensions to All Souls, for the exquisite Clarendon building, and it was also Hawksmoor who drew up the initial plans for the building of the Radcliffe Camera. And although he died a year before work on the Camera began in 1737, the project being completed by Gibbs, much of his original plan was retained with entirely beneficial results. For the Radcliffe Camera as completed in 1747 was the finest building of its age in England, and a work which can stand comparison with any of the baroque monuments of Europe. It stood and stands as a permanent reproach to the increasing orthodoxy and rule-worshipping of the Burlingtonian school.

There were several reasons why Oxford should have particularly favoured the baroque architects. Those very High Church and Tory sympathies which were the source of its reputation as a centre of reaction may have led to the adoption of baroque styles of expression, particularly after the Burlingtonian revolution had led to the equating of Palladianism and Whiggery. It is certainly significant that at the opening ceremony for the Radcliffe Camera, Dr William King, Vice-Chancellor of the University, took the opportunity to deliver a fiery pro-Jacobite speech. But there were certain other favourable circumstances; the proximity of Blenheim, a constant visiting-spot from Oxford, provided not only an essential visual training in baroque architecture and landscape, but also the craftsmen to create it. Work at Blenheim enabled William Townesend, the major mason contractor to work on college buildings between 1706 and 1714, to learn the new techniques of building and so to fulfil his Oxford contracts efficiently and smoothly. But perhaps equally important was the existence in the University of various important men who fancied themselves as connoisseurs of the arts, or as amateur architects: Dr George Clarke, Fellow of All Souls and architect of Christ Church library, William Lancaster, Provost of Queen's and Vice-Chancellor of the University from 1706–10, and Dean Henry Aldrich of Christ Church, author of an unfinished compilation of Vitruvius and Palladio, designer of Peckwater Quadrangle at Christ Church, and of the little baroque church of All Saints.

Another good example of corporate patronage is the commission by the governors of Christ's Hospital to Antonio Verrio to decorate the school hall with a vast portrait group as a commemoration of Charles II's foundation of the Royal Mathematical School in 1674. The prime mover of this scheme was Samuel Pepys, who, as a private individual, would never have been able to patronize art on this scale. We find him in a long letter to the governors, in October 1677, putting forward the idea of providing some form of commemoration of Charles II's munificence. When the governors met in December, it was Pepys who was entrusted with the task of deciding what form this commemoration should take, 'statue, inscription or painting', and it is therefore to Pepys that we owe the decision to commission a large wall-painting 'representing his Majesty and some Chief Ministers of State, The Lord Mayor, the President and some Governors, and the Children of his Majesty's Royal Foundation: a Ship, Globes, Maps, Mathematical Instruments, and such other things as may well express his Majesty's Royal Foundation and bounty to this Hospital', and to Pepys too that we owe the choice of artist.

Other group patrons of some importance were the City of London and the great London companies. After the Great Fire responsibility for rebuilding the civic buildings of the city – principally the Exchange and the halls of the city companies – devolved upon them. In these projects the commercial leaders of London seem to reveal an old-fashioned and very conservative taste, for they naturally entrusted the work to city craftsmen and principally to Edward Jarman who designed the Exchange and four halls of the wealthiest companies: Mercers', Drapers', Goldsmiths' and Fishmongers'. These buildings, it must be admitted, were far removed from the ideas of Wren, yet it is also true that the same companies and individuals who were responsible for the choice of Jarman were, in many cases, also responsible for providing the fittings for the new City churches. In every case those fittings blend so well with the fabric of the church that there is little evidence that different types of group patronage inevitably demanded different modes and styles.

The Church, itself, in previous ages often the most important patron of the arts, had little impact in England at this time, for this was an essentially Erastian age when church building was influenced by lay rather than ecclesiastical patrons. If we consider, for instance, the church of St Lawrence (Whitechurch) at Little Stanmore in Middlesex, which was designed by John James and decorated with wall-paintings by Louis Laguerre and Antonio Bellucci, it is evident that the choice of design was not made by any representative of the Church of England, but by James Brydges, first Duke of Chandos, who paid for the whole project. Even the one major Roman Catholic work of art produced in the late seventeenth century – James II's Whitehall chapel with its brilliant ornate interior – was no exception to the general rule that lay tastes should predominate over clerical ones. The chapel was the creation of James II as king and embodiment of the state, and it was built entirely to the dictates of his artistic tastes. It was James, and not the clergy of his beloved faith, who ordered Wren to build the chapel, Grinling Gibbons and Arnold Quellin to provide the statues and the carving for it, and Verrio to design the decorative oil paintings.

As far as the Anglican Church was concerned, the only major project on which its influence as a patron was felt was the later stages of the rebuilding of St Paul's. Initially, the rebuilding commissions had contained a careful balance of the ecclesiastical and the secular – of the cathedral clergy, the court and the City of London. But, as the years passed, the whole project gradually lost its attraction for the court as well as for the City, and, after 1692, although in theory the Lord Mayor of London still headed the commission, in practice he only came to those meetings where an issue between the cathedral and the City was being discussed, or where his own personal interests were involved. The wealthy City aldermen gradually ceased to sit altogether, while at the Whig court of William and Mary the project was so out of favour and neglected that the only courtier who continued to attend the commissions regularly was Sir Christopher Wren. The commission was therefore dominated by ecclesiastics whose attitude to architecture, as the new building revealed, proved to be very conservative.

One other type of group patronage may also be mentioned in connection with the St Paul's project, and that is the increasingly common practice of raising money for prestige projects of this nature by means of public subscription. Such subscriptions were normally solicited with an accompanying picture of the building concerned. It seems possible that this may have had an influence on the kind of architecture chosen by a group of fund-raising patrons, i.e. that they would endeavour to pick designs which would not offend the artistic sensibilities of those from whom they were hoping to raise money. In this context, therefore, we can talk of a large proportion of the population as being *potential* patrons with the capacity to influence the development of the arts in England.

Group patronage of the English Baroque is a relatively complex phenomenon; patronage by individuals is simpler at least in the sense that a limited stratum of society is involved: members of the English aristocracy were the only individuals wealthy enough to patronize the arts on a grand scale. The aristocracy had long been important both as patrons and as practitioners of literature, and this tradition continued to flourish in the Baroque Age; the relationship between Pope and his patron, the first Lord Bathurst, is an outstanding example. But, as a group, the English aristocracy had tended to be less discriminating and enthusiastic in their patronage of the visual arts. Nevertheless, largely as a result of the efforts of Charles I early in the seventeenth century, the situation by the second half of that century was less bleak than it once had been. During the sixty years between 1670 and 1730 men like Montagu, Exeter, Pembroke, Manchester, Shrewsbury, Bingley, Strafford, Bathurst and Oxford were to prove themselves highly sophisticated patrons, even by European standards. Combining a profound respect for genius with considerable literary, artistic and musical knowledge, they came to treat artists and men of letters almost as their social equals, and surrounded themselves with little artistic courts on the Continental model. They were missionaries on behalf of European culture and civilization and deliberate framers of English taste. Ralph, Lord Montagu and first Duke of Montagu (1705) was, for instance, quite self-conscious in his efforts to introduce French tastes into England. In pursuit of this end he persuaded Louis Chèron, a distinguished French decorative painter, to come to England in 1695 where he employed him extensively at Boughton and Ditton Park. Montagu's Bloomsbury townhouse was first built between 1674 and 1679 in his favourite French manner; when it was burnt down he rebuilt it between 1686 and 1688 in an even more Gallic style, internally as well as externally, its decoration being carried out by teams of French craftsmen under Charles de la Fosse, Jacques Rousseau, on whom Montagu settled an annual pension of £200, Jean Baptiste Monnoyer and Jacques Parmentier. At about the same time, Montagu began the building of his country house, at Boughton in Northamptonshire, which was ostentatiously French in appearance.

Montagu's cousin, John Cecil, fifth Lord Exeter, on the other hand, was completely Italianate in his tastes. He had travelled widely in Italy, where he struck up a lasting friendship with the Grand Duke of Tuscany, a friendship rooted in a shared love of the arts. Exeter's tastes were comprehensive and catholic but always completely up to date. He commissioned paintings in every Italian city he visited, and from every artist he encountered; in England he devoted his energies to the redecoration of Burghley House in the most modern style. One of Verrio's greatest patrons, it is to his munificence that we owe the Heaven room at Burghley, entirely Italianate in its inspiration, and the epitome of baroque wall-painting in England.

The Cecils, of course, had a long tradition of art patronage in their family, and Burghley House was a triumph of an earlier architectural age. A similar tradition existed in the family of the Herberts, Earls of Pembroke, who ever since the reign of Henry VIII had been famous patrons of the arts. This tradition was maintained in the seventeenth and early eighteenth centuries; the fourth Earl was a patron of both Van Dyck and of Inigo Jones who had designed the Pembroke family seat of Wilton House, although the design actually executed is probably by John Webb. The eighth Earl was a prominent patron of the Baroque, a famous collector who specialized in gems and in intaglio. A constant friend to all artists, he had taken the Irish painter, Hugh Howard, on a tour through Holland and Italy in 1696; and in 1715 or 1716 he was responsible for inviting to England Paolo Rolli, the contemporary Italian poet, whose grossly overrated reputation owed a great deal to the fact that his drama, *Alessandro*, had been set to music by Handel, but something to the fact that he had laboriously translated much of Milton's poetry into Italian. Although he was one of the Palladian prophets and, as such, scarcely falls within the scope of this book, we should note that Henry Herbert, ninth Earl of Pembroke, maintained his family tradition of artistic patronage: when only nineteen, he contributed £20 towards the building of Peckwater Quadrangle.

Why should the eighth Earl have been an ardent patron of the Baroque, and his successor an equally ardent promoter of the Palladian dream? Why, indeed, should only some of England's leading aristocrats have favoured baroque art and architecture? What factors governed their choice of artistic style? It is difficult to provide confident answers to such questions. The suggestion frequently made, from the early years of the eighteenth century until the present day, that Tory aristocrats favoured the baroque style because of its association with despotism and popery, while the Whigs favoured Palladianism as the style directly derived from the free spirit of republican Rome, may be true of the later period, once Shaftesbury's aesthetic views were widely known and accepted as a Whig orthodoxy; but such an explanation can hardly apply to the earlier period when, for instance, great Whig aristocrats were the Whig Vanbrugh's most ardent patrons. And what of the case of the first Duke of Manchester, a handsome, cultivated Whig who left England in 1685 because he could not bear to live under the rule of the papist James II, joined William of Orange, and did not return to England until after the battle of the Boyne in which he fought bravely on the side of William and Mary? No man could have had purer Whig credentials, yet this was the man who chose Vanbrugh to devise the alterations to his home at Kimbolton

Castle (Huntingdonshire) – a weird and evocative exercise in medievalism; who subsequently proved himself to be one of Alessandro Galilei's few true English friends; and who was responsible for bringing Pellegrini and Marco Antonio Ricci to England in 1708 to decorate the walls and ceilings of his new staircase. Or what of the case of Charles Talbot, Duke of Shrewsbury, the handsome charmer whom William III nicknamed the King of Hearts? No individual made a greater contribution to bringing Dutch William to England in 1688; thereafter he served twice as Secretary of State, was a prominent member of the Whig Junto of the 1690s, and was well known for his single-minded devotion to Protestant causes. Shrewsbury, who also played a prominent part in arranging for the Hanoverian succession, was a Whig through and through, yet he was also a leading patron of baroque art. He became, for instance, the patron of Thomas Archer, the baroque architect, and in April 1713 was writing to Robert Harley, Earl of Oxford, to urge Archer's claim to a post in the Board of Works and 'to acquaint you that, impartially speaking according to my skill, he is the most able and has the best genius for building of anyone we have'.[3]

Some explanation of the choice of different styles by different men clearly lies in the varying artistic experiences to which they were exposed. As we have seen, it was their French and Italian experiences respectively which made Montagu favour French and Exeter Italian-influenced art. Fortuitous circumstances played a similar role in determining Shrewsbury's tastes. Until well into middle age he showed interest neither in building nor in art collecting but found his relaxation on the hunting field. However, constant ill-health in the end drove him to Italy in search of the sun, and there he underwent what amounted to a total conversion. Within only a matter of months after his arrival in Rome he had caught 'building-fever' and had begun designing both a house for himself and a grandiose scheme for Whitehall. Although nothing came of the Whitehall scheme, Shrewsbury's project for his own house survived to materialize in Heythrop, the beautiful Roman-like *palazzo* which he built on his return from Rome to house both his collection of Italian paintings and the Italian *contessa* of uncertain origins whom he had married on his travels.

Another explanation for the choice of styles, as James Lees-Milne has pointed out,[4] probably lies in the crucial family ties which existed between major aristocratic patrons of baroque architecture. Chatsworth, for instance, was built by the first Duke of Devonshire, brother-in-law of Lord Exeter and related to the fourth Earl of Kingston, builder of Thoresby (Nottinghamshire). William Talman was architect both of Thoresby and of the early works at Chatsworth.

A second family grouping can be traced round Daniel Finch, second Earl of Nottingham, that lukewarm supporter of William III, whom Queen Mary unkindly nicknamed Don Dismallo. Like Montagu and Exeter, Nottingham had had his artistic tastes formed by travel. In 1665, at the impressionable age of eighteen, he had visited Italy and Rome at the very time that Bernini was building the great columns which surround St Peter's square. Those columns clearly haunted Nottingham's imagination, for they reappeared in the front of his spectacularly lovely house of Burley-on-the-Hill (Rutland) which he began in 1696 and of which Defoe wrote:

I say there be some that excel in this or that particular, but I do not know a house in Britain, which excels all the rest in so many particulars, or that goes so near to excelling them all in every thing.

And here was the start of another baroque grouping, for Nottingham was uncle to the wife of Lord Bingley, the builder of Bramham (Yorkshire).

Similar patterns of relationship can be traced between other baroque builders; Sir John Langham, builder of Cottesbrooke, was first cousin to the first wife of the Duke of Chandos, builder of Canons (Middlesex). Canons, which was designed by Gibbs, John James and John Price, and decorated by Thornhill, may well have had the misfortune of being Pope's model for Timon's villa,

> Where all cry out, 'What sums are thrown away!'
> So proud, so grand; of that stupendous air,
> Soft and Agreeable come never there.
> Greatness, with Timon, dwells in such a draught
> As brings all Brobdignag before your thought.
> To compass this, his building is a Town,
> His pond an Ocean, his parterre a Down:
> Who but must laugh, the Master when he sees
> A puny insect, shivering at a breeze. . . .[5]

The Duke of Montagu, as we have noted, was first cousin to Exeter and Montagu's first wife was mother to the Duchess of Somerset, whose husband, in his lavish redecoration of the chapel at Petworth (Sussex) – a house which, as a whole, is very reminiscent of Montagu's second house – proved himself one of the greatest patrons of baroque art in England. The patron of Laguerre, Closterman and of Michael Dahl, a Swedish baroque painter and serious rival of Kneller, Somerset also had close connections with the Marlborough family. Lord Leominster, whose first wife had been a close relative of Wren, and who built the baroque palace of Easton Neston (Northants.), the only country house known to have been designed by Hawksmoor and one of his most attractive designs, was subsequently married to a daughter of Thomas Osborne, first Duke of Leeds, another distinguished patron who had William Talman design and Laguerre and Thornhill decorate his country house at Kiveton (Yorkshire). The link between aristocratic patronage of the Baroque and patterns of family relationship does emerge in a most striking manner.

Patronage by the aristocracy was exercised in a variety of ways. Like the crown, many of the nobility continued to operate a traditional household system, maintaining artists for a period of years within the family circle. Other aristocrats supported men of letters or musicians by appointing them as chaplains of their households or as tutors or companions to their sons. It was in just such a capacity that many poor scholars were enabled to enjoy the pleasures of foreign travel, and sometimes of study at foreign universities. A typical household which supported men-of-letters in such ways was that of George Bubb Dodington at Eastbury, where he surrounded himself with a whole circle of young writers including James Thomson, Edward Young, Fielding, Glover and Lyttelton. Another famous literary household was that of the Duke and Duchess of Queensberry at Ham House, where Congreve, Swift, Prior, Pope, Henry Viscount Cornbury and Bolingbroke often gathered, and which became the witty centre of the opposition to Walpole. Artistic patronage was also extended out from the household to that wider circle of dependents, hangers-on and clients which surrounded every late seventeenth- and early eighteenth-century aristocrat. The custom, widespread at the beginning of the seventeenth century, of paying pensions to promising young men of letters, was continued; the third Earl of Shaftesbury had several such young men on his payroll, in addition to the young men from his estates who were educated at his expense up to university level. Men of letters or scholars were maintained through being presented to livings in an aristocrat's gift, while the same aristocrat might use his political influence to find artists or writers sinecures at court or in the government.

The commonest form of aristocratic patronage, however, was exercised either through straightforward purchase or by granting particular commissions for a specific job or work of art. Aristocratic patrons in this period were great collectors: of books, of manuscripts, of medals, coins, jewels, curios and antiquities, but, above all, of works of art. It was in the seventeenth and early eighteenth centuries that the first great picture collections in England were being formed. Many of these collections made significant contributions to the development of a taste for baroque art in England; Carlo Dolci, Guido Reni, Caravaggio and the Caracci were all eagerly sought after and were represented in all the major collections. Some of these works of art collectors purchased for themselves on trips aboard, but most commonly they were dependent on agents who bought for them, usually on a commission basis. If one was buying works of art in this way, the most satisfactory kind of agent to have was a man who was a practising artist himself, for, in an age in which there was no means of authenticating pictures, and copies, forgeries and imitations were only too common, the patron was totally dependent on the expertise of the man buying for him.

So far only members of the English aristocracy have been considered as individual patrons of the arts. And undoubtedly aristocrats composed the great majority of such patrons. There was, however, another small group of men who were just as lavish in their patronage: *parvenus*, self-made men who had made good, either in trade, or through the civil service or through the profits of war, and who were anxious to demonstrate that they could employ their wealth to create a luxurious environment to rival that of their social superiors. Some of these men, therefore, must be counted as prominent and important patrons of the English Baroque. In the City of London, for instance, there were men like Sir Robert Clayton, Sheriff in 1671–72, who built himself a vast new town-house, with a dining room panelled in the highly fashionable and very expensive cedarwood, and with interior decorations by Streeter; or Sir James Bateman, Lord Mayor of London, 1716–17, who had Thornhill decorate the staircase of his house in Soho Square; or Robert Hooke's most consistent patrons, the City Aldermen, for whom he designed so many town and country houses, and to whose collective interest he no doubt owed commissions for Bedlam Hospital, Merchant Taylors' Hall and part of the Royal College of Physicians.

Typical of the successful career civil servant was William Blathwayt, who eventually rose to be Secretary at War for William III, an office in which there were famous opportunities for profit. Blathwayt used the wealth he acquired in the King's service to build his house at Dyrham Park (Gloucestershire), where, after 1698, he was wealthy enough to employ William Talman. And as a type of the man who made his fortune from war we can instance Admiral George Delaval, who in 1717 purchased his property at Seaton in Northumberland from an impoverished elder branch of his family, and immediately got Vanbrugh to design him a baroque palace to build there. The result – Seaton Delaval – is one of the most splendid of English baroque houses and is regarded by many as Vanbrugh's real masterpiece.

These men, like the English aristocracy whom they were consciously imitating, patronized the whole spectrum of the arts, but easily the commonest form of artistic expenditure in the seventeenth century, and the one practised furthest down the social spectrum, if we discount the purchase of books, sheet music, concert and theatre tickets, was that involved in the commissioning of portraits. Portraiture was the real craze of seventeenth-century England, and its most characteristic art-form. From the very beginning of the century the market for portraits began to expand, beginning in London, but gradually spreading through the whole country. By the end of the century, the demand was so great that portrait painters began to establish themselves in the large provincial towns – York, Oxford and Bristol – where they could make a very good living indeed from their art. So great was the vogue for portraits that in the reign of Charles II William Aglionby attributed the dearth of English history painters to the popularity of 'face-painting'. Certainly portraiture did provide the bread and butter of even the most distinguished painters resident in England. In the first half of the seventeenth century, for instance, Van Dyck, despite the cost of his paintings, managed to build up the largest portrait practice that had ever been known in England. All the principal nobility were painted by him; Sir Kenelm Digby's Lady posed as *Prudence*, the Duchess of Richmond as *Venus*, and the Duke of Hamilton's son as *Love*. So many were painted that we know the faces of the Caroline court better than those of any previous reign. By the 1640s Peter Lely had become nearly as popular as Van Dyck. Throughout the Civil War and the Interregnum the demand for Lely's work continued, and after the Restoration, which brought a whole host of new patrons back to Britain, a positive torrent of paintings began to flow from his studio, making Lely into one of the best known and most characteristic of English painters. Lely, and Kneller after him, turned their portrait painting into little industries, and their characteristic baroque style became known throughout the length and breadth of the country, even among those who knew little else of contemporary cultural shifts and changes. Thus Kneller's style, so beloved of the Churchills and of Queen Anne, his sitters always seen from below as if they existed on some more elevated plane than that occupied by the rest of mankind, symbolizes and dominates the age of the English Baroque, successfully capturing on canvas a whole generation as it wanted to be remembered.

Here, surely, is the major reason why people chose to patronize baroque art; it provided the kind of image of themselves, of their power and influence, that they wished to convey to 'outsiders'. It created, in fact, their 'image'. And the crucial point is that, as the seventeenth century went on, economic prosperity and stability made it increasingly possible for members of the upper level of society to be aware of their 'image' as individuals. For the upper classes as a whole there had been a general increase in standards of comfort, and an improvement in their surroundings. The changes were most obvious at the simplest level in furnishings and furniture of all kinds. Tables were now made with leaves, and chairs and tables began to be covered with velvet or stamped leather, edged, characteristically, with a shaggy fringe. Bedrooms began to contain much more than the traditional four-poster bed and chest: a full-length couch and a mirror, a silver ewer and a basin, often a dressing table, which might now be fitted with drawers and on which stood a toilet box. In the dining room, too, there was to be found a new display of opulence. A man's status had always been partially measured by the kind of table he kept, but in the past what had mattered was the quantity of the viands and the variety of courses offered. Now display had come to include a lavish array of table silver, including the newly introduced and highly civilizing fork. Walls were no longer generally left bare but were decorated with wainscoting, pictures, tapestry or statuary.

In such a world of increasing luxury, people were almost forced to take stock of their surroundings and, essentially, become aware of the environment which they were creating for themselves, no longer for the purpose of defence or of simple shelter against the elements, but as a place to live and divert themselves in. In this situation contemporary cultural and social pressures ensured that they became patrons of the arts, for people rapidly began to judge a man's status by the kind of style in which he chose to live. Once it had been generally recognized that status was epitomized by trappings and surroundings, fashion in patronage of the arts inevitably began to play its part, as the wealthy hastened to keep up with their fellows. One of the truly remarkable features of the late seventeenth and early eighteenth century, for instance, is the speed with which people, of whatever political complexion, rushed to imitate fashions introduced by the court. This speed caught the imagination of Defoe who described the dramatic impact which Queen Mary had on interior decor in England: 'The Queen brought in the Custom or Humour as I may call it of furnishing Houses with China-Ware . . . piling their China upon the tops of Cabinets, Scritoires and every Chimney-Piece, to the Tops of the Ceilings' – a practice which the English have followed ever since.

A similar desire to imitate the successful and to follow the latest fashion played a large part in any decision to employ one artist rather than another for any particular project. But all kinds of other variables might enter into the question: the availability of the artist, his reputation, the knowledge, gener-osity, meanness or simple pig-headedness of the patron, the artist's own manoeuvring. Some patrons, as we have seen, were sufficiently discriminating and knowledgable to know what they wanted and to go out and get it. But others had to rely on paying the highest prices to the artists of the greatest reputation and even then, as often as not, they subsequently complained of the price. Many consulted artists or architects of great stature. Wren was con-stantly being applied to on this basis; it was on his recommendation that

Lord Leominster commissioned Hawksmoor to design Easton Neston house. Vanbrugh was another recipient of such demands for advice; in 1718 Admiral George Delaval wrote to his brother:

> I intend to persuade Sir John Vanbrugh to see Seaton if possible and to give me a plan of the house, or to alter the old one, which he is most excellent at; and if he cannot come he'll recommend a man at York, who understands these matters.

As for the artist, he was not merely a passive recipient of tempting offers but very often a seeker-out of commissions. Begging letters are a common and distressing feature of the age and had been developed almost into a new art-form by the beginning of the eighteenth century. Kinship could be important in getting an artist a start in the world, as is evident in the case of Wren and the commission he was given in 1663 by his uncle to design a chapel for Pembroke College, Cambridge. One patron might breed others; because Mary Beale's chief patron was Archbishop Tillotson many of the leading clergy chose to sit to her and she seems to have become something of an expert in the portrayal of the dignified Anglican clergyman. A chance meeting between Kneller when he first came to England and Mr Vernon, the Duke of Monmouth's secretary, led directly to royal patronage for, through Vernon, Monmouth came to know of Kneller's work and

> The Duke was so charmed that he engaged the King his father, to sit to Kneller, at a time when the Duke of York had been promised the King's picture by Lely. [Charles II], unwilling to have double trouble, proposed that both the artists should draw him at the same time. Lely as an established master chose the light he liked: the Stranger was to draw the picture as he could, and performed with such facility and expedition, that his piece was in a manner finished when Lely's was only dead-coloured.[6]

Political connections could also be used to obtain commissions and, indeed, tended to become more important than other types of connection in the early eighteenth century; the whole structure of eighteenth-century influence might be galvanized into action on behalf of the artist. It was often not enough to have the ear of only one man; Sebastiano Ricci lost the commission to redecorate the Prince of Wales's bedchamber at Hampton Court, which the Lord Chamberlain, Shrewsbury, had promised to obtain for him, because the Lord Treasurer, Halifax, flatly refused to release funds for the project if he was appointed. Social encounters could also be important to the artist if he moved in the right circle. Vanbrugh, here, is the supreme example of the importance of the right contacts, for he never allowed any opportunity to pass which might provide him with employment, and even the contract for Blenheim, the great triumph of his career and England's greatest national monument, he claimed was a direct result of a purely chance encounter with Marlborough at the theatre.

CHAPTER VI

Patronage

Painters, poets and builders have very high flights but must be kept down.
Sarah, Duchess of Marlborough

*

IN THE PREVIOUS CHAPTER the elaborate system of patronage which supported English baroque art has been described. But the profounder question of the consequences for that art of the particular kinds of patronage which sustained it remains to be explored. The central issue is this: to what extent can it be shown that the history of baroque art in England, the development of English taste towards an appreciation of the baroque sensibility, even the shapes and forms of the art itself, were in any way directly affected by the structure of patronage within which English baroque art existed?

In this as in so many connections the crucial example is that of the Stuart court. As we have seen, if there was an English baroque art it largely coincided with the reigns of the later Stuarts who appreciated baroque forms even when they could least afford to patronize them. Even more than before the Inter-regnum, the post-Restoration court became the centre of the social life of the nation and affected the changing fashions of the age very directly. What the court patronized tended to flourish. Household china was not the only artifact affected by the accession of William and Mary. The insistence of their up-to-date Dutch courtiers on replacing mullion windows with double sashes to keep out the English cold, and on the modernization of the old Tudor fire-places in the royal palaces, led to a rash of similar changes in town and country houses throughout England. Even the members of the House of Commons petitioned for double sashes to be installed in their chamber to the contempt of Wren who seems to have regarded such comforts as totally unnecessary. It was only with the accession of George I that the court lost the position Charles I had gained for it as the national arbiter of good taste; after 1714 the centres of fashion moved elsewhere, so that by 1760 the English court could be seen as a cultural backwater and the epitome of dullness and dowdiness.

In the English Baroque Age, however, the role which the court could play in encouraging or discouraging particular arts, art styles or artists remained vital. Consider, for example, the fate of English church music under the later Stuarts. Charles II, who married a personal delight in music to a strong con-viction that good church music enhanced his kingly dignity, was determined to have music of a high standard and magnificence performed in his royal chapels. In consequence, he gave continuous encouragement to his musicians, and the services in the Chapel Royal were the resort of all the fashionable world. In Charles's reign, therefore, church music flourished. But his brother was a practising Roman Catholic, with his own establishment of largely foreign musicians, and therefore had no interest in the Anglican Chapel Royal. The neglect begun in James II's reign continued in that of William and Mary, leading to an irretrievable decline in English church music, a neglect whose effect can be measured by the fact that all but ten of Purcell's anthems were written before 1688.

Patronage, then, clearly had a determining effect on the art of church music. The fact that it happens to be an art that suffered under the later Stuarts does not affect the basic point. In general the Stuart court continued to act as an important educator in the arts, just as it had done in the early seventeenth century. As far as the visual arts were concerned, James II's taste for the Baroque was almost boringly correct and in his Catholic chapel he showed his English subjects what Counter-Reformation art at its greatest could achieve. It is true that William III showed little interest in the arts except in so far as they were able to enhance his political and military prestige; but his wife was passionately interested and 'there were few Arts or Sciences, in which *her Majesty* had not only an elegant Taste, but a Knowledge much superior to any of her Sex, in that, or (it may be) any former Age.'[1]

After Mary's death, William continued to patronize the arts for love of her and completed their joint foundation of the Royal Hospital at Greenwich which 'as a public building of monumental character . . . was to become England's most integrated baroque achievement',[2] and one of the major influences on the next generation of architects.

There can be no doubting the immense importance of royal patronage for baroque art. Nor can the consequences of that patronage be circumscribed in any way. But some of the problems involved in the patronage system are perhaps less clearly revealed in the royal example than in others. Artists, for example, often complained about the general boorishness and ignorance of those who paid them. When, in 1693, Henry Playford dedicated the second volume of his *Harmonia Sacra* to Dean Henry Aldrich of Christ Church, he complained that

> Men are usually so far from Suiting the Subject of their Treatises to the Qualifications of the Person they Apply to, that we may shortly expect to see Music dedicated to the Deaf, as well as *Poetry* to Aldermen, and *Prayer-Books* to Atheists.

Playford went on to explain how fortunate he was in his own patron, but recognized how rare such fortune was. Obviously, Playford exaggerates a little in pursuit of a compliment but he was not completely mistaken. There were inevitably some totally unsuitable patrons of the arts, and the more fashionable the arts became, so the rarer it was that an artist found a patron of real discernment. And whereas the interference of a patron who spoke with knowledge and understanding was reasonable, that of a patron, like the Duchess of Marlborough, who did not, was positively irksome.

The lack of such knowledge and understanding was all the more important in that in certain areas the artist could be at a complete loss without specific instructions from a patron. This was particularly true of decorative wall-painting. No painter working in England in this field was competent to create his own designs *in toto*, with the possible exception of Thornhill. For the contemporary fashion for allegorical and mythological wall-compositions of great erudition required above all a first-class classical education, such as every

English gentleman or aristocrat, but few painters, had been privileged to enjoy. A patron, therefore, either had to design the programme for his wall-paintings or else get someone else to do it for the artist. And so, for example, when Laguerre was decorating Sir John Bridgeman's house at Castle Bromwich, with themes taken from Ovid's *Metamorphoses*, it was not Laguerre, but a relative of Bridgeman's who actually invented the design, and cheerfully changed it even after the work had begun.

In such a context the artist was largely the executive officer of another's ideas. This could often produce extraordinary situations, so that we find, for instance, the devout Catholic artist, Benedetto Gennari, painting a complex allegory depicting William III triumphing over Catholicism, immediately after his work on the Catholic chapel of James II. Yet in such cases it is difficult to see that artistic genius suffered. Rather it seems as if the varying demands put on artists by their patrons often stimulated them into new experiments or techniques. Tension between the patron and the artist seems to have occurred rarely in this area. Both worked together in almost intimate relationship so that the work of art can really be seen as their joint production.

More interesting, from our present point of view, are the instances where the very success of the artist in terms of patronage, in one area, may have prevented him from exploring others, as was probably the case with the great baroque portrait painters working in England. Such a possibility was always a problem inherent in the kind of relationships established by household patronage. Robert Streeter, for instance, despite the versatility and universal genius for which contemporaries acclaimed him, between 1660 and 1667 was largely employed by Charles II in painting the royal coaches and sedan chairs and in carrying out routine repairs at Whitehall and Greenwich. A similar case is that of Francesco Fanelli, who, during his stay in England in the early seventeenth century, largely confined himself to turning out small-scale bronze horses and portraits, simply because that was what his patron and host, the Duke of Newcastle, wanted him to do. In this case one could well argue that the patron not only had a debilitating effect on the artist, but on the whole course of the development of sculpture in England. For had Fanelli had the opportunity to explore more substantial and monumental work, as his talents enabled him to do, he could have provided that Continental model for subsequent native sculptors to imitate which was so clearly lacking in seventeenth-century England.

There may well have been other Fanellis, for few artists were left to get on with a job of work alone, and the majority of patrons showed an obsessive interest in the progress of any work they had commissioned. In this area architects were the most sinned against. Their patrons always seem to have been determined to assert their dominant role in the relationship by constantly insisting on minor alterations, so that the pages of Robert Hooke's *Diary* are full of entries like the following:

July 19th 1675. At Bloomsbury with Mr Montacue. He ordered stables bigger two foot. . . .
July 30th 1675. Drew Sir R. Edgcumb's House showed it him and his Lady. They liked it but to have it a little altered.[3]

'They liked it but to have it a little altered' might well describe the major patrons of English baroque architecture. The most difficult were those who pretended to a little architectural knowledge themselves, like William Blathwayt, who, as a self-made man and amateur architect, was the worst kind of task-master. His first architect, Samuel Hauduroy, a Frenchman who is only known from his work at Dyrham Park (Gloucestershire), complained that in the winter of 1692–93 Blathwayt forced him to get up two hours before dawn and draw plans until two o'clock the following morning, work for which he was paid no more than 10 guineas. Blathwayt's attitude to artists and workmen whom he employed, expressed in 1701, was that 'These people want stirring up soundly and not to be overfed with money.' Poor Wren was a particular sufferer in that royal patrons were not immune to this particular disease; much of his work was done for a succession of monarchs who had pretensions to a knowledge of architecture. If we are to believe the testimony of the *Parentalia*, Wren's work at Hampton Court was seriously hampered both by the perpetual interference of Queen Mary, who 'pleased herself from time to time in examining the Drawings, Contrivances, and whole Progress of the *Works* and to give thereon her own Judgment, which was exquisite',[4] and of William III, who, when the building was widely criticized, had to defend Wren in public 'for not raising the Cloisters under the Apartments, higher; which were executed in that Manner' by express royal command.[5]

An artist who suffered from a difficult or interfering patron had little real choice but to endure the situation. The only artists for whom commissions were so plentiful that they could afford to ignore the wishes of patrons or potential patrons were the very successful portrait artists. Rather than change his working habits and attend the judges in their chambers in order to paint them, Lely let the valuable commission for the portraits for the Guildhall go to Michael Wright, and Kneller's arrogance, even in relation to his patrons, was proverbial. Some artists, however, did at least attempt to cope with difficult patrons by embarking on what may be called a process of educating the patron. There exists, for instance, an interesting letter of 1704, addressed by the decorative painter Isaac Bayley, a specialist in the fashionable art of painting imitation marble and wood graining, to his patron, Thomas Foley, MP for Hereford and Strafford. Foley, who was having the interior of his house redecorated by Thornhill, had attempted to choose a pattern for the panelling in his hall directly from Bayley. But Bayley himself was in sufficient sympathy with baroque decorative ideals to recognize that his own work must be related to what Thornhill intended and tactfully suggested that

> I think it will be best to advise with Mr Thornhill in that point for I may not only put you to more charge but do damage to Mr Thornhill's work for to paint very beautiful colours will take the eye off from his painting which is principal.[6]

Wren and Hawksmoor, also, seem to have regarded it as a self-imposed task to educate their patrons in better taste. Thus we find Wren dealing with consummate and very necessary tact with Bishop Fell of Oxford, who, having commissioned Wren in 1681 to design the completion of Tom Tower, Christ Church, suddenly decided, after the work had already been started, that he would like the design to incorporate an Observatory. With pardonable weariness, Wren confessed that he would 'be glad You should proceed upon the first thoughts', for to make the Tower into an Observatory would mean a change of the whole design,

> for the Loft of the Bell above the ringing loft must be higher considerably and with large Windows and still doubt the Bell will be somewhat low to be well heard: then the Octagonal Tower must be flat on the Top. . . . these things Considered it will necessarily fall short of the beauty of the other way, for having begun in the Gothic manner we must conclude above with flats and such proportions as will not be well reconcilable to the Gothic Manner.

No doubt exercising considerable restraint, Wren remarked that this 'proposition had been much better effected had not the parts formerly built diverted us from beginning after the better forms of Architecture, and I fear we shall make an unhandsome medley this way'. Then he came to his final and most telling point, 'that such a room as this will be when built, is no way necessary for Observations as now they are managed. . . .'[7] By the exercise of such tactful means a former Oxford professor of astronomy and a practising architect got his own way with a very difficult patron.

Some artists, however, were unable to exercise constant restraint, and attempted to resist interference on the part of their patrons, but such an attitude caused considerable strain within the patron/artist relationship. Distinguished artists were naturally more prone to dislike interference. Vanbrugh, for instance, bitterly resented any attempt by the Marlboroughs to dictate to him over the building of Blenheim. They might want Woodstock Manor pulled down, because to them it was an eyesore. Vanbrugh, on the other hand, saw it as an integral part of his overall plan for the Blenheim estate. So when the Marlboroughs went abroad on their self-imposed exile, leaving instructions for Woodstock's demolition, their architect chose instead to profit from their absence, to use some of the money destined for Blenheim to restore and improve the Manor, and to live in it, rent-free, himself. Then we might take the case of Verrio and the governors of Christ's Hospital, for this was another relationship which suffered from high-handedness on both sides. The commemoration project for Charles II,[8] planned in 1681 and initiated in 1684, had still not been completed by 1687, although Verrio had already demanded and been promised a double fee for replacing the portrait of Charles by one of James II, and had also been paid two-thirds of his original fee. The exasperated governors were driven to writing to the artist to warn him that 'if he does not forthwith finish the picture . . . they must be compelled to complain to *His Majesty* of his ill usage.'[9]

Beside the question of the length of time which it had taken to fulfil a contract, at the heart of this dispute between patron and artist lay the question of hard cash. In England there was never a case of an artist being over-rewarded for a work of art. English patrons drove a hard bargain and were totally unaware of the kind of fees which genius could command on the Continent. Agents for patrons, trying to buy pictures in Europe, found it difficult to convince the men they were working for that it just was not possible to pick up an 'old master' at a bargain price, or that it was a bad investment to do what so many English patrons insisted on doing – i.e. to purchase a copy of a work by an established painter rather than to expend money on original work. Painters working in England had similar experiences. Even Van Dyck eventually priced himself out of the English market; in 1640 his sketches for a series of paintings representing the Order of the Garter, which had been intended for the walls of Inigo Jones's Banqueting House, were returned to him by the King, with a hint that his charges were becoming exorbitant. Van Dyck had to leave England in order to realize the fees which he felt his genius could command. Other artists were to tell the same tale and usually it was they who had a just sense of their market value rather than the patron. English patrons wanted a bargain before they wanted great art. So Sarah, Duchess of Marlborough, was scandalized by the fee which Thornhill proposed charging for decorating the Hall ceiling at Blenheim and told him 'that I was very sure that there never was a piece of painting of the size of that in the Hall even of Rubens or the greatest master that cost so much as this had done at the time they were painted, though they were of more value when they were dead.'[10] Yet Sarah was completely wrong in her estimate; Thornhill charged the Marlboroughs £987 for the Blenheim Hall ceiling, while Rubens, as we have seen, had been paid £3,000 for the Banqueting House ceiling.

If time and money could create friction between patron and painter, how multiplied were the opportunities for disagreement between a patron and an architect. Every patron expected to be given an accurate estimate both of the length of time required to complete a building and of its ultimate cost. These the architect would dutifully provide, but, however honest he was, it was virtually impossible for him to take into account all the many imponderable factors which might affect the cost of his project.

He was, for instance, always at the mercy of the elements. In the winter, all building operations had to come to a halt, and a long drawn-out winter could seriously delay a project, just as an early frost could destroy valuable building materials. Work held over from the autumn to the following spring could not always be protected, and it might be found to be cracked or warped, so that it had to be done over again. The price of imported materials, or even those brought by sea from other parts of Britain, might be seriously affected in time of war. The supply of labour was likewise subject to wide fluctuations, and for difficulties of this kind an architect rarely could make allowances, while his patron always expected him to do so.

Although so extravagant in her behaviour as to be scarcely typical, Sarah, Duchess of Marlborough, exemplifies in her relations with the numerous artists and craftsmen who tried to please her all that could go wrong in the artist/patron relationship. Armed with a deep-seated conviction that she knew better than even the most distinguished artist, and neurotically opposed to the expenditure of money on the arts, she was the average artist's nightmare patron. There was scarcely an artist employed by her, not excepting Wren, with all his reserves of tact, who did not leave her employment in disgrace. When, for instance, John Closterman had finally managed to complete a family portrait of the Duke and Duchess with their children, Marlborough remarked with considerable feeling that 'It has given me more trouble to reconcile my wife and you than to fight a battle,'[11] though what occasioned the disputes on this occasion is not known. When Marlborough was not there to exercise a restraining influence on his volatile wife the results were disastrous. Certainly, as far as Blenheim was concerned, Sarah's influence was positively pernicious. She was not possessed of the kind of baroque imagination which could grasp what Vanbrugh was about; so from the beginning she objected to the scale of the project, and to what she called 'the madness of the whole Design'.[12] To Vanbrugh her interference was deeply exasperating for it affected every detail of his beloved building. Even at its earliest stage she was blithely transferring all the skilled masons to work on the garden walls, telling them that the Duke wanted the gardens finished, and that as all the walls would one day have to meet it could make no difference where they began. Doubtless a breach between patron and architect would have happened even at this early stage had it not been for the Duke of Marlborough who both understood and approved of what Vanbrugh was about. He constantly occupied himself, first trying to shield Vanbrugh from Sarah's venom, wrath and prejudices, and then in placating his wife with a series of notes like one of 1705 in which he wrote that he had been advised 'by everybody to have the Portico, so that I have writ to Vanbrugh to have it; and which I hope you will like for I should be glad we were always of one mind, which shall always be endeavoured for I am never so happy as when I think you are kind.' But by 1709, despite a moment of self-revelation in which Sarah admitted to Vanbrugh that

> though you have vexed me extremely, in forcing me to things against my Inclinations; yet I shall always think myself obliged to you . . . because I know, that what I did not like as well as what I did approve of, you intended for the best, and though it is said that in this world there is no perfection, you are not the only Architect that thinks 'tis impossible they can err; I believe it is the opinion of all that Science. . . .[13]

the Duchess was in full cry after the architect. Her complaints now centred on four particulars: the elaboration and expensiveness of the kitchen court, the prodigious scale of the building, the preservation of the Old Manor of Woodstock, and above all else Vanbrugh's great bridge which was designed to span the valley of the river Glyme. Wren had unfortunately suggested a more modest means of approach to Blenheim, but Vanbrugh with, it must be admitted, the full support of the Duke of Marlborough, was determined on a monument reminiscent of a Roman conqueror, and suited to the scale of his great palace. From the beginning that bridge which she described as 'a prodigious expense to no manner of purpose' ate into Sarah's heart. Subsequently she described it in a bitterly sarcastic letter to Mrs Clayton as having thirty-three rooms disposed in 'four houses at each corner . . . but that which makes it so much prettier than London bridge, is that you may sit in six rooms and look out at a window into the high arch while the coaches are driving over your head', and, of course, in the end her obstruction was, from her point of view, successful. The bridge was never completed to Vanbrugh's design, and ended up as an altogether more modest affair.

No relationship could have been more unsatisfactory than this one between a patroness who confessed that she 'mortally' hated 'all Grandeur and Architecture', and whose ideal was 'a clean, sweet house and garden, though ever so small', and her designer and architect with his powerful baroque imagination. Only an eternal optimist could have declared, as the Duke of Marlborough did when writing to his wife about their architect, 'I believe you and he could make the best house in the world if you could agree to work together.'[14]

A total breach in these early years was probably only prevented by the self-imposed exile of the Marlboroughs in 1712 and 1713, and nearly occurred on their return when they discovered that, far from pulling down Woodstock Manor as he had been instructed, their architect had been living in it while he made hay in the grounds and fished in the river. It is probable that only Vanbrugh's powerful friends in the Kit Cat Club saved him from dismissal at this point. By 1716 when Marlborough was already too ill to take any part in the negotiations Sarah was even more irritated and determined, as she put it, 'to prevent if I can having a great estate thrown away in levelling of hills, filling up precipices, and making bridges in the air for no reason that I or anybody else can see but to have it said hereafter that Sir John Vanbrugh did that thing which was never done before'.[15] ' 'Tis time', she wrote, 'to put a stop to such madness', and she finally goaded Vanbrugh into resigning from his dearest project in November 1716. Well might that architect subsequently refer to her Grace as 'that BB: BB: Old B. the Duchess of Marlborough'.

Difficulties then were always inherent in the relationship between patron and artist, difficulties which, in the case of a Duchess of Marlborough, could be multiplied over and over again; but can one say that the patron ever affected the form or style as opposed to the content of the work of art? In literature it seems that we may be able to. Certainly Dryden complained of the tyranny of the theatre audience, whose taste was so inferior that 'a true poet often misses of applause because he cannot debase himself to write so ill as to please his audience.'[16] As for himself, Dryden confessed that he had 'given too much to the people',[17] that he was 'ashamed for them as well as for myself, that I have pleased them at so cheap a rate',[18] and that, 'I never writ anything for myself but "Anthony and Cleopatra". '[19] As far as architecture is concerned, the answer must also be in the affirmative for even an architect as distinguished as Wren found some of his best instincts to be in conflict with the whims of his patrons. The whole history of the rebuilding of St Paul's is littered with stylistic compromises between Wren and the various committees for whom he worked.

However, the effect which a particular pattern of patronage could have on style is most marked in the victory of the Palladians over the baroque artists and architects. That Palladianism was largely the product of the fancy of patrons seems now to be obvious. It was from them that the impetus towards classicism came, as poor Nicholas Hawksmoor, who was destined to see his finest baroque plans being constantly modified in the direction of more simplicity, was to find. As a single example, one might choose his plans for King's College, Cambridge, and his arguments with the Provost, Dr John Adams. By 1713, when he was designing the new building, Hawksmoor had already become totally imbued with the baroque spirit of the Continent, seeing the work of art as a total experience involving the whole environment. So it was inevitable that having been asked to design one work of art – the completion of King's College – he should have gone further and made his designs within the context of a complete replanning of the city of Cambridge, based on the kind of urbanization which Fontana had undertaken for Sixtus V at Rome. But Hawksmoor seems to have realized that these plans, like those he made for a similar remodelling of Oxford, would have to remain within the realm of the imagination. What he does not seem to have anticipated is that even his project for the completion of King's would be considered too grandiose and would be whittled away by Adams in the direction of classicism.

Hawksmoor was but one victim of a contemporary shift in the artistic demands which patrons were beginning to make upon artists. Humility before genius, as we have seen, had never been a marked characteristic of English patrons, and increasing education in the fine arts brought greater self-confidence with a determination to get what the patron wanted from the artist, rather than to get from the artist what he wanted to offer. And what the new generation of patrons increasingly demanded was not baroque art and architecture. Thornhill was to be the last of the great decorative wall-painters, for by his day patrons were ceasing to be interested in baroque history painting on the grand scale. Painting was coming to play a smaller and smaller part in the decoration of houses, being used only over chimney-pieces or in super-portes, as in contemporary France.

In an earlier generation, as we have seen, aristocratic patrons, Whig and Tory alike, had often been enthusiastic patrons of the Baroque. But for the Whigs, the developing influence of Shaftesbury's philosophy and aesthetics, with their emphasis on ideals of harmony, symmetry and proportion, soon had its effect, creating a new generation of Palladian patrons, typified by Lord Burlington. This generation, led by Pembroke and Leicester, as well as by Burlington, all avowed disciples of Palladio, saw in baroque art nothing but the grossest vulgarity. Such men were the new, true-blue, Hanoverian Whigs, men who, as we have seen, believed that they had found in the style of the Italian Palladio a paradoxically *English* style. And these men – the real powers in the land – represented the future, so that all who wished to prove their political orthodoxy rushed to imitate their building projects, with the results which Pope had prophesied:

> Yet shall (my Lord) your just, your noble rules
> Fill half the land with Imitating Fools;
> Who random drawings from your sheets shall take,
> And of one beauty many blunders make;
> Load some vain Church with old Theatric state,
> Turn Arcs of Triumph to a Garden gate;
> Reverse your Ornaments, and hang them all
> On some patched dog-hole eked with ends of wall;
> Then clap four slices of Pilaster on't,
> That, laced with bits of rustic, makes a Front.
> Shall call the winds through long arcades to roar,
> Proud to catch cold at a Venetian door;
> Conscious they act a true Palladian part,
> And, if they starve, they starve by rules of art.[20]

After the Burlington revolution, the artist who wanted material success, or to make a name for himself, had to create what his patrons demanded – the purely, almost frigidly, classical, where no inappropriate column, no lapse from the rules of 'good taste', could either offend or inspire. For, although some work remained for the baroque-trained or baroque-inspired, it was, on the whole, work of little importance. Only the Tories, the Jacobites, the Stuart sympathizers, showed a touching affection for the old ways and favoured the Wren-style country house. James Gibbs was fortunate to find among the Tories continuing steadfast supporters of his work, and Ditchley Park in Oxfordshire, which he designed for the High-Tory second Earl of Lichfield, is the most magnificent example of his work and a brilliant example of late baroque architecture in England, as his memorial to John Holles, Duke of Newcastle, erected by Newcastle's Tory daughter, Lady Harley, in Westminster Abbey in the 1720s, is one of the most thoroughly baroque works of monumental sculpture in England. Yet, for all his importance as an architect, even James Gibbs was forced, at the end of his career, to modify his natural taste for the Baroque in the direction of neo-classicism in order to meet the new demands of patrons. Patronage had created but patronage had now broken the English Baroque.

CHAPTER VII

The Makers of the English Baroque

Si monumentum requiris, circumspice

*

BAROQUE CIVILIZATION was everywhere as much a culture of artisans as of great artists, for baroque art was always cooperative art. Even an artist as important as Bernini was totally dependent on the ability of his craftsmen to carry out designs for which he would often do no more than provide a tentative sketch – a method which we find the Roman-trained James Gibbs employed in England half a century later. The true genesis of baroque art, therefore, was the rediscovery by a few prominent individuals of a basic truth that had been well known in the Middle Ages: any artisan could be trained to carry out techniques successfully within a fixed style.

It was, however, precisely within the area of training that the artists of the English Baroque were faced with their greatest problem. The magnitude of their task can best be understood by considering how late the Renaissance came to England and how limited was its impact even then. For, as the Baroque was a natural development out of the renaissance tradition, the passage to the new style would have been immeasurably eased if a large body of craftsmen and artists, trained in that tradition, had existed. But Torrigiani's tomb of Henry VII is really the first physical evidence of the influence of Italian renaissance art in England, and although thereafter the impact of Italian craftsmen continued to be manifest in English architecture until the 1530s, their traditions had not really taken root when the break from Rome interrupted direct communication with Italy. The breach with Catholic Europe, and with Italy in particular, could not have occurred at a more unfortunate time from the point of view of English style and developing English taste, for it occurred when English craftsmen and builders had learnt how to ornament and decorate in the Italian manner, but had not yet absorbed that fundamental characteristic of Italian architecture and design which blended disparate elements together through harmony into a balanced and ordered whole. The English had not yet learnt the rules against which baroque art was a studied revolt. A bizarre consequence of this situation can be seen at Burford Priory chapel in Oxfordshire which was dedicated in 1662 by the Bishop of Oxford and was clearly the work of a local mason, whose confused mind is reflected in his mongrel style, part Gothic and part classical.

Nor was this unknown mason unique. Even as late as the mid-seventeenth century what the majority of English craftsmen were trained to produce and to decorate was basically Gothic art and architecture. Dependent on local practices and, as far as masonry was concerned, on oral transmission, this tradition was still so strong that, although the portal of St Mary the Virgin in Oxford –

93

which with its barley-sugar columns and standing figure of the Virgin in an ornate pediment is the most unqualified piece of baroque architecture which has survived in England – was built in 1637 by Nicholas Stone, three years later the vestibule and staircase at Christ Church could be erected by native craftsmen in a pure Gothic tradition. Some fifty years later, when Wren and Hawksmoor found it necessary to explain the principles of Gothic architecture to doubtful patrons, they had no difficulty at all in finding craftsmen to build it. And if there were no masons trained in the new styles, there was a similar dearth of native decorative painters, gilders, sculptors, woodcarvers and iron-workers, with the result that imaginative artists were constantly frustrated by their inability to get plans executed to the standards they required.

In the course of the seventeenth century, relentless pressure by enlightened men like Wren – whether architects, artists or patrons – did in the end produce the required changes in style as well as the very high standards of craftsman-ship they demanded. English woodcarving, for instance, was transformed by Grinling Gibbons. Previously such carving had been of importance in interiors, and had been extensively used by Inigo Jones, but it always remained provincial and stiff. Gibbons, however, had been trained in Holland, where the typically baroque aim of woodcarvers was to translate a basically unsympathetic medium into something of great naturalistic grace and beauty. In England, Gibbons was subsequently to train all his assistants in a similar style while his rivals like Jonathan Maine and Edward Pierce were forced to learn from his example if they wished to remain in business.

Time, however, was of the essence in such a process of retraining. Wren, as we shall see, was very successful in teaching his masons new building methods, although he often had to find them out himself by a process of trial and error, and a few brilliant individuals, like Gibbons, could create a revolu-tion in certain crafts. Essentially, however, since a taste for baroque art pre-ceded the native capacity to create it, in the decorative arts England was for a time dependent on foreign craftsmen. Thus in the reign of Charles II, England shared with contemporary Europe a passion for the formal baroque garden, with its parterres, ornamental pools, fountains, architectural cascades like those which Thomas Archer was subsequently to create at Chatsworth, and long avenues of trees – representing the mastery of the disorderliness of Nature by the symmetry of geometry – which was introduced into England at Windsor, Bushey Park, Badminton, Wimpole Park and Stowe. In the early days, this passion for baroque gardens could only be met by Continental experts who had the necessary knowledge of hydraulics, and several French gardeners – de Caux, André Mollett, Huet, Grillet and Beaumont – had to be brought over to England to create them.

Decorative wall-painting was another area in which foreign influence came to predominate, and plasterwork, so prominent and important a feature of baroque interiors, was traditionally the preserve of foreigners and particularly the Italians, who normally worked together in small groups. During the English Baroque Age the most important of these *stuccatori* were Giovanni Bagutti and Giuseppe Artari, who were employed at Canons, and who often worked for James Gibbs. For him they executed what is possibly their finest piece of work: the ceiling of the Cambridge Senate House.

The dominance of such foreign craftsmen inevitably led to a belief that one got quality by buying foreign. As a result, even when a native tradition did exist in a particular art or craft, as in decorative wall-painting – Streeter's Sheldonian ceiling was the first example of baroque illusionistic decorative painting in England – that tradition could be swamped by professional baroque artists from the Continent. The limitations of such foreign artists were revealed in their lack of understanding of the English environment. In the 1670s and 1680s, for example, Verrio established a pattern for decorative painters in treating a large expanse of wall. This, for the next half-century, became the standard for the decoration of staircases and rooms of state; between 1672 and 1702 at least fifty staircases were treated in the Verrio manner. Typically the principal figures were framed by a painted proscenium whose columns supported a false parapet or, sometimes, an open dome surrounding the ceiling which was then decorated as the sky. It is a manner which is entirely typical of the full baroque treatment to be found in contemporary Europe. But decorative painting on this scale is not only more difficult to complete in England, where relatively long winters leave little time in the year when the work can be done, but is also less effective than in Italy, where the light is always so much stronger. Such an example suggests that the English Baroque would not have achieved as much as it did had it not been for the development of native traditions of craftsmanship.

The retraining of native English workmen tended to develop from the offices of English architects largely because architecture, with its concern for art as a total form, was the inevitable pacemaker of baroque art. Thus, an architect did not just design a house, but created an entire environment, and the more baroque the architect the more he included in his total design. Vanbrugh's houses did not merely stand on their own merits, but on their overall settings which many have felt display Vanbrugh's genius to the fullest. 'No architect', Reynolds was to say of him, 'took greater care that [his buildings] did not abruptly start out of the ground without expectation or preparation.' Archer spent as much time designing garden furniture as he did on more conventional architectural projects, and the most interesting section of Gibbs's *Book of Architecture* is that which is devoted to similar projects.

Because the architect was concerned with the totality of his work of art, he regarded each of the component parts as being as important as the whole. He was, therefore, intimately concerned with the minutest details of his buildings and had to be sure that all designs would blend into and work towards his overall conception. So it is that, although we may recognize Grinling Gibbons, Jean Tijou and Caius Cibber as great artists in their own right, we also acknowledge that in the decoration of St Paul's Cathedral this creativity was kept subordinate to the vision of Wren, the real creator. All their designs were worked out in consultation with the architect, and frequently at his direction. The same was true of all the baroque architects after Wren. Gibbs, for instance, frequently included in his contracts a statement that he retained overall responsibility for all the details of design in a building.

The relationships developed in such a situation are essential models for an understanding of the Baroque Age in England, for it is in such relationships that the essential dynamic of baroque art existed. The final work of art was the result of a continuing dialogue between artist and artist, or artist and artisan; in that dialogue all parties had an equal right to speak, so that the artisan could be as much involved in the creative process as the artist. Often the craftsman was left a great deal of latitude; he could make his own designs for work to fill in whole areas for which the architect might provide only a general specification. How fortunate then that this was still an age of flexibility in crafts, when the limits between various trades were not rigidly defined, and the stonemason, for instance, could also be a stonecarver, or the plain painter take over areas of decorative painting. Perhaps no career is, in this context, more typical than that of Edward Pierce (*c*.1635–95). Pierce, who was the son of a painter, worked happily as a baroque sculptor, as a mason and, occasionally, as an independent architect. A frequent colleague of Wren he was employed in the rebuilding of many of the City churches, and his work was especially important at St Lawrence Jewry and St Clement Danes; but he also produced many portrait busts including the outstanding baroque bust of Wren which reveals the great architect in all his genius. Such a situation and such conditions had the effect of producing those high standards of craftsmanship which are the hallmark of the Baroque Age in England, and which have never been surpassed. By contrast, the Palladian Age which followed, when art was fenced round by rules and rote, was one in which standards declined and the craftsman became once more a passive rather than an active participant in the artistic process.

Buildings in the baroque period, therefore, were continuously created by their architects. It was not the moment of design but the process of building which made them. The resultant standards which the architects set themselves demanded constant attention and supervision. Two kinds of project can be helpfully distinguished – the really large, and the medium to small. On a medium-size project an architect did the bulk of organization and supervision himself. Either by himself, or with his patron, he drew up the contracts for workmen. Thereafter he would try to visit the site very frequently in order to keep a constant watch on standards of workmanship. William Talman went even further and normally resided on the works where he directed them entirely himself. The architect would also organize the purchase of materials and keep his eye open for any seasonable bargains which might save a patron money.

In some smaller projects, however, the architect would do no more than provide building plans for a patron who would then hand over the work to a trusted master craftsman. This was particularly true of a country builder who yet wanted the prestige which was involved in employing a London architect like Wren or Gibbs.

But normally when we think of baroque building in England, we are thinking not of buildings of this type but of vast projects, like the building of royal or private palaces, or the rebuilding of St Paul's. The organization of buildings such as these created a whole series of little industries throughout the country, employed vast workforces, and swallowed up great masses of materials from many different sources. Over two hundred men were employed at any one time on the building of Castle Howard, while the creation of Blenheim was not just a matter of building the palace, but also involved the building of the controversial bridge and the causeways, the landscaping of the 2,000-acre park, including the transplanting of full-grown trees to create the long walks and the avenues, and the laying out and planting of the gardens. At any time more than a thousand workmen were employed on the works in one capacity or another, and the creation of this as of all similar projects demanded a highly sophisticated organization.

The most vigilant daily control was essential. Robert Hooke found that if he left his master craftsmen unsupervised for too long they became 'careless and neglectful',[1] and Vanbrugh described how during the building of Blenheim he would 'haunt the Building like a Ghost from the Time when the workmen leave off at six o'clock, till it is quite dark'.[2] In providing this control the most important person was the architect, or his assistant surveyor. If the architect did not do so, the assistant surveyor selected the site, staked out the foundations and supervised the workforce. Once the work was in progress either he or the architect oversaw all measuring work, made up the books, and was generally responsible for seeing that the work went along smoothly and to the required standard, 'not taking a bare care of the goodness of the materials only, but also of the right seasoning, true and due employing and working them'.[3] To assist him with the paperwork the assistant surveyor often had a comptroller, a clerk of the works, who was paid a day-rate which averaged out at the same rate as that of a skilled craftsman, and a paymaster.

The workforce itself could be found in various ways. In London there was normally no problem except in the immediate aftermath of the Great Fire, when there was an important but entirely exceptional shortage of craftsmen, but in the country it was always difficult. At Burley-on-the-Hill, for instance, the Earl of Nottingham initially had considerable trouble in finding labourers and in 1696 he wrote to his father-in-law that although he was well provided with master craftsmen, 'my great want is of freemasons to work and prepare the stone. . . . Mr Sharp of Clipsham can't, as he says, procure men, which makes me trouble your Lordship with this to entreat your favour in recommending this work, to the Weldon men. . . .'[4] Because of the kind of problem faced by Nottingham, workmen had to be brought to projects from long distances and this tended to create social problems. Separated from their families, the men were often worried and anxious and a natural prey for agitators. Nor was it always very easy to find sufficient numbers of lodgings for the men close by the works.

On a small project, or one like Burley-on-the-Hill where patron and architect were the same man, the workforce tended to be found by the patron, but on the larger projects it was the professionals who undertook the search for good workmen, and the patron played little part. Thus Vanbrugh described how he found the workforce for Blenheim:

> I sent to great Variety of Workmen of the same Trade (in different Countreys, and quite unacquainted with one another) for their Proposals. And when by that means I had at last brought the Prices to be moderate Instead of throwing so great a Work into the hands of a few Undertakers, I divided it against many, three, four, or five of each Trade, with different Rates according to the performance expected from them.[5]

Wren, too, normally selected his own workmen.

For a major building workmen were engaged, as we gather from Vanbrugh, through a contractor whose suitability was determined by two factors: solid financial backing and sheer skill. The seventeenth century was notable in England for the emergence of a new kind of entrepreneur – the great mason-contractors, many of whom came into their own after the Great Fire of London; Joshua Marshall, the Strongs, the Wises and the Kempsters were the most important. Marshall, who was Charles II's Master Mason, was important as a linking figure with a former great age of building, since his father, who had been a notable sculptor and stone worker, had worked with Inigo Jones. By the time Joshua inherited the family business in Fetter Lane it was already established as a resort for the fashionable, for in Marshall's yards were to be seen examples of the new marble mantelpieces, of Italian-style portrait busts, and other novelties. A notable mason and employer, Joshua Marshall established a vast business in the 1660s and 1670s, and was employed by Wren on St Paul's, Temple Bar, the Monument, the Custom House, the pedestal for Charles I's monument at Charing Cross and the reconstruction at Windsor Castle. When he died in 1678, he was engaged in contracts worth tens of thousands of pounds and was a great loss to Wren, who never really found a satisfactory replacement.

Some of the great mason-contractors were also quarry owners. Thomas and Edward Strong, for instance, whose father had worked in the 1630s under Nicholas Stone, a colleague of Inigo Jones at Cornbury, possessed a valuable quarry at Taynton in Oxfordshire, whose stone was used in the building of Blenheim. Like so many master craftsmen, the Strongs first came to London after the Great Fire and established their fortune by acquiring a building site close to St Paul's wharf. Here they set up as stone merchants, selling stone from their own quarries which they had floated down the Thames on barges. Christopher Kempster also owned a number of large stone-pits near Burford, Oxfordshire, from which stone was being sent to London after 1668. It was the possession of these valuable quarries, and the constant demand for good stone, which enabled the mason-contractors to build up the capital they needed in order to carry the heavy debts they were owed by those who employed them as masons. For the scale of these debts, even in an age when the court set the tone by never paying for anything until it had to, was truly remarkable. By 1711, the Strongs alone were owed £9,000 for work already completed at Blenheim, and by 1718, when they finally went to court to recover their money, with the addition of interest, this sum had risen to over £12,500.

Important as the possession of capital was, however, it was equalled by the importance of skill and adaptability. A whole new generation of workmen, as we have seen, had to be taught new styles in building, which, although using traditional tools, involved new kinds of stonecutting. The responsibility for getting the right kind of response to the new demands had to lie with the architect, but his starting point was the contractor. Presumably architects normally followed the practice of Wren and Hooke, who, when they wanted anything new from their workmen, would first ask their contractors to construct a model from the architect's design and under his careful directions. This model could then be used to instruct the journeymen who were rarely literate enough to be able to follow a design on paper. Since the contractor and his craftsmen retained possession of these models afterwards, they could be used to pass on the new styles to other workmen.

A further premium was put on the skill – as well as the honesty – of the contractor by the decline in the traditional guild structure, which, in the Middle Ages, had provided some guarantee of good workmanship. The guilds did not, of course, collapse overnight with the coming of the 'early modern world', and, as far as the building trade was concerned in London, the guild structure survived more or less intact until 1666. Master craftsmen from the provinces who wanted to set up on their own in London were only allowed to do so after they had become freemen of the City and members of a guild. To do so they were still expected to serve a seven-year apprenticeship in London, pay their guild fees, and undertake to submit to its rules. This entire elaborate structure broke down in the building crisis brought about by the disaster of the Great Fire of London, for to get the City rebuilt all the rules and regulations had to be relaxed. Henceforth provincial craftsmen were allowed to work in London, although, after seven years, they were supposed to apply for the status and privilege of City freemen.

With the collapse of the guild system which had tried to prevent bad workmanship, architects became even more dependent on the good faith of a contractor for ensuring that honest work was done. As a result a reliable contractor was worth his weight in gold. Wren found such a man in Christopher Kempster whom he described in 1681 as 'a very able man, modest, honest and treatable . . . very careful to work true to his design and does strong well bonded work'.[6]

As an architect relied on his contractor, so a patron relied on his architect. A patron's only protection was his contracts which did increasingly try to provide against shoddy or dishonest workmanship, and these contracts were made on the advice of the architect. Normally each contract was made between the patron and the craftsman, and the patron made himself responsible for the payment of his workmen, but William Talman preferred to engage and pay his own artisans directly, and the patron was left out of the relationship. Several different kinds of contract were common. The first was the daywork or week-work contract under which the contractor would engage to provide a certain number of men on a particular job in return for a fixed allowance for each man for each day or week's work. This allowance obviously varied but averaged out at about 3s a day for the master himself, 1s to 2s 6d for each of his craftsmen, and 10d to 1s 6d for an unskilled labourer. Out of these sums it was then up to the contractor to squeeze whatever profits he could. Clearly under such a system 'the workmen have a great advantage over you, if they be not very honest men',[7] for, as Sir Roger Pratt pointed out, 'if workmen be employed by the day, they will make small haste to finish the building.'[8] This kind of contract, therefore could only usefully be employed for workmen whose activities were unrelated to the actual progress of the building: nightwatchmen, sawyers employed in cutting up timber, or the joiners who supplied masons with templates or patterns to work mouldings by, and even so it became common to appoint an overseer over dayworkmen to see 'that they do not loiter nor misspend their time'.[9]

An alternative form of contract was that for taskwork. This could be of three main types. The employer might, first, contract for a specific piece and type of work at a pre-agreed price. Such a contract was primarily useful in the case of fittings or ornament, particularly if the contract contained a penalty time-clause. The second type of contract, 'by valuation', mentioned no specific price but the contracting parties agreed that the finished work would be valued by an expert and paid for accordingly. Clearly, this type of contract was open to abuse and was only really suitable for particularly skilled work such as woodcarving, decorative painting or wrought iron work. By far the most common kind of contract, therefore, and the one recommended by the experts, was for work to be done 'by measure'. Here the employer agreed to pay for a specified portion of work at a fixed rate per rod or unit. Since the contractor was completely free to employ whatever workmen he thought necessary to carry out the work, and to pay them what he thought fit, it is clear that with this kind of contract it was to his advantage to get the work done as quickly as possible.

From the employer's point of view, however, work done 'by measure' did have two disadvantages. As Evelyn found out to his embarrassment during a visit to the Duke of Norfolk in 1671, it could lead to endless altercation about precise measurements. On this occasion the altercation in question lasted five hours. The more serious disadvantage was the very real risk of bad workmanship, and many contracts accordingly contained penalty clauses to guard against such an eventuality. Clarendon's contract with Streeter in 1667, for instance, provided for the reimbursement of half the fee if Streeter's white paint turned yellow, and the majority of the St Paul's contracts had penalty clauses.[10]

But however carefully worded, a contract was no substitute for good personal relations between the employer, or his architect, and the contractor. It is clear that the new styles of building, and their exploration by architect and workmen together, did lead to highly fruitful relationships. The architects trained in the Board of Works seem to have been particularly successful in creating the necessary spirit of cooperation, for Wren, Hawksmoor and Talman were famous for their ability to create good teams of workmen. Wren, for instance, worked continuously with the Strongs on the rebuilding of St Paul's, which is thus almost as much their creation as the architect's. It was Thomas Strong who laid the foundation stone of the cathedral in 1675, Edward Strong, the elder, whom Wren chose for the most difficult masonry work after 1675, and Edward Strong, the younger, who, together with Wren's son, Christopher, placed the last stone on the lanthorn of the dome in 1707. With other craftsmen Wren's relationships were just as permanent; the master plasterer Henry Doogood and his friend, John Grove, were particular favourites, and either one or both of them were employed in nearly every building which Wren undertook. Hawksmoor, while working with Vanbrugh at Blenheim, trained Henry Joynes, their resident Comptroller and Conductor of the Building, in his work methods, and subsequently used him as his assistant in his building of the exquisite Clarendon building at Oxford. With William Townesend, one of a large family of Oxford masons who worked both at Blenheim and at King's Weston under Vanbrugh, Hawksmoor developed an especially close relationship. William Talman was also notable for creating successful working teams built around Benjamin Jackson, who is known to have been in charge of the masonry, under Talman's supervision, at Chatsworth, Dyrham and Drayton House (Northamptonshire); and James Gibbs always made a point of employing the same workmen on all his major projects.

Difficulties, however, could arise. No architect ever had complete control over the choice of workmen for a project. Apart from the odd case, like Christ's Hospital, which employed its own workmen on a regular basis anyway, architects were always subject to a whole range of social and political pressures. Thus Wren, if he wanted the continued support of the City of London for the St Paul's project, could not afford to ignore recommendations which were made on behalf of workmen by the city fathers. Equally he was unable to ignore representations made by the cathedral clergy. Difficulties between departments brought other problems. When Talman, who was supervising the building of the new lodgings at Hampton Court, wanted to dismiss an incompetent locksmith, 'not brought up to that trade . . . an ignorant fellow',[11] and to replace him with a man recommended by Lord Ranelagh, he was rapped sharply over the knuckles and told not to encroach on the territory of the Lord Chamberlain's office. As the whole apparatus of political influence developed, so the freedom of an architect to get the best man for the job became increasingly circumscribed, for no architect wanted to offend a patron and patrons themselves were under pressure to find jobs for the politically and socially worthy. The full impact of a patronage system of such great complexity broke over the final stage of the rebuilding of St Paul's with the 'Frauds and Abuses' controversy which eventually led to Wren's voluntary retirement from the Rebuilding Commission. This controversy appears to have begun when the Whig-associated Richard Jones appeared before the commission, which had at this time a Whig bias. Jones proposed the erection of a cast iron fence around St Paul's churchyard and provided an estimate of the cost, 'though it was not for himself, but for Mr Gott who had Ironworks in *Sussex*'.[12] Wren objected to Jones's proposal on three grounds: first, that he did not want the fence, secondly, that if there had to be a fence he did not want Jones to get the contract for it, and thirdly, that if a fence there had to be, it should be made of wrought and not cast iron. There was nothing unreasonable in these objections, for the whole basis of Wren's success at St Paul's had been his putting all contracts out to tender, and then making a careful decision which balanced the advantages of cheapness against the dangers of bad workmanship. To give a contract to the first man who offered an estimate was to undo the work of a lifetime, but Wren was overruled and on 20 September 1710, £1,000 was ordered to be paid out to Richard Jones on account of a fence which Wren had never wanted. Thereafter he ceased to attend the meetings of the Rebuilding Commission.

Despite such setbacks and problems, under the tutelage of a group of architects who had largely learnt their trade in England, there developed in the second half of the seventeenth century a whole school of masons, builders, plumbers, carpenters and other craftsmen, whose skill equalled that of their fellows in Europe and may even have surpassed it. The Italian architect, Alessandro Galilei, who was able to judge these matters with an unbiased and professional eye, wrote of English workmen in 1719 that 'they are all excellent, skilled in their craft and work very hard and speedily.'[13]

Nevertheless it would be doing less than justice to England's baroque architects if one failed to point out that, as far as labour relations were concerned, few projects ran completely smoothly. Even Wren had serious problems with his contractors. Operating as they did in a sellers' market, where their skills and money were essential to carrying a project through to the end, and acting only too often as the purveyors of vital building materials as well, the contractors had a solid sense of their own worth. As far as the rebuilding of St Paul's was concerned, Edward Pierce was complaining in 1689 that the prices offered by Wren were so low 'that he is the loser thereby',[14] and he was not the last complainant. Throughout the rest of the rebuilding, contractor after contractor appeared before the commission to demand higher rates of pay. Some even had to be sacked because it was felt they were becoming too exorbitant in their demands, but they were never easy to replace and the progress of the work inevitably suffered.

Yet Wren's problems were minor compared with the labour problems which Vanbrugh faced at Blenheim, where disputes of one kind or another were virtually a daily occurrence. The carters, whose job it was to get the vital supplies to the builders, were often at the centre of the difficulties, but from time to time there was trouble with all the journeymen, accentuated by the fact that the flow of money from the Treasury was always so erratic. By 1706 Vanbrugh was already complaining of labour troubles because of want of money, and by 1710 the debt incurred on pay owed to the workmen was mounting at the rate of £500 a week. In October of the same year, when it was rumoured that no further supplies of government money could be expected, the Duchess of Marlborough stopped the works. The result was predictable; an army of unpaid workmen, thrown suddenly out of work, resorted to the rioting which was their only resource. A night of serious disturbances was followed by more trouble which was only brought to an end when the Treasury Paymaster at Blenheim, Samuel Travers, put his hand into his own pocket and paid out £500 to succour 'the poorer and most distressed labourers'.

The situation of those labourers might well have been very bad indeed. Unemployment and underemployment were common in a trade where all work was halted with the onset of winter, and in which even the highly skilled man earned little enough. The hours laboured were long and, unlike many contemporary occupations, subject to rigid time-keeping. The work was always hazardous for a chance fall or an error in judgment could lead to death, injury or serious maiming. In such circumstances those who laboured on official projects were the luckiest, for they, at least, might look for some relief in the event of disaster, albeit relief which was given as charity to the deserving rather than as a right. At St Paul's collections for the benefit of the workmen were regularly taken from visitors to the upper part of the cathedral, and the accounts of the commissioners contain several references to specific instances of charitable relief; 40s in 1686 went to a woman whose husband had been killed by a fall,[15] in 1692 £10 was paid out to a man who had been employed in the works for upwards of twenty-three years and who had been 'hurt by a great stone falling on him';[16] in 1701 the commissioners were concerned to find some means of providing permanent relief for the family of a man killed on the works; in 1704 £5 was granted to a poor widow 'for her present subsistence',[17] and in 1717 £3 was given 'to a poor Boy, belonging to the Plasterers of the Church, who fell a very great way from the Cupola, and was very much hurt thereby'.[18] In addition, regular pensions appear to have been paid to all the old and disabled who had been employed at St Paul's for any length of time.

Such labourers were almost certainly a lucky minority, and few can have managed to make any provision for old age out of their current income. Even when he was in work, an unskilled labourer in London was paid only between 1s 8d and 2s 3d a day, a paver 2s 6d, a plasterer or joiner 2s 6d to 3s, bricklayers, carpenters and plumbers between 2s 6d and 3s.[19] These 1691 London rates, which in themselves go some way towards explaining the widespread pilfering which bedevilled every building project, were nevertheless certainly considerably higher than those paid elsewhere in the country, and probably twice as high. The high London rates can be partially explained on the grounds that, as we have noted, the building industry was booming in London in the late seventeenth century, but it is also true that craftsmen from the capital were reputed to be more skilled than their counterparts in the country. No doubt the truth of this varied from area to area, and there existed in York, for instance, a very skilled school of masons and joiners, but it is probably the case that the average London workman was more familiar with new techniques and styles and that it was from London that new methods were spread gradually to the rest of the country.

There is some support for this view in the fact that although Hawksmoor complained that London workmen were 'so far from skill or honesty, that the general part of them are more brutal and stupid than in the remotest part of Britain',[20] architects in general always preferred to use London craftsmen. Sometimes they were able to insist on a London workforce, but patrons were normally too concerned to save money to be prepared to pay full London rates. Their preference always tended to local craftsmen although, as Wren pointed out, this could be a false economy since 'Country men are not altogether so handy in plain work, and in good work scarce to be trusted till they are well practised.' It was in defiance of Vanbrugh and Hawksmoor's wishes that the Earl of Carlisle insisted on employing as his principal masons at Castle Howard, William Smith, Manger Smith and John Elsworth of York, and had his stonecarving done by another local man, Samuel Carpenter. Vanbrugh was presumably happier with the choice of William Etty, a member of a famous York building firm, whom he had previously employed as his deputy at Seaton Delaval, and who was made clerk of the works and general overseer at Castle Howard in 1721, for Etty was a man of great competence, who subsequently emerged as an architect in his own right.

Sometimes, as at Dyrham Park during the first stage of the building up to 1698, a compromise was arrived at: the standard and basic work was done by local craftsmen, but the decorative detail was entrusted to specialists with a national reputation. Thus, at Dyrham, John Harvey of Bath was employed to carve the central balcony enrichments and the urns for the balustrade; the plaster ceilings, although relatively simple, were executed by Thomas Porter of London; the marble fireplaces were from the workshop of Thomas Humphries of Bath, and the woodwork in the important Balcony Room was carved by another Londoner, Robert Barker, who subsequently executed a fine Corinthian screen at University College, Oxford. A similar pattern was followed by Nottingham in the building of Burley-on-the-Hill; the major part of his workforce was local, except for one or two expert craftsmen and finishers – painters, glaziers, plasterers, etc. – who were all London men of established reputation. It seems probable, therefore, that the vast majority of baroque country houses in England were the achievement of a fusion of local and London talent.

In this situation, we might note, upward social mobility became possible for the London master craftsman. Patrons who were anxious to give a certain style to a country building would look for Londoners of an established reputation, and place them in supervisory positions in their own works. So we find the London Alderman, Sir John Moore, who endowed a free school for boys at Appleby in Leicestershire, employing Thomas Woodstock, one of the Master Carpenters at St Paul's, 'to direct all things necessary concerning the School and all concerns belonging to it . . . both for brick, timber and stone'. Similarly, during the rebuilding and redecorating of Petworth House, which was proceeding from 1688 onwards, Samuel Fulkes, one of Wren's master masons, was employed as resident supervisor of the works, and the surveyor, John Scarborough, had also been on Wren's staff.

Yet even between master craftsmen, like those who built houses, and the artists who decorated them, there existed a very great disparity in the rewards offered and the status achieved. When we remember the fees of hundreds of pounds which painters of the standing of Verrio and Thornhill could command to decorate these baroque houses, it becomes apparent that the makers of the English Baroque, while they may have shared common artistic aspirations, parted the wealth that went into its creation in no spirit of fair shares for all.

CHAPTER VIII

World Views

All things are artificial for nature is the art of God.
Sir Thomas Browne

In the centre of the court, under the blue Italian sky, and with the hundred windows of the vast palace gazing down upon it from four sides, appears a fountain. It brims over from one stone basin to another, or gushes from a naiad's urn, or spurts its many little jets from the mouths of nameless monsters, which were merely grotesque and artificial when Bernini, or whoever was their unnatural father, first produced them; but now the patches of moss, the tufts of grass, the trailing maidenhair, and all sorts of verdant weeds that thrive in the cracks and crevices of moist marble, tell us that Nature takes the fountain back into her great heart, and cherishes it as kindly as if it were a woodland spring.
Nathaniel Hawthorne, *The Marble Faun*

*

AS A THINKING AND FEELING MAN the artist in any period inherits the same structures of consciousness as the rest of his society. The thoughts and feelings of even the greatest artistic genius, rather than being wholly individual and original, have their origins in a consciousness which the artist shares with the members of the group which nurtured him, and in this sense, if in no other, the individual work of art is necessarily the product of a group consciousness or culture. But this in no way means that the artist is merely to be identified with the society or group which produces him. Art is not to be seen as no more than an expression of the integrated consciousness of the period in which it was created, for art does not merely reflect society. It orders experience; it imposes some kind of pattern on the constant flux of reality; it is a search for meaning, a way of making sense of things. And this is so no matter how much the manner of its ordering, its patterning, it searching – the styles and forms of art – may change and develop as different kinds of sense are demanded and sought for. Rather than reflecting the group consciousness, the artist is working on its frontier, leading it forward, striving perhaps to clarify the direction in which it must go. It is this circumstance that allows Lukàcs and other cultural historians to argue that an important work of art seems to embody in a relatively coherent system and style some of the pressures and problems which a particular society is experiencing in everyday life.[1] Further, since the structures of thought and feeling in any society are themselves the product of how groups of individuals attempt to relate to each other and the world around them, how they understand themselves and their world, these 'world-views' play an essential part in moulding the particular styles and forms in which the most penetrating kinds of imaginative creativity express themselves. Hence, as Lucien Goldmann puts it, 'the decisive factor in cultural activity is constituted by world-views and by the social groups in which they originated and were developed.'² Hence, too, the paradoxical sense in which the history of styles is essentially the history of ideas.

The baroque art of the seventeenth century cannot therefore be under-stood and appreciated unless at least some account is taken of the world-views characteristic of the society of the period. Baroque themes and baroque forms and styles are equally a product of the structures of thought and feeling of the age in which the baroque artist and his audience flourished. The essential nature of that period is well suggested by the fact that historians now quite conventionally write and talk of something they call 'the general crisis of the seventeenth century'. The baroque is the distinctive art-form of that crisis. What historians have in mind in describing the seventeenth century as a period of peculiar crisis is a general and far-reaching sense of breakdown and change occurring over the entire range of human activity. But they all agree that one central dimension of the general crisis lies in the area of world-views, of funda-mental ideas about the nature of the universe and man's place in it. For much of the seventeenth century such central issues remained in a state of unresolved debate and dispute. Doubt and uncertainty were as common as confidence and assurance; sometimes doubt was synthesized with certainty, and assurance often concealed uncertainty. Sir Thomas Browne was not alone in confronting the paradoxes of his most deeply held beliefs with another paradox:

> I can answer all the objections of Satan, and my rebellious reason, with that odd resolution I learned of Tertullian, *Certum est quia impossibile est*.³

In the later Middle Ages there had occurred a fracture of that spiritual and intellectual unity which had been so marked a characteristic of medieval European civilization. The basis of that unity had been the medieval world-picture which still, to some extent, lingered on into the seventeenth century, and which had produced a characteristic faith in the principle of hierarchy. Medieval man had an unquestioning belief in a universe which was inhabited by a graded chain of beings, the chain stretching down from God in the Empyrean heaven on the outermost periphery of the universe, through the hierarchies of angels who inhabited the nine mobile heavenly spheres, to the men, animals and plants, composed of the four terrestrial elements of earth, water, air and fire, who inhabited the base which remained immobile at the centre of the universe. Within this ordered hierarchy the government of the universe was organized in such a way that any given creature had dominion over all below it, while it served all those above it. In the course of centuries a number of refinements had been introduced into this scheme of explanation, but towards the end of the Middle Ages its capacity to command universal acceptance had gradually weakened. The breaking up of this world-picture and attempts to heal the break led eventually to that cultural efflorescence which we call the Renaissance. But renaissance man never succeeded in discovering a satisfactory new paradigm of the universe by which to explain the world. In consequence, the leading men of the Renaissance were characteristically racked by doubt – doubt engendered by their efforts to reconcile completely conflicting beliefs. The same was true of the seventeenth century – the Baroque Age – and thus for two hundred years the intellectual history of

Europe was dominated by attempts to recover the lost coherence and intellectual unity of the Middle Ages, to discover a valid new explanation of existence and its contradictory phenomena.

In the seventeenth century no phenomenon seemed more contradictory than man himself. Even the old, traditional world-view had placed man in a somewhat ambivalent position; he belonged simultaneously to the spiritual and physical worlds. Man's soul linked him with God and the angels, his body with the natural world. In the medieval world, however, man's spiritual nature was alone regarded as important; and in the Renaissance for a time man's sensual nature was sometimes granted a new status and prestige. But in the crisis of the seventeenth century man seemed unable any longer to choose between the two sides of his nature. Willing to reject neither, he seemed most aware of their inevitable conflict, their contradictory pulls and impulses. 'Our souls would go to one end, heaven, and all our bodies must go to one end, the earth', wrote Donne. What an awareness of this kind makes for is above all a sense of tension, a heightening and quickening of the emotions. Such tension could produce great works of art and literature – Donne's *Holy Sonnets*, many of the poems in Herbert's *The Temple*, Marvell's *The Garden* – but it brought no man peace or complete serenity. Like Donne, Marvell saw the dual nature of man banning him for ever from the enjoyment of real happiness; his soul was for ever being drawn to an ideal world of the spirit, but his body was perpetually claimed by the world of Nature, and conflict between the two states prevented man from ever enjoying Paradise. It was his fate to be, in Herbert's words,

> A wonder tortured in the space
> Betwixt this world and that of grace.

But perhaps it is Sir Thomas Browne who best sums up this sense of man's belonging to two contradictory worlds. In *Religio Medici*, Browne recognizes that 'we are only that amphibious piece between a corporal and spiritual essence, that middle form that links those two together. . . . Thus', concludes Browne, 'is man that great and true *Amphibian*, whose nature is disposed to live not only like other creatures in divers elements, but in divided and distinguished worlds.'[4]

But if conflict existed between the two sides of a man's nature, how much greater was the conflict within himself for the salvation of his soul. Seventeenth-century man was perpetually aware of the vast struggle going on in the Universe between the powers of darkness and the powers of light, between God and Satan, a struggle localized in each individual soul, as the two powers wrestled for its eternal salvation or damnation. But man's understanding of even this eternal struggle had become invaded by doubt. Did man's will participate in the struggle or only God's will? No seventeenth-century debate was profounder or more agonizing than that over the status of the will. What was the relationship between the omniscience and omnipotence of God, with his absolute foreknowledge, and the concept of man's free will? Like Milton's devils, seventeenth-century man was only too familiar with the endless debate about 'Fixt Fate, Free Will, foreknowledge absolute' and, like the devils once again, 'in wandering mazes lost', rarely found any satisfactory resolution.

Should man's will be free, how precisely should it respond to God's will? If seventeenth-century Englishmen were united in anything it was in devotion to a principle of liberty, although they might well differ over the meaning of the word. Hence absolute power, whether divine or monarchical, could only be justified when it was reasonable. But the reasonable itself could not be distinguished from the Divine Will; God could not be conceived of as acting irrationally. Hence, to obey God is to obey reason, and such obedience becomes proof of the will's freedom to choose. As Milton puts it in *Paradise Lost*,

> But God left free the will, for what obeys
> Reason, is free, and Reason he made right.[5]

One paradox is piled upon another. But even if the view that freedom is obedience to God's will is accepted, why is there so little evidence in the world of harmony between God's will and man's will? Milton's answer is that of the Archangel Michael to Adam:

> Since thy original lapse, true liberty
> Is lost, which always with right Reason dwells
> Twinned, and from her hath no dividual being.[6]

In this fallen world, rather than submitting his will to God's, man sets his will in opposition to God's. Man's own self-will, Ralph Cudworth proclaimed in 1647, 'is the strong castle that we all keep garrisoned against heaven in every one of our hearts, which God continually layeth siege unto: and it must be conquered and demolished before we can conquer heaven'. Self-will had led to the Fall of Adam, and to that of the angels, 'those *Morning-stars*' who, in consequence, 'kept not their first station, but dropped down from heaven, like Falling stars, and sunk into this condition of bitterness, anxiety and wretchedness in which they now are'.[7] Some thirteen years later John Smith was to describe self-will in similar terms as 'the seed of the Evil Spirit which is perpetually at emnity with the seed of God and the Heaven-born Nature'. The aim of self-will Smith saw as being 'with a Giant-like pride to climb into the Throne of the Almighty, and to establish an unbounded Tyranny in contradiction to the Will of God'.[8] In *Paradise Lost* Milton similarly identified the unrectified will as the source of the Fall of Satan and his angels; in his wilful pridefulness, Satan opposes his 'unconquerable Will' to God's will, failing to understand that freedom in Hell is a delusion, that true freedom is not reigning in Hell but serving in Heaven. It is the paradox of this that once again suggests the characteristic seventeenth-century tone.

Closely associated with the debate about freedom and the will was that over the rival claims of reason and faith. Although never lacking an austere intellectual content, at the time of its origins Protestantism had been sincere in emphasizing the superiority of faith to reason. There were still many who, in the seventeenth century, associated reason with self-will and human pride, and as such saw it as inimicable to true religion. Donne saw the human capacity to erect intellectual arguments around articles of faith as a potential destroyer of man's relationship with God. Grace and faith alone are surer guides than reason:

. . . snatch me heavenly Spirit from this vain
Reckoning their vanities, less is their gain
Than hazard still, to meditate on ill,
Though with good mind; their reason, like those toys
Of glassy bubbles which the gamesome boys
Stretch to so nice a thinness through a quill
That they themselves break, do themselves spill:
Arguing is heretic's game; No liberties
Of speech but silence; hands, not tongues, and heresies.[9]

But there were others in the seventeenth century less willing to set aside
the claims of reason. The proponents of the new science naturally saw reason as
pointing the way forward to increased human knowledge and understanding.
If there was any danger of a collision between the findings of reason and the
claims of faith, then the answer, according to Bacon, was to keep the two areas
strictly apart. In the *Advancement of Learning* he suggested that 'out of the contemplation of nature, or general human knowledge, to induce any verity or
persuasion, concerning the points of faith, is in my judgment not safe. "Da
fidei quae fidei sunt." ' Sir Thomas Browne, whose religious emotions were of
an intensity unknown to Bacon, arrived at a remarkably similar position. There
was enough of the scientist in Browne for him to be unable to do other than
admire the advances in learning being made in his own age. In *Religio Medici* he
wrote, 'The world was made to be inhabited by beasts, but studied and contemplated by man: 'tis the debt of our reason we owe unto God, and the
homage we pay for not being beasts.'[10] And he continues, 'those highly magnify
him whose judicious enquiry into his acts, and deliberate research into his
creatures, return the duty of a devout and learned admiration.' Yet Browne
loves 'to keep the road' and 'follow the great wheel of the Church',[11] insisting
on reason's limitations and its irrelevance to the world of faith. The mysteries
of faith are beyond our understanding; our reason should be 'humble and sub-
missive unto the subtleties of faith'. 'Thus', writes Browne, 'I teach my
haggard and unreclaimed reason to stoop unto the lure of faith.'[12]

Browne seems to have drawn a distinction between the worlds of faith and
reason lest one should seem to undermine the other. By the middle of the
seventeenth century, however, there were those who saw complete reliance on
faith as a guide to ultimate truth as potentially much more dangerous than
any over-reliance on human reason. Trust in faith alone had produced a
situation in which Protestantism had splintered into a variety of sects, each
one zealously proclaiming its unique adherence to the truth. As a result, an
increasingly large number of influential Anglican clergy, dominated by the
Cambridge Platonists, who aimed to revive neo-Platonic philosophy, were
coming to assert that the most serious threat posed to Christianity was not the
growth of rationalism but of the irrational. The essence of their views was later
expressed by Shaftesbury when he argued that man

must surely have an unhappy Opinion of God, and believe him not so
good by far as he knows Himself to be, if he imagines that an impartial use
of Reason, in any matter of Speculation whatsoever, can make him run any

risk hereafter; and that a mean *Denial of his Reason*, and an *Affectation of Belief* in any point too hard for his *Understanding*, can entitle him to any Favour in another world.[13]

And the ultimate logic of their position was expressed in Locke's *Reasonableness of Christianity* and John Toland's *Christianity not Mysterious* (1696).

Any thinking man in the seventeenth century was constantly being made aware of conflicting ideas and beliefs about man's nature, about man's will, and about faith and reason. But even those who did not think deeply could scarcely fail to notice that they lived in a country which was deeply divided by alternative political claims. Despite the popular rejoicings which accompanied the restoration of the monarchy in 1660, that restoration was achieved only by the most hurried papering over of cracks. Such a make-shift settlement never sweetened the bitterness which eleven years before had erupted in civil war, and which, some twenty years later, was to break out in bitter party-factional struggle. It is sometimes forgotten that the English Civil War *was* a civil war, feeding on extant divisions and further dividing against themselves families, interests, towns and villages. The fierce passions it bred rapidly became dignified into issues of principle.

These issues of principle in turn were closely linked to distinctive ways of viewing the universe but they more directly claimed the attention of the seventeenth-century Englishman in terms of the conflicting demands of that political liberty which he found by experience to be necessary, and notions of power and authority vested in monarchical absolutism which many, in theory, believed to be the right ordering of the political world. The major proponent of such absolutist views was Thomas Hobbes, England's first great political philosopher. And it is Hobbes who, because of his pessimistic assumptions about the nature of man, his emphasis on the power of the will, and the central role he accorded to Fancy in the creation of the work of art, has been called 'the philosopher of the Baroque'. Despite the assumed rejection of the Whig idea of history, the story of seventeenth-century Britain is still normally written in terms of ideas of liberty, representation and consent, and in such company Hobbes's important ideas sometimes appear a strange aberration. Hobbes, however, was as much the product of a particular cultural milieu as was Locke, and in fact the seventeenth-century Englishman was far more familiar with coherent, theoretical justifications of absolutism, than he was with cogent arguments in favour of a limited or representative government. It is also true that the trend towards an acceptance of the theory of absolutism grew, rather than diminished, in the course of the seventeenth century, and after 1660 a wave of reaction against ideas prevalent during the Interregnum led to a widespread, if largely unthinking, acceptance of those doctrines of Divine Right, which, during an earlier period, had been preached only by a small band of extremists and sycophants. Such ideas were bolstered by the revival of the practice of touching for the King's Evil in 1660, and by the cult of the Royal Martyr, Charles I, a cult which represents the actual apotheosis of the English monarchy, as it is manifested in baroque painting.

It took a James II to destroy for ever any general acceptance of the theories of absolutism and hereditary Divine Right, but not even the events of 1688 could successfully resolve all the political divisions which for so long had been characteristic of England. After the Glorious Revolution the rival claims of the Whig and Tory parties, permeating the whole of the nation's life, and the resurrection of ancient religious antagonisms, ensured that the country should remain as bitterly divided as at any time since the Civil War.

Such social and political conflicts and divisions are another characteristic dimension of the seventeenth-century crisis. And Hobbes's philosophy is only one attempt to make sense of such a crisis-ridden world. In the second half of the seventeenth century in England three other world-views can be distinguished, each of them an attempt to reorder the universe in a meaningful way. These are Cartesianism, the 'new philosophy' closely linked with the theories of Descartes, and Cambridge neo-Platonism. At the outset it has to be admitted that, in the end, each of these was to be fundamentally antithetical to baroque art and literature. It must also be understood that there is a certain artificiality in separating these three strands of philosophical enquiry since they tend to be found overlapping or nourishing each other at any one time, and Newton may even be seen as having combined all three into one single world-picture by the beginning of the eighteenth century.

Descartes, however, deserves some separate mention for his views were an inspiration to a whole new generation of philosophers and scientists in Europe, although they were of less importance in England with its tradition of Baconian science. Descartes' intention was to jettison completely the old medieval world-picture and to replace it with his own scheme for a universal system of knowledge, based upon his three principles: that he would accept nothing as certain if any doubt about the question were possible; that he would divide the problems he studied into the smallest possible units; and that he would reason always from simpler to more complex questions. Starting from his famous base-point of 'I think, therefore I am', Descartes erected as his paradigm an entirely mechanistic universe, run on purely mathematical principles and devoid of any qualities of colour, scent, taste and sound. The relation of the Divine to this universe was entirely simple; God, in the beginning, created matter and motion, but thereafter the universe was governed by the laws of mechanics or 'the laws which God has put into nature'. From the point of view of later scientific developments, the great value of this Cartesian view was that it continued the trend, begun by Bacon, of separation between the material and religious spheres of thought. Pope in *The Dunciad* sees the consequences for religion in a less favourable light:

> We nobly take the high Priori Road,
> And reason downward, till we doubt of God:
> Make Nature still incroach upon his plan;
> And shove him off as far as e'er we can:
> Thrust some Mechanic Cause into his place. . . .[14]

God, having set his universe in motion, simply ceased to matter and the Cartesians were therefore able to investigate any problem without reference to the Divine, to spirits, to magic, to mysticism, to the Bible or to the Ancients. This was, no doubt, entirely beneficial to the development of science, mathematics and philosophy. Its effect on the arts is more questionable, for what was brought about by Descartes' mechanical view of the universe, and even more by the Newtonian view, was a situation in which the arts were left to do little more inspiring than contemplate the 'Great Machine and Divine Mechanic'[15] and to acknowledge that the only thing which 'elevates us a Degree above the rest of our Species, and distinguishes us in a more eminent Manner from the Brutes', is man's knowledge and contemplation of the fact that 'Every Action is performed by the Laws of Mechanism.'[16] Since the universe was now regarded as stable and perfect, governed by a set of unalterable 'Laws', it was natural to believe in the possibility of discovering similar simple laws to be applied uniformly to the arts, and such a belief surely underlies the rigid authoritarianism of neo-classicism.

The second world-picture which emerged in seventeenth-century England laid emphasis on the value of reason, common sense and experience, and displayed a fundamental belief in progress and the perfectibility of man. Such views at first found but tentative expression – Hobbes's intensely pessimistic views about man's nature are more typical of the first three quarters of the seventeenth century – but were closely linked with the development of empirical philosophy within the context of the seventeenth-century scientific revolution. Such optimistic attitudes were eventually enshrined in the English eighteenth-century world-view. Throughout the seventeenth century, Bacon, Gilbert, Harvey, Galileo, as well as Descartes, all played their part in disseminating this new world-view which would culminate in the work of Newton and the emergence of England as the cultural leader of Europe. These were the scientists who rejected the traditional dependence on Aristotle and the ancients, and argued that no truth could be accepted unless it could be confirmed by experimentation or observation of a mathematical exactitude. Thomas Sprat gave them their watchword: 'It is certain', he wrote, 'that *Experimenting* . . . is that by which all our Actions are to be fashioned', and their method of operation was described by Harvey in 1628 when he wrote that he professed 'to learn and teach anatomy not from books but from dissections, not from the tenets of Philosophers but from the fabric of Nature'.

Rejecting all intellectual authorities, the new philosophers turned their back on the unknowable world of spirit and revelation, concern with which seemed to have produced nothing but social discord and political upheaval, and set out to explore by the light of reason the as yet undiscovered realms of biology, cosmography, physics and the natural world. In their first enthusiasm there seemed to be no area of human enquiry which could not benefit from the new philosophy.

At first, the new science did not even seem to be essentially antithetical to baroque art. As Sprat recognized, it may even be true that there could have been no baroque art as we know it without the early scientific discoveries which could have been applied 'to the improving of the *materials* of building, and to the inventing of better *models* for *Houses, Roofs, Chimneys, Wharfs* and *Streets*'.[17] Among the most notable results of the scientific revolution was the invention of new apparatus with which to investigate scientific problems: logarithms, algebra and the slide-rule. Such inventions were obvious aids to the new architecture, and it is no doubt of fundamental importance that Christopher Wren was a scientist before he was an architect. From the very beginning of his second career he drew heavily upon the first; for instance, his solution to the problem of the Sheldonian roof, with its ingenious hanging construction, derived from calculations published by one of Wren's closest scientific friends, Dr Wallis, Savilian Professor of Geometry. It is also clear that obsessive interest in the problem of light, which is so characteristic of seventeenth-century science, paid artistic dividends. Light and the use of light was a primary interest of Inigo Jones, whose interest in it was aroused by the problems involved in the staging of the masque. It was no less of a concern with Wren, whose admiration for the Gothic architecture of Salisbury Cathedral derived from his observation of the play of light from the windows on to the contrasted surfaces and textures of the fabric. 'Our Artist', he wrote of the architect of Salisbury, 'knew better that nothing could add beauty to light',[18] and it was a principle which he consistently followed in his own architecture.

Yet, for all the advantages which it brought, the new empirical philosophy was to be an undoing of baroque art for it led eventually to the erection of the Newtonian paradigm which, like the Cartesian universe, left no room for the Baroque. The medieval world-picture had drawn an essential distinction between on the one hand, the 'dull sublunary sphere' where all was change and decay, and on the other, the celestial spheres – Heaven – where all was fixed, permanent, perfect and incorruptible. It had been among the major concerns of baroque art to reveal the incorruptible sphere to the corruptible and to attempt the imaginative reconciliation of the two. Dryden, quoting the Italian G. B. Bellori in 1695, described the relevant artistic role:

> the celestial bodies above the moon being incorruptible, and not subject to change, remained for ever fair and in perpetual order. On the contrary, all things which are sublunary are subject to change, to deformity, and to decay. And though nature always intends a consummate beauty in her productions, yet through the inequality of matter, the forms are altered; and in particular, human beauty suffers alteration for the worse, as we see to our mortification in the deformities and disproportions which are in us. For which reason the artful painter and the sculptor, imitating the Divine Maker, form to themselves, as well as they are able, a model of the superior beauties; and reflecting on them, endeavour to correct and amend the common nature, and to represent it as it was first created, without fault either in colour or lineament.[19]

According to these traditional theories, perfection could never be found in any one human body, for all bodies were subject to decay and corruption. The artist, therefore, created an ideal in his mind, taking the best parts from several examples, and it was this ideal which was then represented. Thus no artist could represent life or nature as it actually was, for 'Nature . . . is so much inferior to art, that those artists who propose to themselves only the imitation and likeness of such or such a particular person, without election of those ideas . . . have often been reproached for that omission. . . .'[20] And Dryden concludes that, 'though I cannot much commend the style, I must needs say there is somewhat in the matter'. The new view of the universe, however, completely destroyed the ancient hierarchical system on which such views depended. In consequence, as the new system gained ground, the very spirit which justified baroque art was increasingly undermined.

The new philosophy made the whole idea of the infinite and eternal suspect, and robbed art of what for centuries had been one of its main creative forces. In the light of this philosophy it was increasingly difficult for the arts to concern themselves with the major themes of religion, of death and immortality, or of human life seen in relation to eternity. The significance of such a loss was fully recognized by contemporaries – from Donne, for whom

> . . . the new Philosophy calls all in doubt,
> The Element of fire is quite put out;
> . . . 'Tis all in pieces, all coherence gone;
> All just supply and all Relation.[21]

to John Dennis, the neo-classical critic, who in 1704 suggested that 'one of the Principal Reasons that has made modern Poetry so contemptible, is, that by divesting itself of Religion, it has fallen from its Dignity and its Original Nature and Excellence; and from the greatest production of the Mind of Man, is dwindled to an extravagant and vain Amusement.'

At the same time that it was undermining the basis of baroque art, the new philosophy, like Cartesianism, was having the long-term effect of strengthening the view of the neo-classicists. For what the new philosophy tended to stress was the existence in Nature of order and rationality. It is, indeed, a presupposition of the experimental method that such order and rationality exist. The culmination was reached with the discoveries of Newton, which became the central element in a new physico-theological system demonstrating the existence and the benevolent attributes of God, from the evidence of a created universe, which was governed by a set of unalterable rules and 'laws sublimely simple'.[22] The impact of these discoveries was summarized by Addison in the *Spectator*:

> The more extended our reason is, and the more able to grapple with immense objects, the greater still are those discoveries which it makes of wisdom and providence in the work of Creation. A Sir Isaac Newton, who stands up as the miracle of the present age, can look through a whole planetary system, consider it in all its weight, number and measure, and draw from it as many demonstrations of infinite power and wisdom as a more confined understanding is able to deduce from the system of the human body.[23]

In similar vein, in 1728, Robert Morris, the theorist of the neo-Palladian movement in architecture, could proclaim it as an act of faith that

> we must be degenerated into the utmost State of Perdition and Apostacy, must wholly over-whelm the Faculties of the Soul with total Ignorance and Insensibility, and debase the Dignity of human Nature to Brutality itself, to be dubious and unconvinced of the immediate Beauties of Nature, and the Hand of a Divine Power alone, in the architectural Creation of the World, and all its works.[24]

With this new emphasis on the rules by which the universe was governed, it was inevitable that, since art was believed to imitate Nature, critics – of literature, the visual arts and music – should all come to stress the primacy of order and symmetry in the aesthetic world as well. For a typical expression of this view we can turn again to Dennis who, in his *Advancement and Reformation of Modern Poetry*, argues that

> both Nature and Reason, which two in a larger Acceptation is Nature, owe their greatness, their Beauty, their Majesty to their perpetual Order . . . so Poetry which is an imitation of Nature must do the same thing. It can neither have greatness or Real Beauty, if it swerves from the Laws which Reason severely prescribes it, and the more Irregular any Poetical composition is, the nearer it comes to Extravagance and Confusion, and to Nonsense, which is Nothing.

The rule of Reason had another direct effect on baroque art, for it led to an emphasis on clarity, purity and utility. Art was no longer seen as a means of expressing a man's emotional needs and uniting him with the infinite, but as a useful tool – only one of many – enabling him to lead a rational life. It was entirely to be expected, therefore, that it should be the Royal Society, dedicated to the encouragement of the new scientific framework of thought, which should also foster a new vernacular prose style, 'bringing all things as near the Mathematical plainness as they can' and abandoning the elaborations of baroque rhetoric, with its emphasis on tropes and metaphors, similes and inversions. That such a change could be a genuine conversion is apparent from the history of the publishing career of Joseph Glanvill. The first version of Glanvill's *Vanity of Dogmatizing* (1661) was written in typical baroque style. But when the work was republished four years later under the title of *Scepsis Scientifica*, it also contained an 'Address to the Royal Society' in which Glanvill explained that he had decided to adopt new modes of simplicity for the future: 'I must confess that way of writing to be less agreeable to my present relish and genius, which is more gratified with manly sense, flowing in a natural and unaffected eloquence, than in the music and curiosity of fine Metaphors and dancing periods.' Twelve years later Glanvill included a shortened version of the *Scepsis* in a collection of essays; in this version Glanvill's style has become simple and direct.

In their successful attack on ornate language, the seventeenth-century scientists were taking up that debate about the relative value of the 'Real' or 'Natural' and the 'Artificial' which had first been launched during the Puritan attacks on the court art of the early Stuarts. This debate had been extended to the point where it had essentially become an argument between two prevailing artistic styles – the neo-classic and the Baroque. Thus William Petty, when he spoke in 1648 of those that 'are Friends to the Design of Realities' as opposed to those 'who are tickled only with Rhetorical Prefaces, Transitions, and Epilogues, and charmed with fine Allusions and Metaphors', was essentially attacking baroque style on the grounds that it was 'artificial'. Some seventy years later, on similar grounds, Addison was to attack the painted façades of the baroque palaces of Genoa:

Figures, Perspectives or Pieces of History are certainly very ornamental, as they are drawn on many of the Walls, that would otherwise look too naked and uniform without them: But instead of these, one often sees the Front of a Palace covered with painted Pillars of different Orders. If these were so many columns of Marble, set in their proper Architecture, they would certainly very much adorn the Places where they stand, but as they are now, they only show us that there is something wanting, and that the Palace, which without these Counter-feit Pillars would be beautiful in its kind, might have been more perfect by the Addition of such as are real.[25]

Little separates this artistic judgment from Colen Campbell's ill-mannered attack on Italian baroque architects who

can no more relish Antique Simplicity, but are entirely employed in capricious Ornaments, which must at last end in the Gothic . . . How affected and licentious are the works of Bernini and Fontana? How wildly extravagant are the Designs of Borromini, who has endeavoured to debauch mankind with his odd and Chimerical Beauties, where the Parts are without Proportion, Solids without their true Bearing, Heaps of Materials without Strength, excessive Ornaments without Grace and the whole without Symmetry.[26]

The impact of the 'new philosophy' on baroque art in England has been discussed at some length because its effect was so widespread. But the third world-view to emerge in this period was also not without a considerable effect. This view arose largely as a counterattack on mechanistic views of the universe, and can ultimately be traced back to the revival of Platonism in seventeenth-century England. Platonism had been a powerful influence at the court of Charles I, a source of theoretical strength in the writings of Herbert, Vaughan, Crashaw and Traherne and the basis for all the works of Inigo Jones. Building on this Platonism, or rather neo-Platonism, since it was as indebted to Plotinus as to the master himself, a school of theologians known as the Cambridge Platonists developed a new explanation of existence, and a new paradigm of the universe, which were to be of considerable influence in the late seventeenth and early eighteenth centuries.

United by a common belief that physical objects were not a final reality but a manifestation of a world beyond themselves, the Cambridge Platonists believed that by applying reason to the world around them they could discover God. Fundamentally they assumed that among all the apparent confusions of existence, Nature alone, far from revealing chaos and disorder, was the pattern of reasonableness and order, since it was a reflection of the Divine mind. Nature, in fact, was God's art, making concrete the abstract qualities of Divine Knowledge, Understanding and Wisdom. Since Nature was 'a living Stamp or Signature' of God, all art could be said to be imitating Nature in that it strove towards the same ends – the rational discovery of the Divine. This, Shaftesbury was subsequently to argue, was to raise the practice of art to the level of divine activity, for art, in imitating Nature, was imitating the whole process of creation.

From the point of view of baroque art, the most destructive aspect of the new rational Christianity was its distrust of the kind of religious devotion

based on the senses and sensual impressions, activating a heightened imagination. Such a heightened imagination lay at the core of the Baroque. It was the
faculty which made life tolerable for men like Donne, and was central to their
creative ability:

> But truly [he wrote] wheresoever we are, if we can but tell ourselves truly
> what and where we would be, we may make any state and place such; for
> we are so composed that if abundance or glory scorch and melt us, we have
> an earthly cave, our bodies, to go into by consideration and cool ourselves;
> and if we be frozen, and contracted with lower and dark fortunes, we have
> within us a torch, a soul, lighter and warmer than any without: we are
> therefore our own umbrellas and our suns.[27]

Baroque sensibility was at its strongest in its capacity to create an acceptable
heaven through the power of the imagination and to manifest that heaven to
men in comprehensible terms and images. But to the Cambridge Platonists
such activities could only be deceptive, for

> a man does not direct all his actions to *the Glory of God* by forming a Con-
> ception in his Mind, or stirring up a strong Imagination upon any Action,
> That must be for *the Glory of God*: it is not thinking of God's glory that is
> *glorifying* of him. As all other parts of Religion may be *apishly* acted over
> by *Fancy and Imagination*, so also may the Internal parts of Religion many
> times be acted over with much seeming grace by our *Fancy and Passions*;
> these often love to be drawing the pictures of Religion, and use their best
> arts to render them more beautiful and pleasing.[28]

True beauty did not exist as the fancied product of man's imagination, but was
discoverable in externals – in the symmetry and proportion of Man, the
Universe and Nature, a symmetry and proportion which only Reason could
discover. Imagination could be of little use in this task, for Imagination was
not the fruit of the mind, but of the passions and the senses, the product of
self-will and self-love. The imaginative powers, therefore, are always 'breathing
gross dew upon the pure Glass of our Understandings', which they so 'sully
and besmear . . . that we cannot see the Image of Divinity sincerely in it'.[29]

Such attitudes, which were extremely widespread – the Cambridge
Platonists influenced to some degree most of the major thinkers of the late
seventeenth and early eighteenth centuries, Barrow, Boyle, Tillotson, Locke,
Ray, Shaftesbury, Newton and Berkeley among others – inevitably led to the
critical rejection of baroque religious devotional poetry, of which England
could boast so many outstanding examples, as the type of anti-religious rather
than religious feelings. Equally, the emphasis on the all-powerful role of
reason led to a rejection of all religious and devotional art other than the purely
classical; Gothic art was too emotional to be reasonable and was therefore
rejected.

The reply of the baroque artists to such attacks was based on a reassertion
of the role which Fancy played in the creation of the work of art, and it was
Hobbes who first suggested what this role might be. Fancy, he argued, was
just as important as Reason and Judgment, for Fancy he defined as the capacity

to observe likenesses in things of different natures – an essentially baroque capacity – whereas Reason could do no more than observe likenesses in things of the same nature. Reason might provide the structure of the work of art but Hobbes was convinced that this was not enough, since Reason alone would not appeal to an audience. It was only by playing on the spectator's emotions and imagination by the operation of Fancy that the artist could create his work of art. No argument could have come closer to the central assumptions of baroque sensibility.

Certainly we find echoes of Hobbes's ideas among the practitioners of baroque art. Dryden had argued that 'the fancy more instructs the painter, than the imitation [of nature]; for the last makes only the things which it sees, but the first makes also the things which it never sees',[30] and always regarded the imagination as the prime mover in the creative experience, 'moving the sleeping images of things towards the light'.[31] Like all baroque artists, he saw the role of Reason and Judgment as being to bound and circumscribe 'the fancy. For imagination in a poet is a faculty so wild and lawless, that like an high ranging spaniel, it must have clogs tied to it, lest it outrun the judgment.'[32] Reason and Judgment were essential in the poetic art but ' 'tis fancy that gives the life-touches, and the secret graces to it.'[33]

In England, three major architects – Vanbrugh, Hawksmoor and Wren – would appear to have been in agreement with Dryden. Hawksmoor, for instance, maintained that architecture could never be a simple expression of Reason, and that Reason itself demonstrated this truth. For if architecture *were* merely an expression of rational thought then it would be possible to invent rules and perfect forms which would suit all ages and all societies. But Hawksmoor maintained that, in fact, even the work of the Ancients showed infinite variety, revealing that art and architecture were the product, not of Reason alone, but of Reason, Fancy and Experience, and that they were infinitely adaptable to changes in society. It was only works which combined all three qualities of Reason, Fancy and Experience that had stood the test of time, and 'if we contrive or invent otherways, we do but dress things in Masquerade which only pleases the Idle part of Mankind for a short time.'[34]

So it was that Hawksmoor, Vanbrugh and even Wren found Gothic art attractive for precisely those reasons for which the Palladians rejected it: it appealed to Fancy and the imagination. In consequence, they were never doctrinaire about style since what mattered to them was not the observance of rules, but that a building should satisfy the eyes, head *and* heart of the viewer. So, because Christ Church had been built in late Gothic style, Wren, who lacked Gibbs's faith – manifested in his new building at King's College, Cambridge – that old and new styles could blend satisfactorily if the scale was right, adopted the Gothic in his design for Tom Tower 'to agree with the Founder's work', and today we can scarcely fault his decision. It was Wren's belief in the importance of visual logic, and his sense of tradition and history which, as we have seen, sometimes led him to adopt a 'Gothic' style, but with both Vanbrugh and Hawksmoor the matter went deeper. Their interest in Gothic art was a vital passion. Vanbrugh's most flamboyant argument with a patron resulted from his determination not to pull down Old Woodstock Manor but to lovingly incorporate it into his general design for Blenheim, and both he and Hawksmoor were architects of projects which deliberately simulated Gothic architecture.

In their readiness to build in the Gothic style Vanbrugh and Hawksmoor were running counter to the aesthetic principles closely associated with the different contemporary world-views that have been described. As these world-views tended to merge and gain in authority towards the end of the seventeenth century, the architects were engaged in what was becoming more and more a rearguard action. But they were not entirely lacking in allies. Since the Renaissance, one of the major cultural debates that had swayed back and forth in most of the countries of Europe was that concerned with the Ancients and the Moderns. Did the spectacular achievements of antiquity in literature, science, military techniques, the arts, and almost every field of human endeavour, mean that the Ancients had established a permanent cultural standard which later ages could only hope to imitate; or did the Ancients do no more than provide useful guide-lines which would help the Moderns to achieve new successes of their own? As its name makes clear, seventeenth- and eighteenth-century neo-classicism took its stand on the authority of the Ancients; baroque art, on the other hand, particularly in the context of its sympathy for Gothic styles, was peculiarly modern art.

Neo-classic aesthetics, though originating in sixteenth-century Italy, were most fully developed in seventeenth-century France in the work of such scholars as Rapin, Le Bossu and Boileau. Traditional English aesthetics and literary theory also tended towards a classical point of view, though English writers like Sir Philip Sydney and Ben Jonson did tend to preserve a certain liberalism and pragmatism in their thought, not really to be found in the French exponents of neo-classicism. These characteristics of the English tradition help to explain why French neo-classicism did not succeed in becoming all-powerful in England even in the period after the Restoration. Architecture is the relevant case in point. The purists of the French academy, led by its propagandist Blondel, argued for the existence of certain mathematically based, fixed proportions as the only basis of beauty in the orders, and therefore in the whole of architecture. But it was not so much Blondel as his critics who found favour in England. In 1664 Evelyn published the chief architectural treatise of the early French Modernists – Roland Fréart's *Parallèle de l'architecture antique et de la moderne* – in which Fréart points out that, even in ancient buildings, the proportions of the orders tend to vary. A more fundamental attack came from Charles Perrault in 1683 in the *Ordonnances des cinq espèces de colonnes* of which the first English edition was published in 1708. Perrault's views were extremely radical for he attacked the very concept of beauty held by the Ancients. He insisted that proportions were, of necessity, variable and arbitrary, for they were used to create a whole that was beautiful, and beauty is not an absolute but largely what we are accustomed to.

These arguments were well known to the leading practitioners of the arts in England. At the period of the English Baroque they tended without exception to support the Moderns, being totally opposed to the rule-making of the academicians and Ancients. The views of the English baroque architects are characteristically summarized by Wren's son in the *Parentalia* where he argues that

Those who duly examine by Measure the Remains of the Greek or Roman Structures, whether Temples, Pillars, Arches or Theatres, will soon discern, that even among these there is no general Agreement; for it is manifest the ancient Architects took great liberties in their capitals, and Members of Cornices, to show their own Inventions, even where their Design did not oblige them, but where it did oblige them to a rational Variation, still keeping a good Symmetry, they are surely to be commended, and in like Cases to be followed. We now most esteem the Learning of the Augustan Age, yet, no question there were then many different Styles in Oratory, and perhaps some as good as *Cicero's*. This is not said as an Inducement to Masons, or every Novice that can draw Lines, to fall into crude *Gothick* Inventions, far from the good Examples of the Ancients, no more than to encourage a barbarous Style in *Latin*, and yet surely we cannot but with *Erasmus*, laugh at him who durst not use one word that he could not find in Tully.[35]

Paradoxically the baroque artists found philosophical support where they might least have anticipated doing so – in the new science. For, as Dryden pointed out, since 'in these last hundred years . . . almost a new Nature has been revealed to us',[36] there was no reason to suppose that, given favourable conditions, similar advances might not be made in the arts. Expressing views about architecture, very similar to those expressed by Dryden about literature, Wren, for all his love and knowledge of classical antiquity, refused to accept the authority of antiquity as final or absolute.

Modern Authors who have treated of Architecture, seem generally to have little more in view, but to set down the Proportions of Columns, Architraves, and Cornices, in the several Orders, as they are distinguished . . . and in these Proportions finding them in the ancient Fabrics of the Greeks and Romans (though more arbitrarily used than they care to acknowledge) they have reduced them into Rules, too strict and pedantic, and so as not to be transgressed, without the Crime of Barbarity. . . .

Wren ranged himself on the side of the Moderns because he saw clearly the connection between culture and society – that social change will inevitably be reflected in cultural change and that the function of culture will change in response to functional change in society. Thus, speaking of ancient proportions and orders he remarks that 'in their own Nature, they are but the Modes and Fashions of those Ages wherein they were used; but because they were found in the great Structures (the ruins of which we now admire) we think ourselves strictly obliged still to follow the Fashion. . . .'[37] In expressing such flexibility and responsiveness to social and political change Wren was, in fact, aligning himself with the particular artistic viewpoint which had always characterized baroque artists and architects. Their self-conscious modernism, their desire to adapt, their passion for movement, made them the natural opponents of the neo-classicists and all supporters of the Ancients. Whatever else it was or was not, English baroque art was consciously up-to-date.

The debate over the Ancients and the Moderns was only one of the intellectual and cultural divisions which characterized the seventeenth century.

The different world-views emerging in the period were all, as we have seen, attempts to bring a new sense of order to the chaos of experience. Baroque art gives artistic expression to none of these world-views. Its connection is rather with the world the new systems were attempting to order, or rather with the actual world in which old traditions and attitudes exist side by side with the new. At bottom the Baroque accepts such a self-contradictory world and grows out of it; it is as if, unusually for an art style, the Baroque is its own world-view. But perpetually concerned as it is with illusion, seeming, paradox, flux, time and transience, the Baroque does not merely reflect a world of conflict and uncertainty. Combining elements of art and nature, spontaneity and control, stasis and dynamic movement, transience and permanence, into a unified dramatic whole, the baroque fountain is perhaps the single most expressive symbol of baroque art and baroque sensibility. Yet the central meaning of the symbol is its unity and coherence – the baroque fountain, like the baroque garden or building, painting or poem, unites its disparate elements into a single dynamic whole. The baroque artist, that is, struggles constantly to resolve the conflicts he contemplates, to overcome them and bring order out of disorder. At its finest baroque art succeeds in this aim; the created work of art does overcome the conflict it contains. Use and beauty, harmony and surprise, uniformity and variety, combine into an image that is beautiful and whole. This was true of some of the great baroque works in England: the new royal apartments at Windsor and the new buildings at Greenwich happily combined use and beauty or business and pleasure, and the whole canon of Vanbrugh's works relied on a continuing tension between harmony and surprise, uniformity and variety. No doubt this explains Vanbrugh's success as a landscape gardener for nothing so cleverly combines all these conflicting elements as the great baroque gardens of the seventeenth and early eighteenth centuries.

Baroque painting, music and literature in their forms and themes also reveal the same resolution of tensions within an aesthetic whole. The drama, of course, was an admirable vehicle for such resolution and so was the court masque, frequently thematically concerned with discord and its resolution through the agency of the creative imagination. The form of the masque was as emphatic in its statement about the role of art; in Jonson's *Golden Age* the resolution of discord was accomplished and the Golden Age established through the power of the arts in the shape of poetry – Chaucer, Gower, Lydgate and Spenser were summoned, the darkness of night and the cold of the winter were banished, and Astraea returned to the earth.

Such images of achieved harmony and restoration are by definition, in the context of the masque, fleeting and transitory; they are like flashes of illumination and heightened understanding. In greater and more permanent expressions of the English baroque imagination, the achievement of resolution seems no more final or absolute. In *Paradise Lost*, St Paul's, Blenheim Palace or Seaton Delaval, contradictory impulses and tensions are contemplated and held together by a soaring, monumental imaginative act; they are held in suspension, not dissolved. As attitudes and habits of mind changed, as new assurance was gained, as man came once more to believe that he understood and dominated his universe, it was inevitable that the drama of baroque forms and styles should cease to be expressively appropriate to the English artistic imagination.

CHAPTER IX

The Formation of Taste

Everyone calls barbarian what is not his own usage.
Montaigne

*

IN THE HISTORY of seventeenth-century Europe, perhaps nothing is of greater significance than the changing relationship between England* and the continent of Europe. At the beginning of the century England was an innocent in the European power game, which the ancient kingdom of Spain sought to manipulate to its own ends, or a pawn with which France might toy, a country turned in upon itself and preoccupied with national issues. By the end of the century England was emerging as the dominant European power, strong enough first to challenge and then to overcome the political, economic and cultural stranglehold which the France of the *Grand Siècle* seemed to have imposed on Europe.

The change was gradual rather than revolutionary, and its cultural dimension, like the rest, dependent on the existence of appropriate preconditions. Most important was the fact that England's cultural isolation from Europe had never been complete. In the realm of music, for example, certain links had never been broken; English styles exercised a considerable influence in Europe, just as Continental styles were enthusiastically accepted in England, and English musicians shared in a cultural experience which was common to all Europeans.

Cultural links were also maintained by the many substantial groups in English society who were forced to take an interest in European affairs. In any country even during periods of comparative diplomatic isolation, there have always to be some professionals who are in touch with developments elsewhere – otherwise, it would be impossible for any country to defend its interests or conduct a rational foreign policy. But these professionals, whose job entails some understanding of another society, will also serve as interpreters of that society to their own, as well as a cultural link between the two.

Of such professionals in the seventeenth century the most important was the crown, for the monarch was still the framer of foreign policy and no one as yet had the hardihood or probably the desire to question his right to do so. But even if the Stuarts had not needed a detailed knowledge of European affairs in order to pursue their foreign policies, their European contacts would have been important, for they married into several of the great families of Europe and, with the sole exception of James II's first wife, never with their own countrymen and women. James I had a Danish wife, his daughter married in Germany, his son in France. Charles II and James II had lived in exile in France and the

***

* By England I *mean* England. In this period the relationship of other areas of Britain to the Continent also changed but in differing ways, too complicated to explain in passing only.

Netherlands, the former had a Portuguese wife and French mistresses, and the latter's second wife was Italian. William III was Dutch, and his wife had spent a large part of her life in the Netherlands; even Queen Anne, whose chief pride was in being English, had visited France as a child, Brussels as a young woman, had a Danish husband, and was to be succeeded by a German prince. It is, therefore, scarcely surprising that even in an age of increasing bureaucratization of government much diplomacy remained personal and familial, as the negotiations for the Secret Treaty of Dover show, for there were scarcely two members of the Stuart family who could meet without engaging in international diplomacy at one level or another.

Several of Charles II's councillors, and secretaries, moreover, had an intimate knowledge of foreign affairs, including the Duke of Buckingham, and Henry Bennett, Lord Arlington, who had a Dutch wife, knew Spain well, and spoke several foreign languages fluently. A knowledge of foreign affairs and foreign languages was particularly desirable in the case of the two secretaries of state and their staffs, who were largely responsible for dealings with other powers. And closely linked with the offices of the secretaries of state was the professional diplomatic service. English diplomats abroad, hand-picked servants and friends of the monarch, often developed close associations with the countries to which they were accredited, contacts which were not without significance in the history of Britain's cultural development. Service abroad provided opportunities not only to sample foreign culture but also to invest in it, and many ambassadors used the time of their residence to purchase works of art for their collections.

Another large group of men whose knowledge of European affairs was sometimes profound, and who were to have the greatest impact on cultural developments in Britain, were English travellers who went abroad for a variety of reasons and purposes. By the 1620s such travellers from England could be found all over Europe. They followed, by preference, roads that ran through Catholic countries since, as the Duke of Shrewsbury once remarked to the Bishop of Oxford, 'There is nowhere in Europe a Protestant country favoured with the warm sun.' Mainly upper class, protected by social prestige and wealth, these aristocrats soon found that travel was possible even within the Church-State and in countries like Spain which had an active Inquisition. The European freemasonry of wealth and birth also protected travellers in time of war. When in 1711 the third Earl of Shaftesbury set out on his last trip to Italy he had to pass through the army of the Duke of Berwick. Despite the fact that Britain was engaged at the time in a bitter war with France, Berwick not only entertained Shaftesbury royally in his camp, but conducted him safely through the French army and into the lands of the Duke of Savoy, the ally of England and the enemy of France. The English knew they were safe abroad, because they were popular, and they were popular because they spent liberally. In 1692 Gregorio Lati remarked of these English travellers that they

come over with plenty of cash, plenty of gear, and servants to wait on them. They throw their money about like lords. It is reckoned that in Rome alone there are, in the ordinary way, upwards of six hundred gentlemen, all with people in their pay, and that, taking everything into account, they

123

spend at least two thousand crowns per head every year, so that Rome alone derives from England a yearly revenue of thirty thousand pistoles, good and sound.

Nor was Rome particularly exceptional. In Paris too 'there is never any lack of English visitors; an English business man assured me the other day that he had paid out to Englishmen in France a hundred and thirty thousand crowns in a single year, and he was by no means one of the biggest banks either.'[1]

Some of these vast sums of money were invested in purchasing tangible mementoes of foreign travels, as often as not substantial works of art, which, when brought back to England, helped to familiarize men with changes in European culture. Even the relatively wealthy would purchase prints and engravings, and usually sit for a portrait or two. Collecting mania was in fact so universal that even aristocrats who had previously shown little interest in the arts tended to blossom into important patrons and virtuosi on foreign soil.

The motives for foreign travel were many and varied. An aristocracy wealthy enough to do as it pleased frequently regarded travel merely as a pleasurable pastime. Gradually, however, there also emerged a notion of the Grand Tour not only as pleasurable, but as an essential finish to a gentleman's education. But travel was not only voluntary. In the troubled period between 1630 and 1730, for some of the English aristocracy, as for many other English men and women, a period of residence abroad was politically expedient; exile of this kind accounts for some of the increased intercourse with the Continent. Those exiled included not only the oppressed royalists of the Interregnum, but also the victims of Stuart oppression like the first Earl of Shaftesbury and Lord Montagu, as well as men like John Bushnell, who found it necessary to escape the rigours of the law or the consequences of their own actions. Bushnell, the first English sculptor to acquire a direct knowledge of Continental baroque sculpture, had fled from England after being forced to marry a servant whom his master had seduced. It is probably in this category also that we can place the architect, James Gibbs, who seems to have been driven abroad by the social and legal complications involved in being a practising Catholic in late seventeenth-century Aberdeen. He travelled across Europe, through Holland, Paris, Switzerland, Germany and Austria and eventually reached Rome, where after an abortive attempt at becoming a priest in 1703, he devoted his time to study of painting and architecture under Pietro Francesco Garroli and Carlo Fontana, only arriving in England in 1709.

A very frequent reason for travel and residence abroad was a desire for study of a more or less serious nature. Robert Boyle studied mathematics, history and geography in Switzerland and Geneva, before moving on to Italy in 1641 to pursue his more famous studies in anatomy and science; and Evelyn studied both anatomy and physiology at Padua, although his residence abroad had initially been an enforced one, brought about by his marked Anglican and royalist sympathies in the Civil War. Many people involved in the arts went abroad quite deliberately for the purpose of perfecting their art. Musicians, in particular, had a long tradition of travel for purposes of improvement and education and it was a common custom for a wealthy patron to make this possible for a protégé. Charles II was doing no more than many aristocrats when he sent Pelham Humfrey to France, in order to improve his knowledge of Continental music, and John Abell to Italy in 1681, in order to improve his voice. And, like musicians, architects, artists and writers also liked to travel in order to develop a knowledge of modern modes and techniques at their source. With no adequate artistic training available in England, it was often only by going abroad that the artist could learn what he needed to know. As we have seen, Isaac Fuller studied for many years in France under the history painter, François Perrier, and Robert Streeter studied painting in both France and Italy during the Interregnum. Of visits of this type perhaps the most fruitful was that of Wren to Paris in 1665. He happened to arrive at what was to be one of the most important periods of construction in the reign of Louis XIV, at a time when all the arts had been drafted into the service of the Sun King. Louis Le Vau, the King's chief architect, had already begun remodelling Versailles and had just completed the Collège Mazarin and the river front of the Louvre, which Wren, himself, described as 'a School of Architecture, the best probably at this day in Europe'.[2] Although Mansart was nearing the end of his career, Guarino Guarini had begun the domed church of St Anne-la-Royale by which Wren, who had never before seen a domed building, was particularly fascinated. What was of special importance here, apart from the opportunity to see completed masterpieces of modern architecture, was the fact that Wren was able to observe at first hand all the stages in the construction of a modern building, from the digging of the foundations to the finishing of the plasterwork.

Diplomacy and travel were not the only sources of contact between England and the Continent in the seventeenth century. Religion too played a role. Admittedly the Anglican contribution was not very great. England in 1660 was still regarded by other powers as the leading Protestant nation, and a bulwark against the Counter Reformation triumphant – despite the fact that the Stuart kings, for reasons of principle and economy, had consistently failed to live up to European expectations. The truth was that, except during the Interregnum, the national church of England, although certainly Protestant and to an extent reformed, had consciously adopted an independent stance in religion. The Anglican Church held that it maintained a unique, unbroken link with the medieval past, which set it apart from the other Protestant Churches. Built on the teaching of the saintly Hooker, with its appeal to history and common sense to supplement and correct too great a reliance on the bare letter of scripture, this was the church of Donne and Herbert, of Isaac Walton and Jeremy Taylor. Celebrating the virtues of gravity and dignity in religion, and strengthened by the tribulations of the Civil War and Commonwealth, it had emerged in 1660 as the state Church. As such it remained open to constant attack by extreme Protestants who preferred not to be comprehended in its traditions, and who wished to abolish all that they believed to be unscriptural in its practices, in part at least because they believed such practices had divided England from truly Protestant Europe.

Broadly speaking these critics of the Anglican establishment were right. It is true that the Anglican Church was never wholly separated from Continental thinking and practice. Those changes in the Anglican Church, which were most abhorred by the Puritan opposition in the first half of the seventeenth century, in fact stemmed directly from theological developments in Protestant Europe, and particularly from the work of the Dutch theologian Jacob Hermanns, or Arminius, as he was known, and his disciple, Simon Episcopius. Nevertheless it was not really until the end of the seventeenth century, with the development of the Latitudinarian movement, that Anglican clergy showed very much interest in the Protestant Churches on the Continent or even considered studying abroad.

To one large religious minority in England, on the other hand, a religious minority of increasing social importance, contact with Europe was all-important. This was the sporadically persecuted Catholic community, culturally dependent on Europe and particularly on those Catholic countries with seminaries, universities and schools which could provide an orthodox education for Catholic children. Not just Rome, but St Omer, Douai, Liège, Paris, Madrid and Valladolid were as important and familiar to English Catholics as any place in England. The vast majority of those Catholics educated abroad came back to England, some as missionary priests who journeyed from Catholic family to Catholic family, helping to maintain the cultural links between the outside Roman Catholic world and England. The consequences for the formation of English taste were not unimportant. The baroque conception that seeing, rather than hearing and understanding, was believing, meant that artifacts and works of art were deliberately exposed to as wide an audience as possible in the hope that conversions would follow. Religious pictures and statues, missal books and altar vessels, imported from abroad, could all play a part. It was for this reason that the Barberini had been so willing to dispatch religious pictures to Charles I, and for this reason that they had been so feared by the Puritan opposition. This was one motive which drove James II to employ the best artists in his kingdom to decorate his Catholic chapels in the most beautiful manner possible. And even before he was in a position to advertise his religion to his people so gloriously, James at York House had done his best to display Catholicism in concrete terms. Evelyn, in April 1672, had gone there to see

> the fopperies of the Papists . . . where now the *French ambassador* had caused to be represented our B. Saviour, at the Paschal Supper, with his Disciples, made as big as the life of waxwork, curiously clad and sitting round a large table, the room nobly hung, and shining with innumerable Lamps and Candles, this exposed to the whole World, all the City come to see.[3]

A final large group of individuals, helping to maintain a permanent Anglo-European connection, were English merchants with businesses based on foreign ties and interests. Many of these merchants had residents abroad, and many had themselves been residents in their youth. An English traveller could always reckon on an hospitable welcome from these expatriates who acted as bankers, interpreters and unofficial guides for their fellow-countrymen – like Mr Thomson of Genoa who acted as Evelyn's guide in 1644 – and, sometimes, as agents for the purchase of works of art. It was common for these men to develop strong ties of affection for their countries of residence and to build up wide social and business connections in them. Often culturally enlightened, they included men like John Finch who was resident in Florence between 1665 and

1700 and who commissioned paintings from Carlo Dolci – at that date virtually unknown in England – or Consul Smith, the most famous of all the merchant-patrons, who became the leading patron of painting in early eighteenth-century Venice, and who, up to 1730, was an extensive purchaser of works by Rosalba Carriera, Sebastiano Ricci, Marco Ricci and G. B. Piazzetta, both for himself and for the many Englishmen for whom he acted as agent. *

When all these diplomats, travellers, students, artists, Catholics and merchants are put together, it becomes clear that there was a substantial sector of English society which was likely to be familiar with changes in European culture in the seventeenth century. And, as the century progressed, a general knowledge of European affairs spread to a larger and larger public. In this process the press was an aid; newspapers like the *London Gazette*, regularly published from 1666 onwards, devoted a large part of their available space to foreign news, and reached a wide public. New scientific associations, of which the Royal Society is the most famous, corresponded regularly with similar bodies in Europe, and acted as centres for the dissemination of knowledge about affairs on the Continent. Booksellers began to import more and more foreign books and prints, and the wars with France at the end of the century made whole areas of Europe which had previously been *terra incognita* household names throughout England.

By the end of the seventeenth century, then, England and the English were deeply involved in Europe and in European affairs, and some knowledge of different European societies and cultures, however limited that knowledge might be, was fairly general. This increased understanding and knowledge played a large part in ensuring the success of Continental fashions in England. Whig propaganda subsequently saw the adoption of baroque art in England as a consequence of the importation of French fashions at the time of the Restoration in 1660 – fashions reflected by a court whose spoken language was French and in which the King's mistresses and mother were all French. Certainly after 1660 the English did suffer from over-exposure to French culture; the most recent successes of the French stage were swiftly adapted for English audiences, the aristocracy surrounded themselves with French servants, French dancing, riding and music masters, and learnt to dress in the latest French fashions. When in October 1660 Pepys dined with his relative, Lord Sandwich, always a man with an eye to the main chance, the noble lord spoke of little except about employing a French cook and master of the office, and having his wife and child apply black patches after the French fashion. But Whig propaganda was wrong in attributing this francophilia to the sole influence of the crypto-tyrannical and crypto-papist Charles II, for it derived largely from the natural interests of the English aristocracy who clearly enjoyed travel in France and who found the way of life of the French nobility familiar, congenial and stimulating. It was they, as much as the court, who were responsible for the importation of foreign styles and artistic modes into England.

In any case, it would be wrong to suggest that the importation of such

---

* At his death his collection went to King George III.

styles alone made the English Baroque, for if this were so it would not be the *English* Baroque of which we would be speaking but merely of an imported subculture. English artists and patrons were influenced by Continental models, but they were always selectively influenced, and that very selection of influences was itself an artistic statement. In fact, imitation, although often the most obvious, since it produced some horrendous hybrids, was probably the least important element in English baroque culture. Foreign imports which were not modified or adapted to English traditions had little hope of permanent success.

The best example is the disastrous history of the Italian opera in England in the early eighteenth century. The first attempts at its introduction were made by a group of three entrepreneurs: Nichola Haym, who, although of German parents, had been born and bred in Italy; the French harpsichordist and violinist, Charles Dieuport, who was one of the first interpreters of Corelli's music in England; and Thomas Clayton, a former member of the King's band, who had studied music in Italy. In 1705 they produced at Drury Lane Theatre, where they had established themselves, an 'opera after the Italian manner: All sung'. This was *Arsinoe: Queen of Cyprus*, with music largely by Clayton and scenery designed by Thornhill. It was followed, two years later, by *Rosamund*, with a libretto by Addison. The catastrophic failure of this venture had the unfortunate, if understandable, effect of ranging Addison on the side of enemies of Italian opera in England.

Meanwhile, a rival to the Drury Lane project had developed at the Haymarket where a series of successful operas, culminating in Handel's *Rinaldo* in 1711, were staged. Thereafter the opera in England seemed to be well established, and it found many enthusiastic supporters among the English aristocracy, including Lord Burlington. In 1719 a permanent opera society – the Royal Academy of Music – was formed, and devoted itself entirely to the presentation of Italian opera. Only ten years later the opera society, and with it Italian opera in England, had completely collapsed. During those ten years Italian opera had been subjected to a whole series of persistent attacks from the literary world. It had been condemned as irrational; Steele, on hearing that Scarlatti's *Pirro e Demetrio* had been performed with great success at the Haymarket, complained in *The Tatler* that

> This intelligence is not very acceptable to us Friends of the Theatre; for the Stage being an Entertainment of the Reason, and all the Faculties, this way of being pleased with the suspense of them for three Hours together, and being given up to the shallow Satisfaction of Eyes and Ears only, seems rather to arise from the Degeneracy of our Understanding than an Improvement of our Diversions.[4]

In similar vein, Addison in the *Spectator* remarked that 'If the Italians have a Genius for Music above the English, the English have a Genius for other Performances of a much higher Nature, and capable of giving the Mind a much nobler Entertainment.' Even worse, in Addison's view, was the largely sensual appeal of the opera whose 'only Design is to gratify the Senses, and keep up an indolent Attention in the Audience'; for he feared that the sensual appeal of the music 'would take the entire Possession of our Ears' and 'would make us incapable of hearing Sense' so that, in the end, it 'would exclude Arts that have a much greater Tendency to the Refinement of Human Nature'. Other critics complained of the insuperable barrier of the Italian language, of the subject matter, of the use of *castrati*, or that the opera, being Italian, smacked of foreign tyranny and of popery. Underlying all these views was the fundamental fact that the Italian opera was a failure in England because it bore no relation to native English traditions. It was not that the English objected to music on the stage. Plays which included music and spectacle had always been extremely successful. But, as the *Gentleman's Journal* explained in 1693, 'Operas abroad are plays where every word is sung', and 'this is not relished in England.' The moment of truth came in 1728 with the presentation of Gay's *Beggars' Opera*, an English ballad opera, deeply rooted in all the traditions of the English stage and musical drama. *The Beggars' Opera*, which ran for sixty performances and was the first real runaway success of the English stage, 'exposes', Swift wrote, 'that unnatural taste for Italian music among us which is wholly unsuitable to our northern climate, and the genius of the people, whereby we are overrun with Italian effeminancy and Italian nonsense.'[5] And thus, in the words of Colley Cibber, 'Opera, after one luxurious Season, like the first Wife of a roving Husband, began to lose its Charms, and every Day discovered to our Satiety, Imperfections, which our former Fondness had been blind to.'[6] For, he continued, 'The Truth is, that this Kind of Entertainment being so entirely sensual, it had no Possibility of getting the better of our Reason, but by its Novelty; and that Novelty could never be supported but by an annual Change of the best Voices, which like the finest Flowers, bloom but for a Season, and when that is over, are only dead Nose-gays.'[7]

Increased contact with the Continent, therefore, did not simply lead to a widespread and uncritical importation of foreign fashions. On the contrary it effected something far more vital: it created a climate of opinion in which new ideas could flourish, ideas which were often indigenous and the product of a peculiarly English civilization. For English taste, as far as the visual arts were concerned, was largely conditioned by what people saw and what they therefore came to expect to see. In any civilization, only the artist remains immune from the general rule that it is normal to assume that what is habitual is also right. It is a basic fact of human psychology that led Horace Walpole to conclude that

> When a Frenchman reads of the garden of Eden . . . he concludes it was something approaching to that of Versailles, with its clipped hedges, berceaus and trellis-work. If his devotion humbles him so far as to allow that, considering who designed it, there might be a labyrinth full of Aesop's fables, yet he does not conceive that four of the largest rivers in the world were half so magnificent as an hundred fountains full of statues by Girardon.[8]

Sir Roger Pratt had also distinguished this basic trait in human psychology as being a major cause of the artistic inadequacy of so much English architecture in the early and mid-seventeenth century:

> For many [he wrote] are apt to think nothing well but what is conformable

to that old-fashioned [house] which they themselves dwell in, or some of their neighbours: they little considering that houses were at first built rather for the necessity of men's affairs than for the exact convenience and neat contrivance of them, and that Architecture here had not yet received those advantages which it has in other parts it continuing almost still as rude here as it was at the very first.[9]

Wren agreed with Pratt and argued for the existence of a 'Customary Beauty' which 'is begotten by the Use of our Senses to those Objects which are usually pleasing to us for other Causes, as Familiarity or particular Inclination breeds a Love to Things not in themselves Lovely . . .'.[10]

A similar attitude can be discerned in contemporary beliefs about church building; a general idea existed that Gothic architecture was most suitable for the purpose simply because most of the surviving church buildings in England happened to be Gothic buildings. This, according to the *Parentalia* account, was a chief ground of complaint against Wren's first model design for the new St Paul's, since, 'it being contrived in the Roman style, was not so well understood and relished' by those 'who thought it deviated too much from the old Gothic form of Cathedral Churches, which they had been used to see and admire in this country'.[11] A similar attitude was at work in domestic building; Inigo Jones had held that while the exterior of buildings should be 'solid, masculine and unaffected', their interiors should be rich and elaborate, and such buildings of his that had been completed and survived, and those built under his influence, conformed to this pattern. As a result it became an established norm, fitting in so well with the functional needs of great houses in the eighteenth century that even the strictest of the Palladians could continue to build houses which, however restrained their exteriors, were a riot of elaboration in their interior decoration.

The belief that what exists is necessarily right was both a strength and a danger as far as English baroque art was concerned. It is a strength in that a fundamental aspect of baroque art is its capacity to utilize native and popular idioms. Part of the vitality of Hawksmoor, of Vanbrugh, and even of Wren, as we have seen, came from their constant interest in England's architectural past. One example of this vitality is the baroque steeples of the City churches, a characteristically *English* contribution to baroque civilization and one always admired by foreign visitors throughout the eighteenth century. No Continental models of any importance existed for such steeples, which are virtually unknown to Italian architecture, and they arose from a dialogue between present and past engaged in by England's baroque architects. The results were enchanting; significantly one of the loveliest, that of St Martin-in-the-Fields, was the design of the most Roman-minded of all the baroque architects, James Gibbs. Yet, the danger to the baroque architects from the general acceptance of the existing norm was very real, for it was one factor in the ultimate victory of the Palladians. The baroque architects were in the end, ironically enough, * to be the victims of the posthumous success of Inigo Jones. This success is not difficult to account for: for a long time Jones effectively had no competitors.

---

* If Wren, as Shaftesbury complained, was 'one single court architect' what was Inigo Jones?

Between 1642 and the 1660s there was no public building in England, and very little private building of real importance. Although Inigo Jones had trained one important pupil, John Webb, who lived on until 1672 (and many of his drawings of ideal buildings were to be well known and a source of inspiration to architects for another hundred years), Webb built little, and in terms of actual modern architectural masterpieces to look at, Inigo Jones stood almost alone. For a whole generation, therefore, his were the only really modern buildings seen and known in England; Wren was the first architect of European stature to emerge after his death and by that time Jones's architecture had long been established as the up-to-date English norm. We would therefore expect, what in fact proved to be the case, that Inigo Jones's influence would be fundamental in forming English architectural taste and as a result establishing in that taste a Palladian bias.

Yet Inigo Jones's influence was necessarily limited to those who either knew his work or knew of it from prints or drawings. It tended, therefore, to be dominant in London and the home counties while the new architects were able to have a similar influence in other parts of the country. This was the real importance of the wave of new building by the aristocracy between 1660 and 1730. Those who patronized the baroque architects inevitably set up new standards for imitation within the area of their territorial influence. Great houses spawned little ones, and little houses led to alterations in existing ones even when they did not provoke a total rebuilding. So Vanbrugh's Castle Howard had a remarkable impact on Yorkshire, bringing a rapid spread of baroque building and bearing out Vanbrugh's contention that 'There are several gentlemen in this part of the world that are possessed of the spirit of building.' Duncombe Park, built in 1713 by the amateur gentleman-architect William Wakefield, the school at Kirkleatham built for the Turner family in 1708, Aldby Park, Buttercrombe and Beningborough Hall built in 1716, by the local architect William Thornton, who had worked under Hawksmoor at Beverley Minster, are all directly influenced by Castle Howard. But perhaps the most remarkable example of the spread of a taste for the Baroque in this northern area is Gibbs's remarkable mausoleum – an octagon, crowned by a pyramid – built for the Turner family, which is the very epitome of English baroque style. A similar provincial influence was exercised by Thomas Archer in the Midlands, where he found a faithful imitator of his style in the prolific Francis Smith, who, long after the Palladian victory, continued to produce small baroque 'Palaces' for Tory country gentlemen.

The impact of completed buildings in a particular area could therefore be very great, but a second major influence must be regarded as just as important. This was the printing press which had an immediate impact wherever books were read or prints were looked at. In the first half of the seventeenth century a steady trickle of books on the fine arts had begun to issue from the English presses: Peacham's *Art of Drawing* was first published in 1606; Serlio first became available in English in 1611 when it was translated from the Dutch edition by Robert Peake. This was a particularly influential edition since besides providing information about the buildings of the ancient world, it also gave designs for decorative detail which were in use in mid-sixteenth-century Italy. Then in 1624 came the first English work on architecture – a rather inadequate paraphrase of Vitruvius – by Sir Henry Wotton; in 1648–50, Edward Norgate's *Miniatura*; and in 1658 William Sanderson's *Graphice*.

More important even than these English works were books and prints of Continental origin which were rapidly becoming included in every good private library. Works on architecture – by Vitruvius, Serlio, Philibert de l'Orme – and many modern Italian architectural treatises were all well known. Books of this nature had their primary effect on patrons; they were almost like catalogues of available artistic wares from which the patron could make his own selection. But they were also important for artists. Some of the major English baroque architects derived the bulk of their building vocabulary from prints and illustrations even though they had travelled abroad. Wren, for instance, did not find his inspiration for the steeple of St Mary-le-Bow in France, for there he saw nothing like it. Rather, the ultimate source for that building, as for the dome of St Paul's, must be found in Italian engravings.[12] It is likewise in Italian engravings of works by Borromini, which Wren knew from Falda's *Chiese di Roma*, that the sources of the most baroque of all Wren's steeples, St Vedast, Foster Lane, are to be found – in Sant' Ivo della Sapienza which, like all of Borromini's work, haunted the imagination of England's baroque architects. And if such books and prints were important even to artists who had travelled abroad, how vital must they have been for those who never left England: men like William Talman, who derived many of his ideas from European models but who never travelled overseas, or Nicholas Hawksmoor, who found all his architectural vocabulary in prints and engravings of both ancient and modern Italian buildings, in the works of Jean Marot, and in books of voyages and travel memoirs?

As English horizons widened there was a considerable vogue for such travel books and Wren, Hooke and Hawksmoor were all great collectors and readers of them. In fact their appetite for such curiosities seems to have been unlimited, and the absorption of information gleaned from them may have had some very interesting effects on English architecture; it is known, for instance, that an early plan of Hawksmoor's for the Radcliffe Camera was based on the Sulemanije mosque in Constantinople.

As far as art and architecture are concerned then, it is clear that as the seventeenth century went on, English taste was formed by a conjunction of European example and influence and existing native traditions, spiced by what could be read or seen in existing books or prints. But the study of the development of English taste in the period of the Baroque is complicated by the fact that, even though the forms of baroque art emerged as a revolt against the tyranny of the intellect and the strict rules of construction of the High Renaissance, the grounds for this revolt and the ingredients of the new style were never systematically expounded. It was, in fact, the opponents of baroque styles who were to be vocal in expressing their reasons for rejecting it. And it was only as a result of such attacks that practitioners of baroque art were forced into a partial explanation of what they were about.

It was a peculiar tragedy of English baroque art that it never found its own spokesman – a baroque Shaftesbury, Dennis, Campbell, Morris or Burlington – to show that far from being a corrupt foreign import, it had sprung directly out of English traditions. Without such spokesmen it stood before the blast of the Palladian winter, dumb and naked in the presence of its enemies. In the 1690s Wren was publicly acknowledged 'to be as knowing and ingenious a gentleman for contrivance in buildings, as our age doth afford, who by his works has manifested himself to be'.[13] Scarcely a generation later those same works were looked at with scorn and contempt from the viewpoint of the self-consciously English Whig Palladians, the exponents of the new age of English cultural supremacy, and Burlington would be widely applauded when he criticized Wren's west front of St Paul's by comparing it with that of Inigo Jones and declaring that 'The Jews, who recalled the First, wept when they saw the Second Temple.' A taste for the English Baroque was no more.

CHAPTER X

The Function of the Work of Art

Music herself is lost, in vain she brings
Her choicest notes to praise the best of Kings:
Her melting strains in you a tomb have found
And like Bees in their own sweetness drowned
He that brought peace and discord could atone,
His name is music of itself alone.
Dryden,
To his Sacred Majesty: a Panegyrick

*

MANY OF THE assumptions widely accepted in most current thinking about the status of art and the artist are of fairly recent origin. The autonomy of the work of art, art largely for art's sake, the heroic artist-individual alienated from society: none of these had much currency prior to the Romantic movement. In Europe in the seventeenth century they would not have been understood. Then the arts were seen in highly functional terms, their primary value ultimately often a question of their utility as forms of social control. The papal and French courts stood as living examples of the fact that a pursuit of the arts could tame and subdue even the most turbulent of aristocracies. Equally the arts could stupefy and amaze, and so control, those whom aristocrats regarded as the 'vulgar herd'. In contemporary France Bossuet expressed this view when he argued that while 'God forbade ostentation that springs from vanity and the puffed-up folly of a court intoxicated by riches . . . He was well pleased that the court of the King was brilliant and magnificent, to inspire respect among the peoples',[1] and at the height of the French *frondes*, Mazarin spent vast sums on sponsoring the opera as a means of distracting the people from civil strife, in the fundamental belief that this was the most effective means of bolstering up a particular form of hierarchical society and a particular social system.

The situation was no different in England. Like Mazarin, the Earl of Clarendon saw the theatre, as was only natural in a man whose political education occurred during the reign of Charles I, as an instrument of government, and another arm of the state.

> It is [he wrote] among the greatest and most difficult Mysteries of Government, to bring People together to Recreations and Spectacles, and this Art the Roman senate studied when it was in its most flourishing condition: and the first Institution of the Stage was the Product of that wise Deliberation.[2]

The stage could be used, and *was* used, to portray an imagined reality, to which it was hoped society would conform by imitation. In 1709 Steele was still

recommending 'the apt use of the theatre, as the most agreeable and easy
method of making a moral gentry; which would end in rendering the rest of
the people regular in their behaviour, and ambitious of laudable undertakings'.[3]
Tragedy could instruct by example, comedy by pouring ridicule on folly. In
fact, the purpose of all literature was to educate and to guide, 'To instruct
delightfully', wrote Dryden, 'is the general end of all poetry. Philosophy
instructs, but it performs its work by precept; which is not delightful, or not
so delightful as example.'[4] And Steele concluded that 'Excellent poetry and
description dwell upon us so agreeably, that all the readers of them are made to
think, if not write like men of wit.'[5] So, too, with painting, music, sculpture
and architecture; experience of them could civilize man, refine human nature,
rouse the happy passions and subdue the socially disruptive ones. How could it
be otherwise when good morals and good taste were held to be inseparable?
Or when art was believed to imitate Nature, which itself was a manifestation
of the Divine?

At a more basic level, it was acknowledged that the arts were an effective
means of political propaganda. This, after all, was why governments all over
Europe, and not just in Puritan-hating England, were anxious to control the
press; why, in England, Charles I in particular took so firm a stand on the
question of censorship. As we have seen, Charles and his father were well aware
of the power of the arts for propaganda purposes, and the Jacobean and Caroline
masque had been used to advertise to the court circle those political doctrines
which the Stuart monarchs held most dear, and to show 'the magnificence of
the court of England'.[6]

Nor were the arts only used to form the political habits of mind of a court
aristocracy. The general public, particularly in turbulent London, was subjected to relentless propaganda through spectacle. After the Restoration, as in
former reigns, the public procession propagandized royal attitudes and adver-
tised public policies. For these processions, evanescent works of art were produced by skilled artists on which as much time and money were lavished as on
more durable artifacts. These works of art embodied themes which were at the
same time being enshrined in more permanent artistic forms; the theme of the
Boscobel oak, for instance, which baroque writers and artists were making a
central strand in Stuart martyrology, found constant expression in the Lord
Mayors' Shows in the reign of Charles II.

Baroque themes in these processions and shows were matched by baroque
stylistic devices and a truly 'baroque' expenditure, which indicates their
political importance to the crown. For the coronation procession of Charles II,
the triumphal arches were designed by Peter Mills and Sir Balthazar Gerbier,
the ex-client of Buckingham and friend of Rubens, who had deserted the
royalist cause after the Civil War and who now vainly hoped to regain royal
favour. These arches were strongly influenced by Rubens's arches which had
been built for the entry into Antwerp of the Cardinal-Infant Ferdinand in
1635 and, although painted by Andrew Dakers and William Lightfoot, both
native Englishmen, were completely in tune with Continental Baroque both in
conception and in execution.

Coronations were not the sole occasion for such displays. Royal marriages,
the signing of treaties, the celebration of peace – all were made memorable by

some form of public procession and celebration. On every occasion these celebrations were considered important enough not only to warrant great expense, but also for even the most distinguished artists to be involved. It is probable, for instance, that Thornhill designed the famous firework machine used in the celebration of the Treaty of Utrecht in 1713.

It is not difficult to see why these processions were regarded as being so vital. Similar displays were a stock-in-trade of governmental machinery in every European country, and in an age in which literacy was by no means universal, such visual displays were the most effective way of making a particular policy known, as well as of involving the populace in it. Above all they provided an excellent opportunity to present a monarch dramatically to his people, since the king, in his visible presence, satisfied that most basic psychological need, which predisposes man to a love of the arts, and which Clarendon described as an 'inclination to gazing'. One of the primary functions of royalty at this time was in fact an artistic one – to bring colour and pageantry into an everyday life that was often grim and always humdrum. A king, as James I had remarked, was 'as one set on a stage, whose smallest actions and gestures, all the people gazingly behold'. It was a monarch's duty to entertain his people. The progress and the procession ideally fulfilled this function while at the same time providing an opportunity to impress upon the spectators the particular view of the monarchy which the English crown wished to convey.

Nor was it only successive British monarchs who grasped the significant value of the public procession. In London the annual Lord Mayors' Shows offered an opportunity to celebrate the greatness, and to advertise the pride, of the capital city to its citizens, and so to involve them in its destiny and interests. Similarly, the Whig opposition in the time of Charles II was to advertise its policies through public processions and progresses, while the great pope-burning processions of the later seventeenth century were to a large extent a poor man's pageant.

Processions of this kind were the meeting point of high and popular culture, and both high and popular culture were essentially politicized in the Baroque Age. It was inevitable that all the resources of the higher culture should be used to glorify each British monarch and to raise him, or her, into that pantheon of semi-deities which was being populated already by the baroque imagination of Continental Europe. As in so much else, Charles I was the pioneer, establishing a strong Stuart tradition when he commissioned from Rubens the Banqueting House ceiling, which, in its elaborate allegories, celebrates the peaceful rule of James I. After the interlude of the Interregnum, Charles II and James II took up this tradition, established by their father.

Few emotions ran so deep in the heart of Charles II as admiration of Louis XIV, an attitude which led him into the only political follies he committed during his difficult reign. Admiration led inevitably to imitation. In exile, Charles and many members of his court had experienced and approved the power, prestige and wealth of the French Church and the French system of government, and while Charles II was intelligent enough to recognize that he could never identify England with his own person in the same way as Louis had identified France with his, he was also astute enough to realize the propaganda value of the French king's artistic projects. Louis XIV had founded the Invalides, so Charles, in imitation, could set up his Chelsea hospital for pensioned soldiers;* the projected palace of Winchester, the most baroque of all Charles's schemes, embodied in the most French of all Wren's designs, was, with its proposed dramatic recession of wings narrowing towards the centre, nothing more than a Versailles writ small; and the royal band of twenty-four violins was a direct imitation of that of the French king.

Yet Charles II never lost sight of political reality. However much he might desire to emulate his cousin Louis, he always recognized that England was not France. With a monarchy limited *de facto* as much as *de iure* by the acts of 1641–42, the Civil War and its aftermath, monarchy in England could not be celebrated as absolute. Yet art could be used to do the next best thing, to elevate the monarch above other mortals, to depict the Stuarts and their consorts, less as they were, and far more as the nature of their office would have had them be.

In the case both of Charles II and his successor, this apotheosis could most easily be achieved by associating them, as in Verrio's ceiling for the Henry VIII chapel at Windsor, with the royal martyr, Charles I, whose tragic story lent itself so exceptionally well to the full baroque treatment. It was a theme which Verrio was to return to more than once, but one which was most successfully treated by the Anglo-Scottish painter, Michael Wright, in his ceiling-piece for the bedchamber of Charles II. In this allegory of the Restoration – the most attractive piece of baroque decorative painting ever executed in England – the figure of Justice points to a medallion-head of Charles I, while *putti* bear up the Boscobel oak.

Such constant references back to the disasters associated with the execution of Charles I and 'the iniquity of the late times' were one of the most powerful devices of social manipulation and control ever devised by any government. Every disaster could be seen as divine punishment for the murder of the royal martyr and often was so regarded by the popular imagination. There can be no doubt that Charles II, always acutely attuned to public opinion, was aware of this popular emotion and deliberately played upon it. But we should not underestimate his character to the extent of denying him his fair share of Stuart family piety. It was not merely a matter of form which caused Charles to declare his intention of rebuilding St Paul's 'in pursuance of' the 'royal and pious intentions' of his royal grandfather and father. The Stuarts were always a most closely united family,† and filial devotion played a large part in the countless remembrances of Charles I which are associated with the reign of Charles II. It was, for instance, such an emotion which underlay the proposed building of the mausoleum for Charles I at Windsor, projected in 1678.

The theme of Charles I, King and Martyr, was then often present in works commissioned by or for Charles II, and offered an ideal theme for the imagina-

---

* Incidentally, also a permanent, unfortunate reminder that Charles II was the first English king to maintain a permanent army.

† Two possible exceptions to this generalization are Queen Mary and Queen Anne, whose attitude to their father in 1688 can scarcely be regarded as filial in any conventional sense. Their attitude to their brother is even more problematical.

tion of the baroque artist. But the circumstances of Charles II's own early life, his restoration, and the political upheavals of his reign, also proved excellent subjects for allegorical treatment. All were alluded to in the remarkable series of paintings which Verrio completed for Hugh May's remodelled interiors at Windsor and which were much admired by Mary of Modena, the Duchess of York. The ceiling of the Audience Room was decorated with a painting of the Restoration of the Church of England, which was linked to the ceiling in the Withdrawing Room. This represented the Restoration of the Monarchy, symbolized by a picture of Charles II riding the sky in a triumphal car, and attended by a variety of obligatory deities and allegorical figures. On the ceiling of St George's Hall, the Rye House plot was recorded, with a portrait of Charles II in his garter robes, enthroned in glory attended by various allegorical persons, and with the first Earl of Shaftesbury, among the forces of Evil, 'dispersing Libels'.[7] Although the reign of Charles II is not one which is normally remembered as one of great military successes, nor even one when British influence in Europe was particularly great, the same series of paintings makes it clear that Charles II wished to see himself in the tradition of the European absolute monarch; the King's bedchamber was decorated with a portrait of the King in his garter robes, to whom the four continents paid homage, while the ceiling of the Queen's gallery showed Perseus and Andromeda and symbolized the liberation of Europe by Charles II.

While the reign of James was too short for the completion of a large body of work, the quality of that which was commissioned by the King makes it clear that he also saw art as primarily serving the purpose of magnifying his own person. During this reign, one of Verrio's few completed works was the ceiling of Henry VIII's chapel, which had for its subject matter the glorification of James II, shown attended by various figures, symbolizing the restoration of Catholicism in England. The powerful agency of this change was monarchical authority, religion being portrayed as very much the handmaid of secular authority.

Perhaps surprisingly the Glorious Revolution made very little difference to this tradition of court art. William and Mary came from a court where the necessary allegorical vocabulary was well understood and where art had been employed for much the same purpose as at the courts of Charles II and James II. In the Netherlands, by long tradition, the House of Orange had frequently been associated with the symbolism of Hercules, and this tradition was now imported into England. On the King's staircase at Hampton Court, in a complicated painting representing the triumph of Protestantism, William was portrayed by Verrio in the guise of Hercules, while the ceiling decoration also included the lions of Hercules and the sign of Leo from the Zodiac. More lion-skins – this time in stone – decorate William Emmett's enchanting round window-frames in the Fountain Court, the south side of which displayed the Labours of Hercules by Laguerre in *grisaille*. The most outspoken statement about the rule of William III, however, was in Cibber's garden-front pediment, where William, portrayed as Hercules, is shown trampling on Superstition, Tyranny and Fury, and is led by Fame to the Arts of Peace.

The glorification of William's reign was also taken up by Thornhill in his decorations at Greenwich Hospital. Here, in the Great Hall, he painted the

Triumph of Peace and Liberty, with William presenting the cap of Liberty and trampling on Arbitrary Power. William and Mary were surrounded by various allegorical figures to represent Peace, Piety and the Cardinal Virtues, while above them the Vices and their destruction by Minerva and Hercules were depicted. This complicated painting, completed in 1717, was complemented by the rest of the Greenwich series which illustrated the landing of William at Torbay and of George I at Greenwich, and the consequent inauguration of a Golden Age. The last of the series was painted on the ceiling of the Upper Hall: Queen Anne and George of Denmark, attended by Neptune, to whom the World paid homage as the rulers of the seas.

It was completely in accord with the spirit of the Baroque Age in Europe that, as we have seen, painting did not stand alone in its celebration of the monarchy. Architecture, above all, had to be impressed into royal service. In contemporary France Richelieu had stressed the importance of palaces in impressing visitors with the grandeur of France as embodied in the person of the king. Beginning with James I, the Stuart monarchs all shared this view. The first building in England whose essential service was to display royal secular might, power, prestige and glory was the Banqueting House at Whitehall, built for the express purpose of entertaining foreign royalty, for receiving ambassadors, and as a physical and permanent setting for the ephemeral but on-going entertainments, spectacles, 'magnificences' and events which were an integral part of the art of government of the early Stuarts. After the Restoration, Charles II's grandiose schemes for the building of a new royal palace at Winchester, and that of William and Mary for the rebuilding of Hampton Court, had a similar underlying purpose. At the same time, musicians within the court circle were expected to contribute to the apotheosis and celebration of the monarchy, producing compositions not only for the great state occasions, victories and peace treaties, but also for royal weddings, coronations and even royal birthdays. Nor would any of the later Stuarts have needed that reminder, which Pope would have to provide for a less enlightened age, of the important role which the poet could play in the state:

> Sages and Chiefs long since had birth
> E're Caesar was, or Newton nam'd,
> These raised new Empires o'er the Earth,
> And Those new Heavens and Systems framed;
> Vain was the chief's and sage's pride
> They had no Poet and they died.
> In vain they schemed, in vain they bled
> They had no Poet and are dead.[8]

Poets were maintained on the royal pension roll because poetry was well recognized to be an excellent medium for propaganda and advertisement. The literary counterpart to Verrio's Windsor decorations was Dryden's libretto for the opera of *Albion and Albanius* which celebrated the apotheosis of Charles II, Dryden's 'best of Kings'. Dryden wrote many other poems in praise of Charles, his policies and his reign, and if Charles II had his Dryden, Queen Anne had her Colley Cibber. In his description of the Duke of Marlborough and celebration of the glories of Blenheim, Cibber also presents the apotheosis of Queen

Anne whom he describes as 'A Gentle Goddess' animating Marlborough's Mind.[9]

The arts, therefore, were a necessary adjunct of royalty in the Baroque Age, and the amount of control which the crown was able to exercise over them is a clear indication of the very great powers which were still enjoyed by the British monarchy. But just as the aristocracy of Britain was beginning to dispute those powers with the crown, so also they were beginning to dispute the crown's control of the arts. They began by imitation. Like the crown, they demanded that the arts should glorify them as individuals and celebrate their political and territorial power. As a result, the Restoration was followed by a positive mania for building among the upper classes. The renewal of court life restored to the aristocrats a position of social ascendancy which they had lost during the Interregnum. They were powerful, wealthy – particularly those individuals who had managed to maintain a royalist stance and to retain a hold on their property – and immensely arrogant. Their building projects were designed to consolidate their position, to advertise their territorial power, and to provide a permanent setting for a way of life which was conceived of as necessarily different from that of every other class in society.

This Restoration building boom was temporarily halted with the accession of James II, for the political uncertainties of his reign were not very conducive to large-scale artistic projects, but the interruption was only temporary. For the Glorious Revolution followed – that Revolution which the English aristocracy subsequently came to see as their greatest creative work of art – and by the Revolution and its aftermath the aristocrats reached that summit of political authority which they were to maintain for another two hundred years.

After 1688 the Fates continued to conspire in favour of the already great. The wars with France, which William III brought in his train when he became King of England, brought countless new opportunities for those who had money to make money. These wars were financed both from loans and from taxation, principally from that notorious land-tax to which the Tory country gentlemen took exception. Both these means of raising finance inevitably increased economic disparities among the upper classes. Those who derived their income from sources other than land found that money begot money and prospered. The small men, solely dependent for their income on their estates, at a time when rent levels remained steady and sometimes even declined, suffered just as inevitably. It is true that between 1660 and 1692 taxation on land had already been a main source of governmental income, but, even at its highest during that period, the land-tax had never absorbed more than a fifth of income, and that was only in the peak years of 1667 and 1690. By contrast, the war taxation between 1692 and 1715, which was both heavier and continuous, was nearly as ruinous as the Tory squires always maintained it was. The inevitable consequence was a steady drift towards the large estate and the great landlord. Thus, before 1740, lands which changed hands tended to be purchased by families who already owned large estates, or by men, like the Duke of Marlborough, who, although newcomers to the aristocracy, were rapidly building up large territorial agglomerations for prestige purposes.

In this connection one other consequence of the changing patterns of wealth, landowning and taxation should be noted, since it had a clear impact on cultural development. This was the undoubted fact that, while rents remained steady or even declined in the country as a whole, in London they were booming, and those who could invest their wealth in building houses for rent in the metropolis could look for enormous profits. To this may be attributed the vast expansion of the 'politer' areas of London in the later seventeenth and early eighteenth centuries, from which the English baroque architects, and particularly James Gibbs, who was commissioned to develop the Marylebone estate of the Harleys, greatly profited. In the City of London alone from 1660 onwards a number of important building developments were going forward; the area south of the Strand was developed after 1674 by the shady and unscrupulous speculator, Dr Nicholas Barbon, an entrepreneur from Leyden in Holland; the area around St James's was being redeveloped by the Earl of St Albans from the 1660s onwards; and Soho was laid out and built up in the subsequent decades. Mayfair was also opened up in the same period; it was here that Clarendon's house was built, here, in 1664, that Hugh May built a mansion for Lord Berkeley, and here that in 1664–65 Sir John Denham built the first Burlington House. Further expansion followed. From 1675 onwards Lord Berkeley had become deeply involved in the property business and was laying out a square and several streets in the area immediately to the north of his own mansion. And it was for these new fashionable areas that subsequent demand came for new churches, a demand from which, again, the baroque architects were to profit.

It was those English aristocrats who had large landholdings as well as profitable investments elsewhere, the wealthy Whig oligarchs, who now disputed political power with the crown. At the same time they began to challenge the court's dominance in cultural matters. The first symbol of this change was the building of Chatsworth, the first great Whig palace which, by its scale and magnificence, was a direct statement about the changed relationship between the crown and the aristocracy. Chatsworth had many successors as the great aristocrats moved beyond a mere imitation of prevailing court tastes and modes of living, and, in a remarkable wave of building, even more spectacular than that which had followed the Restoration, began to create their own characteristic country-house culture. 'All the world is running mad after building as far as they can reach', wrote Sir John Vanbrugh in a letter to the Duke of Manchester in 1708.

What the aristocrats demanded of their architects was that they should build on their estates country houses which would have all the appearances of palaces. These would emphasize what so many of the English aristocracy really were – princes within their own provinces. The great house had become a status symbol in an age which interpreted a man's position by his external surroundings. It was a setting for a particular way of life whose emphasis was on expenditure and magnificence, as the great lords who divided England between them vied with each other to have the most extravagant table or the greatest number of servants. There is considerable truth in Horace Walpole's complaint that 'art in the hands of ostentatious wealth', as expressed in the formal baroque garden, 'became the means of opposing nature; and the more it traversed the march of the latter, the more nobility thought its power was demonstrated'.[10] For the magnificent country house surrounded by magnificent gardens distinguished its owner and his descendants from lesser men, as Vanbrugh emphasized to the Duke of Newcastle when he was trying to persuade him to rebuild Welbeck in 1703:

> I believe [he wrote] that if your grace will please to consider of the intrinsic value of titles and blue garters, and jewels and great tables and numbers of servants etc. in a word all those things that distinguish Great Men from small ones, you will confess to me that a good house is at least upon a level with the best of them.[11]

Great houses on this scale were designed to awe and impress and so, 'since men tire of expense that is obvious to few spectators',[12] from the first, it was of their essence that they were meant to be seen. They were conceived of as works of art, showpieces rather than homes, where sightseers and visitors were positively encouraged. Indeed, for a period in the 1720s at Canons, the proceeds from visitors were sufficiently large for them to be earmarked in the household accounts for specific purposes. It is in this kind of context that we can intelligently place the most brilliant gem of early eighteenth-century art – Gibbs's Octagon Room at Orleans House, Twickenham, built for the important Whig politician, James Johnson. The room was built for one purpose only: to entertain the Princess of Wales as splendidly as possible, and it is to this occasion that we owe a fine example of late English baroque art.

It is not surprising, therefore, that the new aristocratic palaces were distinctive neither for their rationality nor for any consideration of domestic comfort, convenience or cheerfulness. The external appearance mattered far more than the interior. Although Vanbrugh was to maintain that he always bore in mind the fact that people would have to live in his houses, and that Castle Howard was so well designed that the 'Passages would be so far from gathering and drawing wind . . . that a Candle would not flare in them . . . not even in the Hall, which is as high (though not indeed so big) as that of Blenheim', and that all the 'rooms, with moderate fires are ovens',[13] in fact he usually seems to have been peculiarly careless about the purposes to which the interiors were to be put. At Blenheim, whose whole building covers three acres, his major concern was to build a national monument which would be the pride of England and the envy of Europe, 'an Intended Monument of the Queen's Glory'. Duchess Sarah was therefore quite right in maintaining that he cared little that a family also had to live there or that it was 'a private Habitation of the Duke of Marlborough'.[14] Voltaire, who some years after Marlborough's death visited the Duchess at Blenheim, declared roundly that the last thing Vanbrugh had considered in designing the building was comfort, for he had sacrificed everything to effect and to the 'Majesty of Size'.

Castle Howard also suffers from similar defects. From the beginning it was planned on a scale which had previously been the preserve of royal palaces, but the only room in proportion to the building as a whole is the magnificent entry hall, thirty-four foot square and reaching to the full height of the dome, with lavish decorations by Pellegrini. All that mattered lay in the area of external display. It is as if the whole building was a statement intended only for the Earl of Carlisle's social inferiors, who could be dazzled from afar, but would rarely cross the threshold of his palace, and never penetrate beyond the public rooms.

At Castle Howard, the Earl of Carlisle also showed how the arts could serve the aristocracy in death as well as in life. This was an age in which men typically craved personal immortality, and were anxious to ensure a permanent reminder of themselves as individuals, rather than as bearers of their family name, or mute representatives of the blessed anonymity of the grave. They wished to be remembered, and to be sure that they would be remembered in a particular way. Pepys, who wished posterity to remember him as a musician, had his portrait painted with a lute. Sir Robert Walpole, who wanted to be remembered as he was at the height of his power, on receiving the Order of the Garter, had its star and ribbon painted into all the portraits he had previously sat to. Marlborough, also, wanted to be remembered as he was in his vigour, as England's greatest general, and consequently loved the flattery of Kneller's portrait of himself which hung at Blenheim. Once, as an old man, he walked with slow and faltering steps to this portrait and stood looking at it for some time before turning away with a sigh, exclaiming 'That was once a man!' The aristocracy of England scarcely needed Shaftesbury to urge them into a munificent patronage of the arts since this 'more than all other Labours would procure them an immortal Memory'.[15] Magnificence, they knew, could be used to defeat the grave and to preserve the memory of the dead. So, at Castle Howard, Carlisle commissioned from Nicholas Hawksmoor the famous, circular colonnaded mausoleum, which, when it was begun in 1731, at once reassured the Earl that even if he did not have the grandest house in England to live in during his life, he would have its greatest monument to repose in after death. His mausoleum remains one of the finest surviving pieces of funereal architecture in Europe. In true baroque style Carlisle aimed to preserve his own fame after death by an ostentatious display of wealth, and, in so far as he is now remembered largely as the patron of some of Vanbrugh's and Hawksmoor's best work, we can say that his ambition was largely fulfilled.

It was not only the individual whom the arts could serve. Collective bodies also wished to celebrate their wealth, power and prestige in this status-conscious age. Prime among these collective bodies was the state. For just as we can distinguish between personal and official patronage by the crown at this time, so we can distinguish between art designed to serve the person and the family of the monarch, and that designed to serve and glorify the State. It was a shrewd move on Wren's part to appeal to the spirit of patriotism in the bosom of the commissioners for the rebuilding of St Paul's when, in 1666, he begged them to accept his proposals in order that the new cathedral might become 'an ornament to his Majesty's most excellent reign, to the Church of England and to this great city which it is a pity in the opinion of our neighbours should longer continue the most unadorned of her bigness in the world'. According to the *Parentalia* account many people had indeed objected to the first model design on the grounds that 'it was not stately enough, and contended, that for the honour of the Nation, and City of London, it ought not to be exceeded in magnificence by any church in Europe'.[16]

State works of art could be simply commemorative; of such a nature is the Monument to the Great Fire of London – Wren and Hooke's elegant fluted

Doric column, surmounted by a golden globe rising from the flames – for which parliament voted money in 1667, 'the better to preserve the memory of this dreadful visitation',[17] or Blenheim which was devised as a great memorial to a great victory by a great general and to honour the queen he served. Commemorative statues as public monuments were an innovatory feature of the Baroque Age. A typical example was the statue of Charles II by Cibber, erected in Soho Square. But state patronage was happiest and most successful when it was concerned with objects of a utilitarian or charitable nature, that is, when the function of the work of art could be shown to be a generally useful one. Contemporaries believed that it was incumbent on the state, whether in its monarchical or collective guise, to patronize and encourage projects that were for the good of the people as a whole, but which no single individual could undertake for himself. In this connection many, like Hawksmoor and Dryden, were to recognize that in such projects Louis XIV had been not only a good but a great king to his people, and to praise, above all, 'his rectifying the irregular and ill Management . . . of Great Cities', which 'had been of Apparent Service to the Public'.[18] For, in the words of Wren, 'Architecture has its political use; publick Buildings being the Ornament of a Country; it establishes a Nation, draws People and Commerce; makes the People love their native Country, which Passion is the Original of all great Actions in a Common-wealth.'[19] By the 1690s the lost opportunities of 1666 were being regretted and in particular the failure to rebuild London 'in such a Manner, as to have stood foremost at this Day amongst the Wonders of the World, for Extent, Symmetry, Commodiousness, and Duration, at much less Expense than the Citizens have been at, in the Rebuilding it. . . .'[20]

By the 1680s and 1690s the promotion of such useful projects was widely regarded as being an important function of government. Of course, there was a sense in which all patronage of the arts by the state could be regarded as useful, either by helping to prevent unemployment and consequent social unrest, or by providing an effective means of encouraging new or ailing native industries, like the Mortlake tapestry works, which only survived because they were constantly being rescued by the injection of official capital. Nicholas Hawksmoor argued that on these grounds public buildings in effect cost nothing 'but the Labour and Industry of our own Poor; and their Productions are lasting Memorials of the Care and Industry, as well as the evident Marks of a Polite Government'.[21] Many business pressure groups existed precisely to bring the interests of their members to official notice and all had to be placated. Thus, in 1707, when the Committee for the Rebuilding of St Paul's finally decided to cover the dome of the cathedral with lead, they did not neglect the disappointed copperworkers, who had hoped that their product would be chosen. Indeed the Committee publicly recognized its obligation to encourage the native copper industry, and accordingly promised 'the buying of . . . the Society, or Undertakers of these Copperworks, what Copper shall be wanted for the West Towers and Lantern of St Paul's'.[22]

Building projects could therefore serve an indirect charitable purpose but many of the state's undertakings were more openly utilitarian projects. Typical of these was Charles II's new School of Mathematics at Christ's Hospital to encourage the 'art of navigation'; or the Greenwich Hospital for sick seamen, begun in the reign of William and Mary, deliberately designed to call attention to England's naval glories and also to promote the 'Encouragement and Improvement of that most important branch of the national Defence, the naval arms of Great Britain'.[23]

The state was not alone in the promotion of architecture for utilitarian or charitable purposes. Many men and women chose to spend their money either during their life or after it in this way. Thus, Sir Edward Hunnes left £1,000 in 1708 to be employed 'in erecting a building for the lodging of forty Queen's Scholars for the time being in Westminster School', but Sir Edward was perhaps less than typical in specifying that Wren, Dean Aldrich or Christ Church were to be consulted over the design of the building.[24] Charities of this kind served both as a memorial to their founders and a salve to their conscience. Another great benefactor with whom Wren was closely associated was Sir John Moore, alderman and merchant of London, who paid both for the new Writing School at Christ's Hospital, designed by Wren, and for a free school for boys in Appleby, Leicestershire, of which he wrote to his nephew, 'Is not all my charge done for the good and benefit of you and posterity, your parish and the country round about you, and will not this be a living benediction to you and yours?' It was his insurance with heaven, 'for the good seed we sow in this world we shall reap the fruit in the world to come.'[25]

State, private and public charities came together to finance the great ecclesiastical projects of this age – the rebuilding of St Paul's, of fifty-one out of eighty-eight City churches destroyed by the Fire of London, * the building of 'fifty' new churches for expanding London, and of St George's, Tiverton, and of Archer's St Philip's, Birmingham. But above all else, these projects were the cultural expression of Toryism with its devotion to High Church principles. Thus the commission set up, under the New Churches Act of 1710, to build new churches for London out of the proceeds of coal duties, was entirely Tory. The positive attitude of the Tories to such projects – that they should be public advertisements of Anglicanism – was clearly expressed in their decision that St Mary-le-Strand – Gibbs's 'fair daughter in the Strand' – should be lavishly built and decorated both because it was the first of the new churches and because it was in a 'very public place'.

Given such attitudes, we might expect to find in these projects full-scale baroque art of a European nature. On the Continent much baroque art was undoubtedly ecclesiastical or religious in inspiration, largely because it co-incided with the triumph of the Counter Reformation. Serene in their knowledge that the advancing tide of Protestantism had been checked, and was even being driven back, ecclesiastical patrons were prepared to invest money in the truths of the Roman Catholic Church as defined by the Council of Trent, and this coincidental conjunction best explains why baroque art has sometimes been seen as quintessentially Counter-Reformation art.

The situation in England, however, was very different. Here Catholic art was virtually non-existent. It is true, as we have seen, that Catholic chapels had to be provided for successive Stuart consorts, but initially the aim was to make them as unobtrusive as possible in order to avoid scandal. The cases of James II

* All fifty-one were designed by Wren.

and his Queen, Mary of Modena, were different, for their chapels, at least in their full-blooded baroque interiors, were intended as flamboyant advertisements for the religion James would sincerely have loved his subjects to share with him. As soon as she became Queen, Mary of Modena impressed the arts into the service of her religion. From her favourite painter, Benedetto Gennari, she ordered a Holy Family and a Crucifixion for the large chapel at St James's Palace. Another imposing series by the same painter, and a lavish Verrio ceiling, went to decorate her Whitehall chapel which was first opened in 1686. But James II's ill-judged attempts to convert his kingdoms abruptly ended with the departure of the King, Queen and their infant son into exile, and even this fleeting Catholic influence on English artistic development evaporated.

On the other hand, unique historical circumstances determined the fate of ecclesiastical art within the Anglican Church. At no time since the Reformation had Anglican divines really considered what a church should look like, and, in the same period, with the exception of Inigo Jones's St Paul's, Covent Garden, there had been virtually no church building in England. Even St Paul's, Covent Garden, although influential in artistic terms, was no real guide to up-to-date church building, for in no sense had it been purpose-built to the needs of the Church of England; it was more an intellectual exercise than a functional work of art.

Since the Reformation, the only group within the Anglican Church who had seriously considered the question of church building had been the Puritans, who always saw the problem in the most strict of functional terms. On such grounds, in the reign of Charles I, they consistently opposed the restoration of St Paul's which they saw first, as the ultimate symbol of episcopacy, and secondly, as far too large to be useful. 'The rules of piety', they considered, argued that it would be better 'to demolish such old monuments of superstition and idolatry than to keep them standing', and a fellow of Pembroke College, Oxford, was forced to recant for declaring that 'he would rather give ten shillings towards the pulling down of that church to build other churches where they want them, than ten shillings towards the repairing of it.'[26]

Puritan sentiment was clearly opposed to ostentatious expenditure on church building, just as it was opposed to ostentation in the setting of religious worship, and Puritan attacks at least had the positive merit of forcing the High Church party into defining its own position in these matters. The Anglican Church was driven into maintaining the importance of the setting of worship, of what it termed 'outward things', since Anglican divines believed, in the words of Donne, that 'outward things apparel God; and since God was content to take a *body*', that body should not be left 'naked, or ragged'.[27] But although Anglican divines might be anxious to provide a seemly and beautiful setting for worship, they were normally at a loss when it came to describing the precise nature of such a setting. For High Church thinking and theology were drawing the clergy in opposing directions; in the first place, as we have seen, the Anglican Church claimed to be unique among the Protestant Churches because it maintained an unbroken link with the medieval English Church. This indeed was the Church of England's major distinguishing feature. Such considerations, combined with an attachment to the customary, drew the Anglican clergy to Gothic and traditional forms, and, in particular, to the adoption of the Latin cross as a ground plan. But equally important, in some eyes, was the fact that the Anglican Church was a Protestant Church, and, as such, its buildings must be participatory and auditory, where the congregation must be able to see and hear all that was going on. One further consideration has to be born in mind in this connection. We are talking about a post-printing age, when familiarity with the printed book had become a norm, and churches had to be light enough for people to read in. Wren, who considered his St James's Piccadilly as the most successful of all his churches, in terms of its suitability for Anglican worship, recognized all these problems and limitations in designing his churches:

> In our reformed religion [he wrote in 1711] it would seem vain to make a Parish Church larger, than that all who are present can both hear and see. The Romanists, indeed, may build larger Churches, it is enough if they hear the murmur of the Mass, and see the Elevation of the Host, but ours are to be fitted for Auditories.[28]

To combine the optimum size, which baroque architectural opinion favoured, with facilities where a whole congregation could participate in the service, could best be achieved by building within a centralized church plan. And a centralized church plan was also suited to a public taste which was shifting in favour of buildings designed in the idioms of classical architecture.

The demands of the Anglican liturgy contributed their own additional architectural problems. For that liturgy demanded that during services equal emphasis should be placed on altar, reading desk and pulpit. Neither Catholic nor Protestant European models could be of any use here and the solution worked out was essentially English. Additional problems arose as a result of the disastrous tradition, drawn from Protestant experience of Huguenot and Dutch churches, of adding galleries to an existing structure. But whereas the Protestant churches of Scotland and Europe had no altar and could, therefore, be galleried on four sides, in England automatic asymmetry was created by the existence of an altar which was normally sited against the east wall. And, as Gibbs pointed out, galleries 'as well as Pews, clog up and Spoil the Inside of Churches and take away that right Proportion which they would otherwise have'.[29] For this reason his own favourite of the churches he built was All Hallows, Derby, which contains no galleries. Yet so much were galleries a part of the Protestant experience in the early eighteenth century that normally no architect could afford to omit them. All these difficulties made it less than likely that English baroque architects could design or build a church in a pure baroque tradition.

From the point of view of interior decoration and church furnishings, European Catholicism again had the advantage over Anglicanism. Protestantism regarded as superstitious trappings, reeking of popery, even the most seemly of church decorations, and extreme Puritans had rejected not only ornaments of any kind in church, but organs as well. The adoption of such ornaments, their impressment into service by the Laudian and High Church clergy, became, therefore, a theological statement. When James I wished to introduce into Scotland that Anglicanism which he found accorded better with his notions of kingship than the faith he had been nurtured in, it was done not so much by teaching and instruction but symbolically by sending up to Edinburgh 'a pair of organs costing £400 . . . besides all manner of furniture for a chapel', designed by Inigo Jones, 'with pictures of the apostles, Faith, Hope, and Charity'[30] – more than would have been found in the vast majority of churches in England. For while a Puritan lecturer could be prosecuted in High Commission for preaching that 'pictures were no more ornaments in the church than stews in a Commonwealth',[31] it was harder to get at humbler or more insignificant people, who had become accustomed to the bare churches which England had inherited from her reformation, and who petitioned against innovations, whether altars, images, pictures, statues or even crosses. As late as 1680 Ralph Thoresby was horrified to see, during a visit to Durham Cathedral, 'the exceedingly rich copes and robes', and 'was troubled to see so much superstition remaining in Protestant Churches; tapers, basins, and richly embroidered I.H.S. upon the high altar, with the picture of God the Father like an old man; the Son, as a young man, richly embroidered upon their copes'.[32]

It is remarkable how rapidly the Reformation and the changes wrought during the reigns of the Tudors had obliterated all traces of the medieval past within English churches. Expensive church furnishing was totally unfamiliar to the experience of Stuart Anglicanism. Iconoclasm, Protestant principles, and economy had combined to create in the Elizabethan period a tradition by which Anglican churches were, with the occasional rare exception such as the chapel in Hatfield House, built by Robert Cecil in 1612, kept simple and bare. From the sixteenth century right through the eighteenth century, the typical Anglican church had whitewashed walls, symbolizing the recovery of the true faith from error and superstition. With only two exceptions in interior decor, churches were normally devoid of colour. These two exceptions were, first, the sculpted tombs, often containing the remains of the local aristocratic patrons of the church, and secondly, painted boards, bearing the Royal Arms, the Lord's prayer, the Creed and the Ten Commandments. This last was often flanked with the traditional figures of Moses and Aaron. By the second half of the seventeenth century baroque artists were beginning to allow themselves a little latitude in this area, gradually elaborating on the basic design and providing more exuberant frameworks. Edward Bird, for instance, the decorative painter frequently employed by Wren in his City churches, created two such illusionary frameworks; at St Benet's Church, Gracechurch Street, his commandments were supported by the traditional figures of Moses and Aaron, with, above them, 'a large piece of Architecture, painted in perspective, representing the Arched roof and Pilasters of a Building' which appeared 'from under a Purple Velvet, Festoon Curtain, elevated by two Cupids';[33] and, at St Mildred's Church, Bread Street, his design was surmounted by a 'Glory proceeding out of an equilateral Triangle, at each of which Angles, in the Rays, is a Cherub well painted all within Clouds'.[34]

Even in those places where experimentation in ecclesiastical decoration was both possible and probable, such as at Oxford and Cambridge and in other private chapels, the long arm of Puritan prejudice often prevented decoration in a Continental manner. A sense of decorum in church decoration was very strong and must have had its effect. In the 1660s Isaac Fuller had been able to decorate the east end of three Oxford college chapels, All Souls, Magdalen and Wadham, but Evelyn, whose views on the arts were as advanced as those of any of his contemporaries, felt that Fuller's *Resurrection* at All Souls was still 'too full of nakeds for a chapel'.[35] It was doubtless in order to prevent the unfortunate appearance of any such nudes or other elements of Catholic decorative painting that the Commissioners for the Rebuilding of St Paul's insisted that the figures painted to decorate the Dome should be confined to 'Scriptural History taken from the Acts of the Apostles'.[36]

If visual ecclesiastical art suffered because of the chronic inability of members of the Church of England to make up their minds as to what constituted a suitable framework for worship, church music fared no better. The Puritan position was, of course, only too clear; since adornments of any kind, visual and audible included, were unsuited to religion, the only permissible church music was psalm singing. In particular, organs and cathedral choirs were anathema. The organ, the Puritans compared to 'the whining of pigs' and choir singing to 'a jovial crew in a blind alehouse'.[37]

The Anglican position was marked by its usual hesitancy and uncertainty. Although at the Restoration it could still be claimed that 'the first and chief use of *Music* is for the Service and praise of God whose gift it is',[38] the Anglican clergy were dubious about the precise function of music in the church. They began to fall back on increasingly utilitarian justifications for music in the liturgy, of which the favourites were that music encouraged concentration during a long service and that good music was an inducement for people to attend church. While no doubt true, such attitudes could do little to develop a strong tradition of church music. Nor did church music benefit from the ideas of decorum, which were infiltrating music just as they were church decoration. For it was in the baroque period that people first became conscious of style in music, and it was perhaps an inevitable though regrettable consequence that the idea should have grown up that only a particular style of music was suitable in church.

Many of the Puritan objections to the use of music in church were associated with the idea that music gave great sensual pleasure, and we should not forget that of all the functions of the arts that of giving enjoyment was as important in the Baroque as in every succeeding age. Baroque music and painting, baroque architecture, decoration and furnishings, baroque procession and display: all of these gave their audiences pleasure. But even pleasure may have its functional dimension, for it may well include awe and wonder before the signs and symbols of a culture's power and glory.

CHAPTER XI

Money and Materials

*'Tis with a Poet, as with a man who designs to build, and is very exact, as he supposes,
in counting up the cost beforehand; but, generally speaking, he is mistaken in his account,
and reckons short of the expense he first intended.*

Dryden

✳

ONE INESCAPABLE FACT about baroque art is that it was outrageously expensive.
This was partly because it depended on rich materials and a lavish scale for its
impact, but largely because it characteristically expressed itself in the complete
artifact – in the palace and garden, in the masque or opera, or in urban planning
and the rebuilding of cities in a total and uniform style. Considerations of
cost must therefore come into any account of baroque art in any country even
though they will never be a sufficient explanation either for the adoption or for
the rejection of baroque styles. For even the most cursory examination of
baroque art in Europe shows that its cost was never a primary consideration;
at Venice, for instance, the votive church of S. Maria della Salute was built as a
thanksgiving for recovery from a plague epidemic which had in fact seriously
contributed to Venice's economic decline. At the same time the papacy was
acting as a flamboyant patron of the most expensive forms of baroque art
although it was suffering from one of the most serious of the Church's financial
crises in modern times; popes such as Urban VIII had so great a commitment
to baroque art that they preferred to commission it even when it led to the
long-term impoverishment of the Church and the Papal State. Even in
England, we have already noted, James I's greatest expenditure on the arts
occurred at the period of gravest financial difficulties in his reign. Yet in
England it must be confessed that the level of commitment to baroque art was
such that those who had once experienced its expense were rarely subsequently
tempted into similar projects.

The truth is that there were circumstances in England which prevented
expenditure on the arts on a Continental scale. In Europe, baroque art was
normally court art, and, in France in particular, the crown was the chief
financier of prestige projects. In England the crown never had similar resources
at its disposal and its expenditure was always carefully monitored by parliament. As we have seen, had he had the means Charles II would indubitably
have spent on the same lavish scale as Louis XIV, but his income never matched
his tastes.

During the Interregnum, the Commonwealth governments had spent
money with complete recklessness, to a point where the resultant financial
chaos contributed to the restoration of the monarchy. Eighteen years of
political instability and civil strife, coupled with an expensive foreign policy,
brought virtual bankruptcy. From the Commonwealth, therefore, Charles II

inherited a deficit of some three million pounds, to which he had to add his own personal debts as well as those of his father. In the first flush of royalist enthusiasm at the time of the restoration, parliament voted the King an annual income of £1,200,000, believed to be adequate to cover all the ordinary expenses of government. But not only did the cost of government grow considerably, the projected proceeds of taxes also proved to be gross over-estimates. The consequent financial morass only entangled Charles in a series of squabbles with his parliaments, which made the voting of additional supplies difficult, particularly as the King's explanation of his financial problems sounded singularly unconvincing to a House of Commons which had heard that Lady Castlemaine had appeared at the theatre wearing jewels worth £200,000.

It was never the King's mistresses, and always the arts, which suffered during periods of retrenchment, although, if we are to believe Colley Cibber, even Charles's mistresses had little success in trying to persuade him to reward artistic merit. For Cibber recalls a performance of music in Nell Gwynn's lodgings, attended both by the King and the Duke of York, and that

> When the Performance was ended, the King expressed himself highly pleased, and gave it extraordinary commendations: Then Sir, said the Lady, to show you don't speak like a Courtier, I hope you will make the Performers a handsome Present. The King said, he had no Money about him, and asked the Duke if he had any? To which the Duke replied, I believe, Sir, not above a Guinea, or two. Upon which the laughing Lady, turning to the People about her, and making bold with the King's common Expression, cried, *Od's Fish! What Company am I got into.*[1]

This well-meaning attempt by the 'Protestant whore' to recall the King to a sense of his obligations to those artists who served or delighted him, had, apparently, little effect. At his death, Nell Gwynn's fellow-actors were owed about £1,500 by the crown 'for Plays commanded etc.',[2] but they were in no way exceptional. Music, the King's own special love, always suffered first in times of retrenchment, as in 1668 when Charles was forced to reduce the number of royal trumpeters. Employment in the Chapel Royal might be prestigious, but it was not a very reliable means of support; the salaries of the gentlemen of the chapel, although substantial – they were raised from £40 to £70 in 1662 – were largely notional for they were always in arrears. Even those wretched Catholic musicians who were forced to flee the country at the time of the Papal Plot had first to petition for the payment of some of their arrears of salary in order to meet their travelling expenses. At the time of Charles II's death the Gentlemen of the Royal Chapel were owed a total of £2,484 16s 3d, while Captain Cooke, who had been in charge of the Chapel, was owed at least £1,709 13s.

Essential royal and state building projects were also constantly being put off for lack of money. In July 1671 the Council for Foreign Plantations was in urgent need of a building to accommodate a council chamber and essential offices, but the King could hold out no hope of its getting one, and his only positive suggestion was that the council should raise a forced loan from each of its members to finance the project. At no time during the period 1660–1715 was even the Board of Works supplied with adequate funds. The paymaster never knew from year to year what sums would be made available to him. That the office continued to function at all, that important building projects did not simply come to a halt, was simply because the Works managed to exist on credit for months and years at a time by the careful system which Wren expounded to the Treasury in 1691:

> What money from time to time is Directed is equally Divided to every Creditor by a pound rate, and we pay ourselves [the Officers of the Works] no otherwise: by which means we keep up a Credit for His Majesty's Service. . . .'³

Inconvenient accounts, that is, were always being postponed, while the most pressing creditors were palmed off with a share of whatever monies happened to be available, so that it sometimes took decades for their accounts to be finally cleared.

Costs in the Board of Works were pared down and then pared down again, so that there was little room for corruption in this austerely run department. Materials were carefully husbanded and sought after. Excess materials were auctioned to the highest bidder, and expenditure was saved by using materials over again. Under William and Mary, Charles II's Winchester Palace, which had never been completed, was pillaged for materials for the alterations to Hampton Court. This kind of saving Wren also employed during the rebuilding of St Paul's; stones from the old building were either sold off – some went to Clarendon House, some to the City of London to repave the burnt areas – or were used on the new cathedral, and it was not until 1675 that the commissioners had to buy any new materials.

Although the commissioners for St Paul's and the crown were driven to desperate measures to continue to operate as patrons of building enterprises, this does not seem to have curtailed expenditure, for, as we shall see, both at St Paul's and at the Board of Works, expenditure tended to increase. The Board of Works spent an annual £20,000 in the reign of Charles II, a sum which rose to £30,000 in that of his brother, and £45,000 in the reign of William and Mary. It was an expenditure which was normally regarded with intense disapproval by a highly critical House of Commons which tended to regard it as a manifestation of court extravagance.

Such extravagance was, after all, as we have already seen, a consistent object of attack in 'Country Party' opposition throughout the seventeenth century, and little ground separates Prynne, as the author of *Histriomastix*, from Sir Charles Sedley who in the House of Commons in 1691 attacked the size of the civil list, and the luxurious habits of a court which he believed was responsible for cutting the King off from his subjects. 'His Majesty', Sedley reminded the House, 'is encompassed with and sees nothing but plenty, great tables, coaches and six horses and all things suitable, and therefore cannot imagine the want and misery of the rest of his subjects. . . .'⁴

Sedley's real concern was with the cost of the wars against France, which so perturbed the English in the reigns of William and Mary and of Queen Anne. 'We must save the King money wherever we can', he continued, 'for I am afraid our work is too big for our purses if things be not better managed with all the thrift imaginable.'[5] He was touching here on a very significant difference between Britain and some of the smaller countries of Europe where baroque art flourished. Unlike several small German principalities, where the local opera company might represent the largest single item in the state budget, British financial commitment to the arts at this time could not be very great. At the turn of the century Britain was beginning to emerge as one of the great powers in Europe, engaged in a life and death struggle with France which meant a perpetual drain on the country's financial resources. Britain's first concern in a time of almost constant warfare had to be the financing of her armies, navies and government, and the garrisoning and protection of her overseas possessions.

From neither crown nor state, therefore, could unlimited support for baroque art on the Continental scale be looked for. Nor would such support come from the Church, for in England the state Church was notoriously impoverished, shorn of its great medieval endowments by the Tudor monarchs, and, even among the Anglican bishops, there were few who could afford to support expensive prestige projects. As for the English aristocracy as a social class, certainly they were immensely wealthy, but there was an infinite number of calls on their wealth in this period so that expenditure on the arts required a positive commitment on the part of the patron. Evelyn had noted how in the contemporary Netherlands the lack of opportunity for investment had actively encouraged the arts, and, commenting on the public sale of easel paintings in the markets of Rotterdam, had remarked that

> The Occasion of this store of Pictures and their Cheapness proceeds from their want of land to Employ their stock; so as 'tis an ordinary thing to find a Common Farmer to lay out 500 or 600 pounds and more in this Commodity, and that keep Painters at work in their house.

In Genoa he again noted the same factors at work; the absence, above all, of an extensive Genoese *contado* in which to invest in land drove the Genoese to spend their money on 'Costly-houses of Marble, and adorning them with statues, and costly furniture'.[6]

But England was no area of economic stagnation; this was an age of land improvement, of fen drainage and of developing opportunities for investment in land, building speculation, trade and government stock. Equally, it was an age of heavy expenditure in less productive areas; the wars had been largely financed out of the land, by, as we have noted, that notorious land-tax which caused one backbencher to remark bitterly of the great national victory at Blenheim that it represented 'more for their four shillings in the pound than they had ever seen before'.

Meanwhile there were increased demands on the purses of the aristocrats and gentry produced by the general rise in their standard of living. As new tastes spread into the provinces from London, and the local gentry began to imitate the fashions of the capital, expenditure, rather than the careful husbanding of wealth, was seen as the mark of an aristocrat, gentleman or leader of society, so that, as Lady Hartford lamented in 1740, 'the fortune which should be increasing . . . is often decreasing in dress, equipage and sometimes in worse things.'[7] There are instances of men being forced to mortgage their estates in order to keep pace with the new fashions. Marriages, funerals and younger sons could all be ruinous. Dowries and settlements were rising steeply. Lawrence Stone has provided an example of what this could mean to one family with his examination of the finances of the Salisbury family. In 1667 the Salisbury estate of under £12,500 a year was burdened with permanent annual outgoings amounting to £3,420. Of this £400 went as pin-money to the Countess, £1,800 to Diana, Dowager Lady Cranbourne, £920 to younger children and £300 in pin-money to the wife of the Salisbury heir, Lord Cranbourne.[8] Yet such payments were necessary to maintain the dignity of a great family. So were lavish funerals, and, although it was admittedly exceptional in its magnificence, Marlborough's funeral, with its music specially composed by Bononcini and a display of baroque splendour costing at least £5,265, was in line with a general trend. A career in politics required constant expenditure, particularly at the time of an election when voters had to be bribed and the panoply of influence made apparent. New amusements and diversions were beginning to require heavy financial outlays. Horse-racing and horse-breeding were prestige pastimes, but very costly ones; even in the early eighteenth century a good racehorse could cost as much as £1,000 and was as unsafe an investment as it is today. Gambling was universally popular and among the upper classes amounted to a passion; the Duchess of Marlborough reckoned that her grandson lost £100 a week in one game of chance or another.

Yet despite all these varied claims on their resources, very many of the aristocracy did embark on expensive building and rebuilding projects only to recoil in horror when they realized the expenditure involved. Even a tolerably modest town-house like Clarendon House or Marlborough House cost between £30,000 and £50,000, while a country house was always a more expensive proposition. It is true that Lord Nottingham spent only £30,000 on Burley-on-the-Hill (Rutland), but the purchase of the estate had already cost £50,000. And this sum is a relatively small one compared with the expenditure on some of the great baroque country palaces which involved not only the actual building of the house, but the laying out, planting and landscaping of the grounds as well. The £80,000 spent on Castle Howard between 1699 and 1737 seems almost modest when considered beside the £140,000 spent by Bubb Dodington on Eastbury Park, or the more than £300,000 spent on Blenheim. And, although Blenheim was largely created with public money, in the end at least £60,000 had to be found from the Marlborough estate. Small wonder that the Duke of Marlborough came to the conclusion that as a general rule it was always better to buy than to build.

Marlborough's Blenheim is the outstanding example of a private house which could only be carried out through a particular financial windfall, but there were others. James Brydges, Duke of Chandos, made the fortune that went into the building of Canons, and supported its continued existence as a cultural centre, as paymaster of Marlborough's forces; the fortunes made by the acute in the South Sea Bubble enabled some to complete or to begin coveted projects; and the hanging gardens at Powis Castle, one of the most perfectly conceived and Italianate of the baroque gardens of Britain, were made possible by the fortuitous opening of the rich lead mines of Llangynog on the Powis estate.

But even more projects, like the first projected building of the Senate House at Cambridge in 1674, came to nothing simply for lack of funds. Some projects were rejected out of hand because they were too expensive; Hawksmoor's original designs for All Souls were rejected because he 'Designs Grandly for a College';[9] Gibbs's circular design for St Martin-in-the-Fields was thrown out on grounds of cost, and Wren's plan to decorate the interior of St Paul's dome with mosaic was also largely rejected because it 'was imagined . . . the Expense would prove too great'.[10]

Other projects were begun and then were never finished; in this connection we can cite the Cambridge Senate House again. The present Gibbs building which was begun in 1722 is justly admired and famed throughout the world, but it is not precisely what Gibbs intended and its full baroque potential was never realized. Gibbs had actually designed, not just a single block for Senate meetings, but a complete four-sided scheme for an administrative centre for Cambridge University. Presumably the University found the £16,386, which the one building alone cost, a sufficient strain on their resources. Certainly they treated Gibbs very shabbily for they paid him only £100 for eight years work, although his travelling expenses alone came to £60. Another of Gibbs's Cambridge projects suffered a similar fate; the Gibbs building at King's represents only about a third of an intended building which could not be completed because money was never available. For similar reasons, at Castle Howard only one of the side wings was completed as Vanbrugh had intended and, at Blenheim, the famous bridge which had caused so much controversy was left unfinished. And what was made could also be unmade for financial reasons. Chandos lost so heavily in the South Sea Bubble that his role as an eighteenth-century Maecenas was brought to an abrupt halt and, after his death in 1744, his showpiece palace was broken up and sold for the marble, iron and stone which it contained.

The cost of building was as much a problem for the corporate body as it was for the individual. When he first began his designs for the new St Paul's, it was Wren's intention to design a building on a scale for which funds were already certain. Fortunately he was overruled, the commissioners for the rebuilding showing more faith in the forthcomingness of Mammon than did their architect. As Sancroft reported to Wren on 2 July 1668,

> the only part of your Letter we demur is the Method you propound of declaring first, what Money we would bestow; and then designing something just of that Expense: for quite otherwise the Way their Lordships resolve upon, is to frame our Design, handsome and noble, and suitable to all the Ends of it, and to the Reputation of the City, and the Nation, and to take it for granted, that Money will be had to accomplish it.[11]

We may be grateful today that Wren was overruled, but in the course of the rebuilding, successive commissions may well have regretted that that decision was taken. For, throughout its construction, the problems of financing the cathedral bedevilled the project. Although the costs averaged about £10,000 p.a. until 1692, thereafter they began to climb steeply to £17,000 p.a., and then to £19,000. In peak years of activity the expenditure was even higher; in 1693, when there was a great drive to get the roof leaded before winter, the works cost £30,000, and in 1706 this rose to a record £37,000. The sources of income, meanwhile, were never reliable. The major source had been provided by act of parliament: a levy of 1s per cauldron on all coal shipped into London, 'to enlarge Streets, rebuild Churches and other works'.[12] In 1670 the levy was raised to 3s per cauldron which was divided between the rebuilding needs of the City of London, the City churches and St Paul's, the cathedral getting only 4½d out of every 3s. In 1687 a fresh act was passed: for three years the levy would be 1s 6d a cauldron and of the sums thus raised a fifth was to go to the City churches and four-fifths to St Paul's. By the 1690s new problems connected with the coal levy had arisen; lay interest in the whole project was waning and the City of London which, because of mismanagement and embezzlement of its Orphans' Fund, was in financial difficulties, was again demanding its own share of the coal duty. Since the City possessed valuable friends in a House of Commons where the cathedral had virtually none, it was London which won the day; an act passed in 1694 imposed an extra duty of 4d on the existing dues, which was to last until September 1700, and this money was to go into the Orphans' Fund. Thereafter parliament decreed that the coal duty was to revert to 1s 6d but that the City was to have a priority claim to 6d. In 1697 parliament again grudgingly consented to extend the duties from 1700 until 1716, but only at a reduced rate of 12d of which the first sixth was to go for the repairs to Westminster Abbey, a total sum of £3,000 was to be devoted to St Thomas Southwark, and of the remaining monies a fifth was to go to the City churches and the rest to St Paul's. In addition, the Whig House of Commons took the occasion to mark their disapproval of the whole project, and their dissatisfaction with the Tory Wren, by ordering that until the cathedral was finished the architect was to be paid only half his salary, receiving his arrears only after its completion. Fortunately, after the accession of Queen Anne there was a Tory revival and parliament agreed to impose a higher coal duty again. On this security the commissioners were able to borrow enough money to complete the project. It was the great advantage of this regular tax-based income voted by parliament that it made it possible to raise sums of money in this way – borrowing in anticipation of income.

The bulk of the rest of the money, apart from a small amount which came in from a proportion of fines imposed in ecclesiastical courts, came from donations and gifts. Wren had always believed that 'a fair building may easier be carried on by contributions with time than a sordid one',[13] and events served to justify this conviction. In a real sense the rebuilding of St Paul's became a national effort in which the people as a whole acted as a collective patron. The National Appeal for St Paul's was launched in 1677 with letters patent from the King recommending the cause. This was followed by a long letter from Bishop Compton which detailed the work so far carried out, explained the present finances of the building fund, and sought to deal with two objections to contributing which he anticipated. First he spoke to the Puritans who would surely object that sumptuousness and magnificence in church building was contrary both to the letter and to the spirit of the gospel and the primitive church. 'The public worship of God', he replied, 'though it doth suppose and require inward and spiritual devotion, yet, as public, is necessarily external and as such ought to express in the best manner we are able that inward honour and reverence we pay to the Divine Majesty; and therefore the circumstances of it should not only be decent but very solemn and magnificent.'[14]

Secondly, Compton dealt with the possible objection that the City and diocese of London ought to pay for their own cathedral, by pointing out the considerable trials which London had recently undergone. Appealing to his countrymen's nationalistic feelings, he tried also to cash in on their anti-papal prejudices by recommending the project to them in the following terms:

> Everyone ought, with more than ordinary zeal, to be concerned for the carrying on of this work, not only for the honour of our nation and the credit of our common Christianity but also of our reformed religion; that there may be no pretence to upbraid us that error and superstition could make men more zealous of good works than the doctrine of true religion; and that our adversaries of Rome may be more convinced that our piety is as generous and charitable as theirs but would not be so arrogant and presumptuous and that whilst we declaim the merit yet we do most steadfastly believe the obligation and necessity of good works.[15]

Sermons on this and similar themes were, accordingly, preached up and down the country so that the appeal must have reached the majority of the population. Nor was the response disappointing for contributions came in from all conditions and classes of men. The clergy, as we should expect, were generous, the bishops in particular placing the weight of their authority behind the cause. New bishops were required to subscribe £50 on their appointment to sees, but many gave more and in seventeen years over £16,000 was collected from the episcopate as a whole. Sancroft himself, as Dean of St Paul's, gave £1,400, and there were substantial gifts and bequests from other individuals; Lady Williamson of Haleshall in Norfolk left the cathedral £4,120 when she died in 1686. Other donations came from the artistic community including Wren and the elderly Peter Lely who gave £50. The only real disappointment was the King who, in a first flush of enthusiasm, had promised £1,000 a year which he could not afford. By the time of his death he had paid over no more than £3,154 to the building fund.

But, despite all this money, the building fund was always in difficulties and usually heavily in debt. This could not fail to affect the progress of the building for, as Wren reported in June 1688, 'since the Debt grew considerable, he found not a little difficulty in contracting and settling prices with the Masons, which hitherto he had endeavoured to keep to the same sort of prices for the same sort of work which they formerly had.'[16] By the end of that year the building fund had debts of £14,225 of which some £9,000 was owed to contractors for work already completed. The commissioners were therefore hardly in a position to refuse demands for increased rates of pay for the more dangerous work involved as the walls of the cathedral gradually rose to their full height. Determined as they were that the 'Work should go vigorously on',[17] their only resource was to borrow more money and by December 1693 they had to confess that 'the Church is now almost £23,000 in Debt, which Debt must of necessity increase next year by fitting up the Choir or the work must stand still.'[18]

Heavy financial problems therefore dogged all large-scale projects undertaken in England between 1660 and about 1740. This, no doubt, is one reason why by the beginning of the eighteenth century, with the increase of the land-tax and the financial disaster of the South Sea Bubble, people were beginning to apply to building that same attitude of rationality which they were already applying to the running of agricultural estates or commercial enterprises. One might almost say that the spirit of capitalism was being applied to the arts. In actual fact, the face of capitalism was not even always hidden. The Royal Academy of Music which was launched in 1719, as we have seen, in order to promote Italian opera, was in fact a joint-stock company, whose stocks were listed on the Stock Exchange, and many of the investors had no interest in opera at all, but were merely interested in a speculative investment.

Whatever the reasons for it, and we have suggested some, by the beginning of the eighteenth century there was a general trend towards economy and saving which was bound to have an effect on the arts. The impact of such attitudes was initially seen in a rapid decline of enthusiasm for the baroque garden, manifested in a movement away from the formal layouts and settings of the seventeenth century satirized in Pope's description of Timon's villa where

> Grove nods at grove, each ally has a brother
> And half the platform but reflects the other.

The baroque garden was rapidly replaced by the 'Natural' parkland of the eighteenth-century landscape movement, largely because the formal garden with its 'Minute Forms and Compositions . . . the great collections of Orange and other Exotic Trees, Plants and Flowers that are kept in very great beauty . . . and the many kinds of Evergreen Trees and Espaliers'[19] was so expensive. At a time when land was increasingly seen as a vital productive industry, and a source of profit as well as of prestige, it became hard to justify an annual expenditure of between £50 and £60 an acre on formal gardens and parks.

Similar principles of rationality were at work in relation to building projects. On grounds of economy, utility and a form of humanitarianism – the provision of local employment – it became the aim of every large-scale builder to supply as many of the materials as possible from his own estates. For the largest saving to be made was not so much in the actual cost of materials as in the cost of their carriage which, with the existing very inadequate system of communications, was very high indeed. The cost of all buildings in this period was increased by between a tenth and a half by the expense of carriage and cartage.

A desire to curtail cost was bound to affect the finished appearance of a building, since the materials of which it was built so often depended on what was locally available. The plentiful supply of good clay in England, coupled with the comparative scarcity of good stone, particularly in the vicinity of London, meant that the bulk of domestic building was done in brick, a medium with which Wren fortunately enjoyed working. And considerable additional savings could be effected if bricks were produced on the actual building site; Pratt reckoned that the bricks for Lord Clarendon's house, which would have cost 8s 6d per thousand had they been made on the estate, were in fact bought for 15s the thousand. Nor did the price remain at this level. Wren noted that 'the mighty Demand for the Hasty Works of thousands of Houses at once, after the Fire of London, and the frauds of those who built by the great, have so debased the Value of Materials, that good Bricks are not to be now had, without greater Prices than formerly, and indeed, if rightly made, will deserve them.'[20]

A large house of the type of Lord Clarendon's was not left with a brick façade, although smaller houses were characteristically finished with a facing of brickwork based on stone. Larger houses and all public buildings were normally also faced with stone, and the choice of what stone again depended on what was locally available. The only exception to this were London buildings for all stone had to be transported to the capital and it came from all over the country. In the 1730s, Ralph Allen, who owned quarries near Bath, nevertheless thought that he would be able to break into the London market by transporting his stone cheaply by the river Avon to Bristol and thence by sea to London. He had enough faith in the commercial possibilities of his product to advertise it, in a somewhat expensive way, by offering to supply it at his own expense for the new buildings at St Bartholomew's Hospital which were to be built by James Gibbs.

Normally, however, it was rare for building operations to draw stone from very far afield; Castle Howard, which was constructed of freestone from quarries in its own park, Burley-on-the-Hill, which made use of the local stone quarries at Clipsham and Ketton, and Shotover Park (Oxfordshire), built from local Haseley stone, are in this sense typical; Blenheim, which drew materials from far afield and from twenty-two different quarries, was not. And, even at Blenheim, Vanbrugh originally intended to use mainly local stone, and it was only during the first winter, when that from the park and the neighbouring village of Glympton was found to be unsatisfactory because it was not frost-resistant, that he turned to alternative sources. Yet, to choose from alternative sources was not an easy task. An architect would find it necessary to balance quality against cost, for the difference between the cost of two stones could be substantial. The Trustees for the Building of the Radcliffe Camera wisely chose Burford rather than Headington stone for their project, but that choice increased the cost of building by £1,600. Dartmoor granite was 'the most lasting of all that has yet been tried, in waters for resisting the Frost',[21] but the cost of its transport made it prohibitively expensive.

⟋ Because builders used local materials, a major result of every large-scale building enterprise was the encouragement of local industry and craftsmanship. Although the great monumental houses of the late seventeenth and early eighteenth centuries were built to elevate one social class, and to emphasize their distinction in relation to the rest of society, for one and often two generations such buildings provided local employment, and generated some local prosperity. There was, therefore, a certain propriety in the joint celebration which followed the laying of the foundation stone at Blenheim on 18 June 1705 when the gentry drank sherry and claret while the 'common people' made do with eight barrels of ale and 'abundance of cakes'.[22]

But with the best will in the world, economy in building baroque palaces could only be very limited. The new standards of luxury and comfort continued to make headway so that at Canons even the rooms of the servants had chimney-pieces of Portland stone, something which would have been un-thinkable but a generation earlier. Such demands of fashion, combined with local shortages, continued to force costs ever upward. As we have seen, the demand for building materials after the Fire of London inevitably led to a rise in their basic cost. Other natural disasters had similar effects; the terrible storm of 26 November 1703, for instance, led to an increase in the cost of tiles in London in one month from 50s a thousand to 65s a thousand. Many impor-tant building materials had to be imported or transported over large distances within Britain. Thus England as a whole was short of good timber from the mid-seventeenth century onwards and that which was available was channelled towards the navy. Wren was phenomenally lucky at St Paul's in that the Duke of Newcastle gave fifty oak trees from his Welbeck estate for the vital roofing timbers, for in seventeenth-century England, where oak covered with lead was regarded as the most satisfactory roofing material, this represented a gift of truly princely magnificence. The necessity of replenishing the depleted wood-lands was rapidly becoming a national obsession and no thinking landowner would leave his house without a pocketful of acorns to plant as he surveyed his lands. In the meantime, despite heavy import duties, much wood had to be imported from the Continent; oak came from Flanders and from Germany, and was greatly appreciated by woodcarvers because it had a straighter grain and was freer of knots than the native variety. Marble for monumental and decora-tive work also had normally to be imported; different coloured marbles were extensively used in monumental tomb sculpture and England produced marble in small quantities and virtually none of first-class quality.

English participation in baroque civilization was, therefore, closely related to the Commercial Revolution, which, with its vast expansion of world trade, made the import of foreign goods possible:

> . . . and from a thousand shores
> Wafts all the pomp of life into your ports.[23]

A builder had become the centre of worldwide enterprises and his raw materials were coming from more and more specialized centres of production. The mason-sculptor, Nicholas Stone, for instance, at one time or another made use in his domestic work of black and white marble from Italy, Purbeck marble, Portland stone, Taynton and Headington stones from Oxfordshire quarries – Oxfordshire was particularly rich in rewarding building stones – Reigate stone from Surrey, Ketton stone from Rutland, and Kentish stone. Deal, for wain-scots, was imported from Norway or Prussia, and shipped into Hull or London; bricks redder in colour and cheaper than English ones came from the Netherlands brought in as ballast on transports between Holland and Dept-ford. Marlborough House was built entirely of these Dutch bricks. Imported cedar was used for staircases as early as the 1670s and by the end of the century timber from America, including the much-admired Virginia walnut, was being shipped into Bristol for the building trade. From Italy, besides marble, came the valuable damasks and velvets in which the Italians still specialized, and which were extensively used in internal furnishings, while silk for bed-hangings and coverlets was being brought from India and China, together with the ornamental ceramics which Queen Mary had made fashionable.

(37) The ceiling of the Sheldonian Theatre, Oxford, painted by Robert Streeter, whose work was much admired by Wren. The subject is an allegory of *Truth descending on the Arts and Sciences*; the network of ropes represents the open roof of a Roman theatre with the awning rolled back to reveal the sky.

UNIVERSITY ARCHITECTURE. (38) The Senate House, Cambridge. Part of Gibbs's uncompleted scheme. (39) St Mary the Virgin, Oxford. A vigorous baroque design by Nicholas Stone grafted on to a medieval church. (40) Tom Tower, Oxford, by Wren. A deliberate Gothic revival. (41) Interior of the Radcliffe Camera by Gibbs, based on designs by Hawksmoor.

LONDON CHURCHES. (42, 43, 44) Three Wren steeples. St Mary-le-Bow, Cheapside. St Bride, Fleet Street. St Vedast, Foster Lane. (45) St Lawrence Jewry by Wren and (46) St Martin-in-the-Fields by Gibbs.

(47) St Stephen Walbrook; Wren's most complex and accomplished interior.

ST PAUL'S CATHEDRAL. (48) Detail of the south pediment. The symbolic phoenix was carved by Cibber. (49) Interior of the Great Model. Said to have been Wren's favourite design, it was rejected by the clergy. (50) The west front. Lord Burlington, the champion of Palladio, compared it unfavourably with Inigo Jones's design (26).

(51) *The stoning of Stephen*. A woodcarving by Grinling Gibbons.

(52) Blenheim Palace, Oxfordshire. A gift from the nation to the victorious Duke of Marlborough. Designed as 'an intended monument to the Queen's glory' by Vanbrugh in almost continuous conflict with Sarah, Duchess of Marlborough, who dismissed him before the work was completed.

THE BAROQUE GARDEN. (53) Wrest Park, Bedfordshire. Thomas Archer's garden pavilion (1709–11). (54) The Satyr Gate, Castle Howard. (55) The spectacular hanging gardens at Powis Castle, designed for the Earl of Rochford with statuary by Van Nost.

THE BAROQUE COUNTRY HOUSE. (56) Easton Neston, Northamptonshire. Hawksmoor's only known country-house design. (57) Burley-on-the-Hill, Rutland. Probably designed by Daniel Finch, 2nd Earl of Nottingham, with flanking colonnades inspired by Bernini.

THE ARCHITECTURE OF DISPLAY. (58) Castle Howard, Yorkshire. Designed for the Earl of Carlisle by Sir John Vanbrugh. (59) The Octagon Room at Orleans House, Twickenham. By James Gibbs for the Whig politician James Johnson as a setting for the entertainment of the Princess of Wales.

THE GRAND MANNER. (60) Seaton Delaval, Northumberland. Vanbrugh's dramatic scheme consists of a central block flanked by two wings. The one on the left of the photograph contains the monumental stables (61).

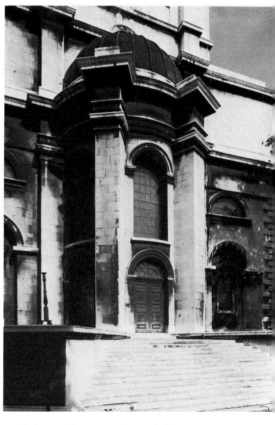

(62) Hawksmoor's Mausoleum at Castle Howard, begun in 1731. One of the finest pieces of funereal architecture in Europe. (63, 64) Two views of St Anne, Limehouse (1714–30). Hawksmoor's London churches skilfully combine Italian Baroque and English Gothic elements.

MUSICAL CONTRASTS. (65) A manuscript page from Handel's *Messiah*, first performed in 1742. (66) William Hogarth: a scene from *The Beggars' Opera*, first performed in 1728. This immensely popular ballad opera exposed, according to Swift, 'that unnatural taste for Italian music among us which is wholly unsuitable to our northern climate, and the genius of the people, whereby we are over-run with Italian effeminancy and Italian nonsense'.

Of all the stones which were available to the English architect, builder and patron, the best and the most popular came from the Isle of Portland which, 'having the largest blocks of stones and the most proper for Magnificent Buildings',[24] was used for St Paul's, the City churches, all major public works, for the docks of Plymouth and Portsmouth, and in all fortifications work. Although very durable and easy to work with, Portland stone did have some drawbacks. The major of these was the fact that it could only be found in limited sizes, and the largest Portland blocks could not be regularly supplied but had to be waited for: 'the Artificers were forced sometimes to stay some Months, for one necessary Stone to be raised for their purpose, and the further the Quarry-men pierced into the Rock, the Quarry produced less Stones than near the Sea.'[25] But there was no effective alternative; durable good quality stone came also from Yorkshire and Oxfordshire, but it was no larger than the Portland block.

The Portland stone industry was highly developed, with its own long-standing traditions, and provided the living of hundreds of families in Portland itself, in London, where it was shipped to, and in the south coast shipping ports of Weymouth and Brighthelmstone. At the quarry Portland stone cost 10*d* a foot, but, after carriage to London, it cost (in normal times) between 9*s* and 24*s* a ton dependent on the size of the block. And times were rarely normal. During periods of warfare the transport of stone from Portland to London was always liable to interruption. Although by the end of 1693 the stone was desperately needed for the St Paul's works, it could only be got through a French blockade by the Admiralty's introduction of a primitive convoy system. Even this could not prevent the sinking of some of the slow-moving stone-ships by French privateers, and stone thus lost had to be paid for by the cathedral rebuilding fund even though it was never received.

Labour disputes such as those in 1693 and 1699 were also common at Portland and could seriously affect the flow of stone for vital works. Throughout the latter year the St Paul's commissioners had constantly to apply their minds to resolving a dispute between the quarrymen of Portland and their current overseers, Mr Gilbert and Mr Russell. In March they ordered Gilbert 'to endeavour as much as in him lies to accommodate the differences between him and the Islanders, and persuade them by all fair means to work again in the Quarries as formerly, and to behave himself civily amongst them. . . . And that Mr Gilbert shall not continue Mr Russell, his Partner, in the Quarries any longer than the 25th May next, at which time their present agreement of co-partnership will expire, and shall not for the future make any such agreement with any other without the consent and approbation of the Commissioners.'[26] Matters did not improve, however, and just over a month later the commission dispatched their own man, Lawrence Spencer, to the island, 'for accommodating the differences aforesaid' and to 'make such regulations as are best for preserving the Quarries and settling the same for the future'.[27] Then, in the spring of 1696, further trouble arose: a landslide at Portland destroyed the roads, cranes and piers on which the regular shipping of the stone depended. Supply became erratic, and the disaster happening to coincide with a sharp increase in freight charges, the price of stone which was available rose steeply.

What is remarkable about the history of the problems connected with the

Portland stone industry is that every difficulty was overcome. The strength of the commitment to the creation of great and monumental and, above all, *lasting* buildings was enough to determine that this should be so. The Baroque Age is remarkable in the determination which was shown that its monuments, whether of architecture, painting, literature or even of landscaping, should survive for ever as a perpetual memorial to a period of brilliant civilization. Its moving spirit is, perhaps, most characteristically enshrined in the magnificent column of victory erected in Blenheim park, rising to 130 feet, and surmounted by a colossal figure of Marlborough in Roman costume. On this monument Duchess Sarah, despite all the bitter disappointments of her life, recorded that

> The Acts of Parliament inscribed on this Pillar shall stand as long as the British name and language last, illustrious monuments of Marlborough's glory and of Britain's Gratitude.

CHAPTER XII

Conclusions

When George in pudding time came o'er,
And moderate men looked big, Sir;
My principles I changed once more,
And so became a Whig, Sir.

The Vicar of Bray

*

THIS STUDY OF THE BAROQUE AGE in English culture produces a variety of paradoxical conclusions. Baroque art, it emerges, is at once essentially popular in its appeal to man's emotional and sensual nature, its reliance on visual display and outward splendour, and highly elitest in its courtly origins, its aristocratic patronage and its sheer expensiveness. English Baroque is at once a submission to and a triumphing over European cultural values; it is native English art in its employment of local traditions and skills, and a foreign import in its reliance on foreign models. It is a culture dominated by a few great names but it is also a culture totally dependent on an army of known and unknown artisans. Even more confusingly, it is impossible not to see the English Baroque as simultaneously a style and a period. It may be objected that such paradoxes should be resolved rather than merely registered. But would resolution be more than the imposition of one more subjective pattern on the complexities of the past?

Culture resists such patterning more effectively than many other areas of human activity, since by its nature culture is a process; it is dynamic rather than static. It is the premise of this book that culture changes as society changes, that it even contributes to social change itself. Hence as the entire social, political and intellectual structure of English society underwent significant changes in the eighteenth century, so the age of the English Baroque, with which we have been concerned, came to an end. It did not end abruptly of course; the normal pattern of cultural change is clearly one of development and evolution out of what has gone before. It is obvious that in the years we have been considering a strong classical current existed, and existed quite happily, side by side with a more baroque style. Wren, after all, always considered himself a true imitator of the classical past, and not as a baroque artist, and the neo-classical quality of his architecture is often more apparent than any baroque manner. As a whole, his work was sufficiently ambiguous for it to be admired by baroque and neo-classical architect alike. Nevertheless, in the early eighteenth century there was a definite quickening of the classical pulse, and a generally enthusiastic reception of the idea of 'RULE' as the guarantee of good taste. In these cultural changes architecture became the pacemaker: Colen Campbell, the Venetian Giacomo Leoni, Henry Flitcroft, James Paine,

179

William Kent, Robert Morris – the theorist of the movement – and their enthusiastic leader the third Earl of Burlington

> Jones and Palladio to themselves restore,
> And be whate'er Vitruvius was before.

It was Burlington's second visit to Italy in 1719 which, if anything, symbolized the beginning of a new style for a new age, for it was on this journey that the architect-Earl spent some time in Vicenza studying Palladio's works and began to purchase original, important sketches by Palladio and his followers. By the time of his return to England Burlington had become determined to revive Palladianism and to restore it to that position of pre-eminence which it had held in the time of Inigo Jones. He began by dismissing the baroque James Gibbs as architect of his Piccadilly house, and replaced him with the entirely orthodox Campbell.

Burlington's interest in neo-classical architecture seems to have been aroused by two important works – Leoni's magnificent *Architecture of A. Palladio in Four Books* (1715) and Colen Campbell's *Vitruvius Britannicus*, the first volume of which appeared in 1715. These works, together with Kent's *Designs of Inigo Jones* of 1727 and Leoni's *Architecture of L. B. Alberti* (1726), formed the basis of the neo-classical programme. Their purpose was to provide illustrations of the physical setting for a certain way of life – that of the aristocratic, poet-philosopher. The ultimate source of this ideal was to be found in Roman civilization, in Horace, in Martial and, above all, in Virgil's second Georgic, a hymn in praise of the Italian farmer, whose simple virtues, hardihood and piety, according to the great Mantuan, joined man to man and man to nature and so formed the greatness of Augustan civilization. This aristocratic poet-philosopher had captured the imagination of Palladio, who clearly had him in mind when he described the purpose of the villa as being to re-create the mind of its owner, who, fatigued by the trials of city life, there might

> apply himself to the study of Books or the contemplation of nature, in imitation of those ancient sages, who, on such accounts, used frequently to retire to like places; where being pressed by their virtuous Friends and Relations, and possessing Pleasure-houses, Gardens, Fountains and such other objects of diversion, but above all their own virtue, they could easily attain the highest pitch of a happy life that on this earth can possibly be enjoyed.

A physical expression of this Palladian dream is to be found in the landscape gardens and in the Palladian villas which, between 1715 and 1750, were erected all over England by the Whig aristocrats: Burlington's own Chiswick House, built between 1725 and 1729 and closely modelled on Palladio's Villa Capra; Leoni's Clandon Park, built for the second Lord Onslow between 1731 and 1735 in pure classical style, and his Lyme Park (Cheshire); Campbell's Houghton, and a host of others. The antithesis of this dream the Palladians saw in Blenheim which Shaftesbury had condemned in 1712, calling it 'as false and counterfeit a piece of magnificence, as can justly be arraigned for its Deformity', and which Horace Walpole was to describe as 'execrable within, without and almost all round'.

Nor was it only the builder of the private country house who gave his patronage to the Palladians. Their public successes were equally important and Burlington's own first public work – the Dormitory of Westminster School – represents a substantial victory over Wren. For drawings had already been made for the building by Wren and his assistant, Dickinson, and their rejection in favour of Burlington's design represents a conscious move towards more classical ideals in architecture.

For a complex combination of political, philosophical and financial reasons, Palladianism was an instant success, with the result that the baroque architects and artists were forced more and more on to the defensive. None seems to have suffered more than Hawksmoor who had little sympathy with Burlington's ideas. 'I would not have mentioned Authors and Antiquity', he remarked wryly to his patron, Lord Carlisle, 'but that we have so many conceited Gentlemen full of this science, ready to knock you down, unless you have some old father to stand by you.'[1] Yet even Hawksmoor's designs for the Castle Howard Mausoleum, which he built for Carlisle, had to be submitted to Lord Burlington for approval and were given a set of steps copied from the Chiswick Villa. However much they might resent the necessity, in the end the baroque architects were forced to conform to the new cultural pattern. Once patrons demanded Palladianism then artists had no alternative but to provide Palladianism. In consequence, we see that, for instance, Gibbs's classicism became much more marked in the 1720s and his baroque mood was reserved for the design of monuments and church furnishings. As time passed his move towards classicism continued: the *Rules of Drawing the Several Parts of Architecture* of 1732 is far more classically orientated than his *Book of Architecture* published only four years before. And Gibbs's gradual shift from baroque to neo-classical styles may well be seen as accurately reflecting the *general* pattern of cultural history in England. For while it is true that the spirit of neo-classicism never took entire possession of any of the arts in England, the neo-classic temper was strong enough for a time in the early eighteenth century to bring the era of baroque culture in England effectively to an end.

It is, no doubt, ironic that the fate of England's neo-classic culture was in the end to be the same as that of her baroque culture, for both were destined to be ignored and depreciated. To the romantic and post-romantic sensibility neither was particularly appealing, and even today one may wonder whether the cultural achievements of the later seventeenth and early eighteenth centuries are fully appreciated. Part of the trouble is, of course, the assumption that this period was one wholly dominated by neo-classicism – the assumption that led Matthew Arnold to describe it as 'our age of prose'. It is the burden of this study that a baroque dimension characterized English culture as a whole before the onset of neo-classicism, and for a long time co-existed with it, so that if the period is to be called an age of 'prose', then the architecture of its prose, if one may use Hemingway's phrase, should be seen as possessing a strong infusion of the Baroque.

In conclusion, it remains for us to make some summarizing suggestions, drawing on what we have already observed, concerning the particular conditions in society which produced England's baroque culture. In general terms it may be argued that the second half of the seventeenth century was remarkable in that all the conditions necessary for a cultural flowering were present in England. The economy was flourishing with a vast expansion of trade. New areas of investment were opening up, engendering new forms of wealth. England was ceasing to be an unknown country inhabited by an unknown people, as the English began to travel more and the number of foreigners who found their way to Britain also increased. A knowledge of the arts and a general appreciation of them had come to be seen as natural for a gentleman, while increased travel and closer contact with foreigners had led to the development of interests not specifically insular. As a result cultural barriers were lessened and the educated and wealthy elite of Europe, including England, came to share in the appreciation of a civilization which was common to all. At the same time, the English aristocracy came to expect the same standards of comfort and to enjoy the same leisure pursuits as their equals on the Continent. An aristocracy with more leisure and increasing wealth, an aristocracy of wider cultural horizons and greater sophistication, was in a position to patronize the arts on an unprecedented scale: equally, artists and designers, architects, writers and musicians, both English and foreign, were in a position to interpret the whims of their patrons in a European idiom. That the two groups should come together was more or less assured by the enlightened lead provided by the court and crown, at least until the change of dynasty in 1714.

Most vital of all, perhaps, was the sense of self-conscious newness characteristic of the culture and society created at the Restoration. Like Italians at the time of the Renaissance, men in England after 1660 were very aware that they were a new generation, a generation that approached problems in ways which differed from those employed by their ancestors. It saw the ages that had preceded it as barbaric, unpolished and unscientific. So men cultivated polish, a sense of form and style, and complete modernity, rejecting the immediate past and its ways of life. 'We live', wrote Dryden in 1672, 'in an age so sceptical, that as it determines little, so it takes nothing from antiquity on trust; I profess to have no other ambition . . . than that poetry may not go backward, when all other arts and sciences are advancing.'[2] Such attitudes are compatible only with a rather heady sense of cultural excitement and a confidence in the cultural future. Such confidence was not misplaced. It is difficult to point to many other periods in English cultural history when so much was achieved by so many in so many different areas. The age of Wren, Vanbrugh, Hawksmoor and Gibbs, of Lely and Kneller, of Grinling Gibbons and Caius Gabriel Cibber, of Clarendon and Bishop Burnet, of Hobbes, Locke and Newton, of Dryden, Swift and Pope, of Purcell and even of Handel, if England may claim him as her own, can never be regarded as anything other than a Golden Age. Some of these figures would of course feature in a rollcall of England's great Augustan or neo-classical geniuses, and it is true that not all of them expressed themselves in a distinctly baroque style. But once again this problem is less real that it seems. Swift's brilliantly satirical fantasies frequently reflect a powerful baroque imagination; the wit of Dryden and Pope, at its best and most imaginative, has a characteristic seventeenth-century, baroque flavour. The example of these major English 'classical' writers in fact reveals how it is possible for the neo-classic temper to co-exist with the baroque impulse within the single gifted individual. Nor is such co-existence surprising, for, as we have seen, neo-classicism and Baroque co-existed in society as a whole, and that period of co-existence was a necessary instrument of cultural change and shift. Yet there was and is no reason to regret cultural change and the necessity for it. Man's capacity to bring such change about is his gamble on the future. Art is an ordering of the present even when it is looking to the past for its sources of inspiration; but it may also be a herald of the future. Like Dryden we should be ready to conclude:

> 'Tis well an old age is out
> And time to begin a new.

The Creative Elite

Listed in alphabetical order below, with some brief biographical notes, are a number of artists, artisans, sculptors, painters, architects, writers and musicians who are mentioned in the text and who were working in England *c.*1630–*c.*1730. They were not all baroque artists but all did have important connections with baroque culture in England, even where that connection was a negative one.

ARCHER, Thomas(?1668–1743): baroque architect, strongly influenced by Borromini; Trinity College, Oxford; Groom Porter 1705; Comptroller of Customs, Newcastle 1715; commissioner for building fifty new churches 1711; most important works – north front of Chatsworth, Heythrop House, Hurstbourne Priory.

BAYLEY, Isaac(fl. 1692–1706): decorative painter who probably specialized in baroque marbling and graining.

BERCHET, Pierre (1659–1720): French Huguenot refugee, baroque decorative painter; came to England 1681; most famous work – chapel ceiling Trinity College, Oxford.

BIRD, Edward (fl. 1678–93): decorative painter; did a great deal of work for Wren at Chelsea Hospital and in the City churches.

BIRD, Francis (1667–1737): baroque sculptor; only native-born sculptor to have worked in both Flanders and Rome; major work – *The Conversion of St Paul* for west pediment of St Paul's.

BROWNE, Thomas (1605–82): baroque prose-writer, physician, antiquarian; his *Urn Burial* is a study of burial customs, *Religio Medici* a confession of religious faith.

BUSHNELL, John (d. 1701): baroque sculptor; apprenticed to Thomas Burman; fled to the Continent and worked his way to Italy; returned to England *c.*1670; many important commissions – royal figures on Temple Bar, Sir Thomas Gresham for the Royal Exchange, etc. His best work is the tomb of Viscount Mordaunt in Fulham church.

CAMPBELL, Colen (d. 1729): born Scotland; accomplished Palladian architect; *Vitruvius Britannicus* (1715).

CHÈRON, Louis (1660–1723): French Huguenot; decorative painter; in England 1695; employed at Boughton, Burley, Chatsworth.

CIBBER, Caius Gabriel (1630–1700): baroque sculptor; born Denmark; came to England *c.*1659; Sculptor in Ordinary to Crown 1693; worked at Chatsworth 1687–90; most important work – phoenix on south pediment of St Paul's.

CIBBER, Colley (1671–1757): actor and dramatist; son of above; Grantham school; writer of artful comedies of which *The Careless Husband* is the best; *Apology for the Life* is an irresistible self-portrait; poet laureate 1730.

CLOSTERMAN, John(1656–1713): baroque portrait artist; born Osnaburgh; came to England 1681; employed by Riley to paint draperies; after Riley's death emerged as Kneller's chief rival.

COUSIN, René (fl. 1675–94): French; Verrio's chief gilder at Burghley and Windsor.

CRASHAW, Richard (1613–49): baroque poet; greatest work – *Steps to the Temple* – a collection of religious poetry.

DAHL, Michael (1656/9–1743): Swedish baroque painter; came to England first in 1682 and settled permanently in 1689. His style, although baroque, is much softer than that of Kneller.

DONNE, John (1573–1631): baroque poet and theologian.

DRYDEN, John (1631–1700): poet, dramatist and critic; Dryden is an ambivalent figure, an important influence on both the Baroque and on neo-classical literature.

FREEMAN, John (fl. 1686): decorative painter said to be a rival of Fuller; scene-painter at Covent Garden.

FULLER, Isaac (d. 1692): baroque wall-painter; trained in France; worked mainly in Oxford.

GAY, John (1685–1732): poet and dramatist; most famous work – *The Beggars' Opera* (1728).

GENNARI, Benedetto (1633–1715): Bolognese decorative painter; came to England about the same time as Verrio; strongly French-influenced.

GIBBONS, Grinling (1648–1728): baroque sculptor; born Rotterdam of English father; in England c.1668; best work is naturalistic woodcarving of fruit, flowers, small birds, etc; as sculptor often worked with Quellin.

HANDEL, George Frideric (1685–1759): German; baroque composer; naturalized English.

HAWKSMOOR, Nicholas (1661–1736): baroque architect; born Notts.; trained by Wren in Board of Works; subsequently assistant to Wren and Vanbrugh; never left England; of his own works, the most important – Easton Neston, Queen's College, All Souls' College, Clarendon Building, Worcester College at Oxford, Mausoleum at Castle Howard.

HENDE, Nicholas; French Huguenot refugee; baroque decorative painter; imported baroque art into Scotland; most important work – Caroline Park, Edinburgh.

HOBBES, Thomas (1588–1679): English political theorist and philosopher whose greatest work, *The Leviathan*, expounds his theories of the state.

HOOKE, Robert (1635–1703): important scientist and mannerist/baroque architect; born Freshwater, Isle of Wight;

curator to experiments of R.S. 1662; F.R.S. 1663; pioneer in almost every branch of scientific learning; Surveyor for Rebuilding of London 1666; strongly influenced by contemporary French and Dutch architecture; most important works – Bedlam, Royal College of Physicians.

HUMFREY, Pelham (1647–74): baroque musician and composer; strongly influenced by French music; trained in Chapel Royal and then sent abroad to study by Charles II.

JONES, Inigo (1573–1652): architect, designer, etc.; his most important works of architecture – Whitehall Banqueting House, The Queen's House, Greenwich, St Paul's, Covent Garden.

KNELLER, Sir Godfrey (1646 or 1649–1723): born Lübeck; arrived in England 1674/5; leading baroque portrait painter; Principal Painter to the Crown, jointly with Riley, 1688; succeeded to whole office 1691; knighted 1692; Bart. 1725.

LAGUERRE, Louis (1663–1721): French baroque wall-painter; came to England 1683/4; worked for Verrio at Christ's Hospital 1684; with French architectural painter Ricard worked at Chatsworth; major works in other houses – Burghley, Blenheim and Marlborough House, London.

LAWES, Henry (1596–1662): baroque musician and composer.

LAWES, William (1602–45): musician and composer; brother of above.

LELY, Sir Peter (1618–80): born Germany of Dutch parents; major English baroque portrait painter; Principal Painter to Crown 1661.

MARVELL, Andrew (1621–78): English poet in the classical tradition; turned to satire in later life.

MAY, Hugh (1622–84): baroque architect; royalist gentry family; Paymaster of Works 1660; Comptroller of Works 1668; friend of Evelyn, Roger North, Lely; his houses remarkable for their full-blooded baroque interiors; often worked with Gibbons and Verrio; most important work – Windsor Castle, remodelling of Upper Ward, 1675–83.

MILTON, John (1608–74): baroque poet of European stature; his masterpiece the epic *Paradise Lost*.

MONNOYER, Jean Baptiste (1634–99): French history and flower painter; widely travelled; in England *c.*1690; worked at Montagu House, and for William and Mary.

PARMENTIER, Jacques (1658–1730): French decorative painter; came to England 1676 or 1677; 1678/9 in Italy; returned to England *c.*1680 where he worked with Berchet and Closterman among others; most important work in England – Montagu House.

PELLEGRINI, Giovanni Antonio (1675–1741): Venetian decorative painter in the Continental grand baroque tradition; came to England 1708; director of Kneller's academy 1711; important decorations at Kimbolton Castle.

PIERCE, Edward (*c.*1635–93): baroque sculptor and mason; son of a painter; much employed by Wren in rebuilding City churches, especially St Lawrence Jewry and St Clement Danes; portrait busts include the very baroque and singularly attractive bust of Wren; architect.

PURCELL, Henry (1659–95): one of the greatest of English composers whose work was of European stature.

POPE, Alexander (1688–1744): poet and satirist in the neo-classical tradition, whose ideals he enunciated in his *Essay on Criticism*.

QUELLIN, Arnold (1653–86): baroque sculptor; born Antwerp; greatest work – altar for James II's Roman Catholic chapel in Whitehall in which he collaborated with Gibbons.

RICCI, Marco (1676–1730): Venetian baroque wall-painter; in England 1708–10; returned 1712–*c.*1716.

RICCI, Sebastiano (1659–1734): uncle of above; in England 1712–*c.*1716; major work in England his *Resurrection*, painted in apse of Chelsea Hospital chapel.

STONE, Nicholas (1587–1647): one of most successful sculptors of his day; son of Devon quarryman; most famous work – baroque in conception – is monument to John Donne, now in St Paul's.

STREETER, or STREATER, Robert (1624–80): baroque wall-painter; sergeant-painter 1663; his best-known work – the ceiling of the Sheldonian Theatre, Oxford, 1669.

TALMAN, William (1650–1720): major baroque country-house architect before Vanbrugh; born Wilts.; Comptroller of King's Works 1689; major works – Thoresby House, Chatsworth south and east fronts, Kiveton Park, Canons.

TEMPLE, Sir William: diplomat, critic, supporter of neo-classicism and the ancients; friend of Grand Duke Cosimo of Florence; Secretary of State 1679.

THORNHILL, Sir James (1676–1734): the only English-born decorator in the full grand baroque style; knighted and Sergeant-Painter 1720; MP Melcombe Regis 1722; F.R.S. 1723. Most famous works – dome of St Paul's Cathedral 1715–17, work at Greenwich Hospital.

THORNTON, William (d. 1721): carpenter-joiner of York; restored Beverley Minster under Hawksmoor's direction 1716–20.

VANBRUGH, John (1664–1726): playwright and architect; author of *The Provok'd Wife*; dominated English architecture from 1701 until his death; England's greatest baroque genius; architect of Castle Howard, Blenheim, etc.

VANDERBANK, John (1694–1739): born London; son of tapestry weaver; member of Kneller's academy; important baroque portrait artist.

VAN DYCK, Sir Anthony (1599–1641): born Antwerp; trained by Rubens; visited England 1620; Italy 1621–25; at court of Charles I 1632; enormous practice as portrait painter.

VAN HONTHORST, Gerard (1590–1656): leading master of Utrecht School; visited England to paint for Charles I 1628.

VAUGHAN, Henry (1622–95): Welsh baroque poet, writing largely religious poems.

VERRIO, Antonio (1639–1707): Neapolitan who had worked in France; reached England *c.*1672; succeeded Lely as Court Painter in 1684; a baroque wall-painter brought up in the full-blooded Italian tradition; was immensely successful in England.

WAKEFIELD, William (d. *c.*1730): Yorkshire gentleman who enjoyed considerable reputation as an architect in his native county.

WEBB, John (1611–72): architect; born Somerset; Merchant Taylors'; pupil of Inigo Jones; design of King Charles Block at Greenwich 1663; assisted Jones at Wilton House; reconstruction of Belvoir Castle after 1654. Webb is most important for the impact of his drawings and designs on the Palladian architects.

WOTTON, Henry (1568–1639): minor poet and diplomat: lifelong friend of Donne; *Elements of Architecture* (1624) – a paraphrase of Vitruvius.

WREN, Sir Christopher (1632–1723): one of the most brilliant of all European architects; of vital importance in both the baroque and the neo-classical traditions; designed among many other buildings about fifty churches in London, the Royal Exchange, Chelsea and Greenwich Hospitals, Temple Bar and his masterpiece, St Paul's Cathedral.

WRIGHT, John Michael (1617–1699/ 1700): brilliant baroque wall-painter; born London, son of a tailor; apprenticed to George Jameson of Edinburgh 1636; in Rome after 1647; member of *Accademia di San Luca*; back in England 1658; as portrait artist one of Lely's greatest rivals; Catholic; most important work – *Apotheosis of Charles I.*

An Alphabetical List of Some Major Baroque Works of Architecture

This list is representative rather than comprehensive. The reader who would like such comprehensive information is referred to the works cited in the bibliography.

Beningbrough Hall (Yorks.): built *c.*1716 for John Bourchier, architect possibly Archer; a large house of stone and brick containing baroque woodcarving of exceptional quality.

Blenheim Palace (Oxon.): gift of a grateful nation to the first Duke of Marlborough; Vanbrugh's most famous design; built 1705–22; baroque palace of two storeys arranged around three sides of a gigantic courtyard. The large central building has four turrets and a portico supported by Corinthian columns; colonnades of Doric columns connect the main buildings to pavilions on either side – a typical baroque device; landscaping and gardens by Vanbrugh and Henry Wise, Queen Anne's gardener; ceilings by Thornhill (*Marlborough presenting a plan of the battle of Blenheim to Britannia*) and Laguerre (*Apotheosis of the Duke of Marlborough*).

Bramham Park (Yorks.): built 1698–1710 by Robert Benson, Lord Bingley.

Burley-on-the-Hill (Rutland): architect unknown but probably the owner, Daniel Finch, second Earl of Nottingham; begun 1696; one of the prettiest of all the English baroque palaces built.

Cambridge, Senate House: designed by James Gibbs, 1722; the only part built of an original massive, baroque design for a whole complex of university buildings. Building of two storeys, nine bays; upper windows roundheaded; lower windows alternating straight and curved pediments; bays divided by giant Corinthian pilasters; three central bays beneath a pediment; interior plasterwork by Artari and Bagutti of exceptional quality.

Canons (Middlesex): palatial mansion built for the first Duke of Chandos; demolished after his death.

Castle Howard (Yorks.): built 1700–14, for the Earl of Carlisle by Vanbrugh, aided by Hawksmoor. First of Vanbrugh's buildings; one of largest and most spectacular of English country houses; original plan was for central domed block flanked by two smaller side wings, but one of these wings was only completed after Vanbrugh's death and is to a meaner scale; Hawksmoor's famous mausoleum erected on nearby hill in grounds.

Chatsworth (Derbyshire): work of several architects; south and east fronts (1687–96) by Talman for the first Duke of Devonshire; baroque gardens by George London and Thomas Archer; *Temple of the Cascade* by Archer; chapel decorated by Cibber, Samuel Watson, Laguerre, Ricard, Verrio.

Claremont House (Surrey): built first as a villa for his own use by Vanbrugh; sold to the Duke of Newcastle *c.*1715 and vastly extended; demolished *c.*1763.

Dyrham Park (Glos.): country mansion built for William Blathwayt; west front designed by Samuel Hauduroy and built 1692–94; east front designed by William Talman and built 1700–3.

Eastbury (Dorset): one of Vanbrugh's greatest designs, built for the Dodingtons; all but one wing of Eastbury was pulled down in 1795 after Lord Temple had vainly offered £200 a year to anyone who would live in it.

Easton Neston (Northants.): designed by Hawksmoor; built 1696–1702.

Greenwich Palace and Hospital (London): old Tudor palace replaced 1662–69 by King Charles Block, designed by John Webb; hospital designed by Wren for Queen Mary. Jones's famous Queen's House made central feature, with two magnificent colonnades leading towards house from palace; elegant dome above each colonnade; hospital built 1696–1705; one of the finest baroque buildings in Europe; interior decorations by Thornhill.

Hampton Court: original Tudor palace greatly modified and extended by Wren for William III; state apartments lavishly decorated by Laguerre, Verrio, Thornhill; sculpture by John Nost, Gibbons, Cibber; ornamental ironwork by Tijou. The Lower Orangery was built for Queen Anne.

Heythrop House (Oxon.): built for Charles Talbot, twelfth Earl and first Duke of Shrewsbury; designed by Archer; built by Francis Smith of Warwick; begun 1706; blockline design with straight balustrade and giant order – typical of an Italian baroque palace front; strongly influenced by work of Bernini and Borromini.

Hurstbourne Priory (Hants.): designed by Thomas Archer; demolished *c.*1785.

Ingestre Church (Staffs.): begun 1676; probably designed by Wren.

Kimbolton Castle (Hunts.): when part of the original medieval mansion collapsed in 1707, the first Duke of Manchester commissioned Vanbrugh to rebuild it. Vanbrugh designed a quadrangle round an inner courtyard and gave it a 'Gothic' battlemented exterior; a portico added by Alessandro Galilei in 1719; staircase decorated by Pellegrini.

King's Weston (Glos.): built by Vanbrugh for Hon. Edward Southwell 1711–14.

Kingston Lacy (Dorset): built for Sir Ralph Bankes whose previous home, Corfe Castle, was destroyed during the Civil War. Designed by Pratt; built 1663–65; gardens also designed by Pratt; stone building surmounted by cupola and lantern, main front with a great porch and fine pediment. This is Pratt's only surviving country house. It shows French influence, baroque features and is a building of very great charm.

Kiveton Park (Yorks.): rebuilt by Talman for the Duke of Leeds *c.*1698–99, demolished 1811.

London, Church of St Benet: Wren church, rebuilt after the Great Fire 1677–85; exterior, apparently Dutch-inspired, of red and blue brickwork; hipped roof; tower has lead spire on lead dome.

London, Church of St Martin-in-the-Fields: original sixteenth-century church unsafe by 1720 and replaced; designed by James Gibbs; built 1722–26; Gibbs's masterpiece, widely copied in Britain and USA; it is a rectangular church approached by a broad flight of steps with a great Corinthian portico; above the portico the very attractive steeple rises in Ionic pilaster form; Corinthian columns above clock are capped by spire.

London, Church of St Mary-le-Bow: rebuilt by Wren after the Great Fire; one of the most baroque, but most characteristically English of Wren's steeples; largely destroyed 1941.

London, Church of St Mary-le-Strand: built by James Gibbs between 1714 and 1717; a very Roman design.

London, Church of St Paul's: Old St Paul's, one of England's largest and finest Gothic buildings, destroyed 1666 in Great Fire of London. Present building erected by Wren 1675–1711; decorated by Bird, Cibber, Pierce, Gibbons, Tijou, etc.

London, Church of St Stephen Walbrook: Wren church, rebuilt after Great Fire 1672–77; exterior plain; interior, in its use of light and space, among the most baroque of Wren's designs; large dome supported at ground level by Corinthian columns, three in each corner.

London, Ham House: famous in early eighteenth century as centre of literary opposition to Walpole; original house built 1610; enlarged and redecorated for the Duchess of Lauderdale 1673–75 in flamboyant, baroque style.

London, Kensington Palace: purchased by William III 1689; greatly altered and extended by Wren; during Anne's reign further enlarged with addition of the Orangery, one of Wren's masterpieces.

London, Marlborough House: built by Wren for Duke of Marlborough *c*.1705; decorated by Laguerre.

London, Monument: a fluted Doric column, surmounted by a golden globe rising from flames; designed by Wren and Hooke as a memorial of Great Fire, built 1671–77.

London, St Bartholomew's Hospital: designed by James Gibbs *c*.1730.

Lumley Castle (Durham): substantial alterations by Vanbrugh.

Moor Park (Herts.): house built for the Duke of Monmouth *c*.1670; flanking wings added by Thornhill in 1727 show a shift towards Palladianism.

Oxford, Radcliffe Camera: first designs by Hawksmoor; design actually erected that of James Gibbs; magnificent circular building, one of the finest in Britain; erected 1737–48; rusticated base, surmounted by Corinthian columns which support a parapet topped by urns, always favoured by Gibbs as a decorative feature; surmounted in turn by dome with lantern; one of the great triumphs of English baroque architecture.

Oxford, Sheldonian Theatre: created as a university theatre and to house the University Press, 1664–69; paid for by Gilbert Sheldon, Archbishop of Canterbury; designed by Wren; based on a Roman theatre and roughly semicircular; the famous flat ceiling was decorated by Streeter's *Truth descending on the Arts and Sciences*, a very fine, baroque, illusionistic painting.

Petworth (Sussex): built for Charles Seymour, sixth Duke of Somerset, 1688–96; woodwork by Gibbons of very great quality.

Seaton Delaval (Northumberland): a superb baroque country palace; built by Vanbrugh *c*.1718–28; comprises a massive central block between two arcaded and pedimented wings.

Stowe House and Park (Bucks.): home of the Dukes of Buckingham; Vanbrugh, Grinling Gibbons and William Kent all worked there.

Thoresby House (Notts.): built by Talman for Henry Pierrepoint, Marquis of Dorchester, 1671; destroyed by fire 1745.

Uppark (Sussex): designed by William Talman for Lord Tankerville; built 1680–1750; red-brick baroque house of great charm.

Vanbrugh Castle (Greenwich): built by Vanbrugh for himself 1717.

Wilton House (Wilts.): home of the Pembrokes; the old house was largely destroyed in 1647 and the fourth Earl asked Inigo Jones to reconstruct it. When Jones died in 1652 it was completed by John Webb. The most important room in the house is the double cube (60 ft. long, 30 ft. high and 30 ft. wide), designed to hold the family collection of paintings by Rembrandt, Van Leyden and Van Dyck.

Wimpole Park (Cambs.): originally built in early seventeenth century; subsequently greatly enlarged and lavishly decorated by James Gibbs for the first Earl Hardwick.

Wrest Park (Beds.): strongly influenced by French building; garden furniture by Archer of exceptional baroque beauty.

Notes

CHAPTER I

1. J. Duvignaud, *The Sociology of Art*, 29
2. P. Charpentrat, *Le Mirage Baroque*, 17–18
3. L. C. Martin, ed., *Religio Medici and Other Works of Sir Thomas Browne*, 70
4. J. Dryden, *The Art of Painting by C. A. du Fresnoy, with Remarks*
5. The phrase is taken from an article by Morris W. Croll, 'The Baroque Style in Prose', which was first published in 1929 but is most readily accessible in S. Chatman and S. R. Levin, eds., *Essays on the Language of Literature*
6. James Lees-Milne, in *English Country Houses: Baroque (1685–1715)*, suggests as possible dates for the baroque country house in England the period *c.*1670–*c.*1730. K. Downes, in *English Baroque Architecture*, takes as his starting point the King Charles Building at Greenwich, designed in 1663 by Jones's pupil, John Webb
7. G. Kitson Clark, *The Making of Victorian England*, 179. The evidence in question is hymns
8. I do not accept the judgment of V. Le-Tapiè in *Le Baroque*, 122, that 'the participation of England in the Baroque, although marked by several masterpieces, remained episodic and limited'

CHAPTER II

1. Quoted in E. Waterhouse, *Painting in Britain 1530–1790*, 35
2. Quoted in E. Croft-Murray, *Decorative Painting in England 1537–1837*, I, 43
3. Ibid.
4. F. Haskell, *Patrons and Painters*, 179
5. See, for example, *Calendar of State Papers Domestic, Charles I, 1637–8*, 49, with its reference to the Queen's 'Billiard Board'
6. J. Harris, S. Orgel and R. Strong, *The King's Arcadia*, I, 37

7. E. Gosse, *The Life and Letters of John Donne*, I, 166
8. Harris, Orgel and Strong, II, 543

CHAPTER III

1. *Wren Soc.*, VII, 228
2. J. Webb, *A Vindication of Stone-heng Restored*, 27
3. *The Diary of Ralph Thoresby, F.R.S.*, I, 428
4. Shaftesbury, *Characteristicks*, I, 219
5. Ibid.
6. Ibid., 403
7. J. Richardson, 'Discourse on the Science of a Connoisseur', in *Works*, 192
8. Shaftesbury, *Characteristicks*, III, 400
9. Ibid., 401
10. Ibid., I, 217
11. Ibid., 265
12. Ibid., 223
13. Ibid., III, 399
14. Ibid., I, 223
15. Robert Whitehall's poem 'Urania', quoted in E. Croft-Murray, *Decorative Painting in England 1537–1837*, I, 45
16. J. Evelyn, 'De Vita Propria', in *The Diary of John Evelyn*, I, 88
17. I. Toesca, 'Alessandro Galilei in Inghilterra', *English Miscellany*, III, 215
18. Ibid., 208–9
19. *Calendar of Treasury Papers 1714–19*, 448

CHAPTER IV

1. See L. Stone, 'Social Mobility in England, 1500–1700', *Past and Present*, 33 (April 1966), 16–17; P. Mathias, 'The Social Structure in the Eighteenth Century', 30–45
2. Pope, *Poem to Mr. Jervas with Fresnoy's Art of Painting translated by Mr. Dryden*
3. Walpole, *Anecdotes*, III, 11
4. Ibid., 12
5. Quoted in E. Croft-Murray, *Decorative Painting in England 1537–1837*, I, 55
6. Walpole, *Anecdotes*, III, 47

7. Ibid., 51
8. Pepys, *Diary*, 20 October 1660
9. Walpole, *Anecdotes*, III, 46
10. *Wren Soc.*, IV, 19
11. Walpole, *Anecdotes*, III, 224
12. *Wren Soc.*, VI, 77
13. Walpole, *Anecdotes*, III, 19. It must be confessed that Streeter died soon after the operation.
14. J. Gibbs, *A Book of Architecture*, p.ii
15. *Wren Soc.*, XVI, 97
16. *Calendar of Treasury Papers 1714–19*, 67
17. Ibid., 309

CHAPTER V

1. T. Sprat, *History of the Royal Society*, 78
2. Ibid.
3. *Wren Soc.*, VII, 215
4. J. Lees-Milne, *English Country Houses: Baroque (1685–1715)*, 11
5. Pope, *Moral Essays*, III, 100–9. Many modern scholars believe Timon's villa to have been Walpole's Houghton, but at the time it was widely assumed that it was Canons that was being referred to Walpole, *Anecdotes*, III, 222–3

CHAPTER VI

1. *Wren Soc.*, IV, 19
2. J. Lees-Milne, *English Country Houses: Baroque (1685–1715)*, 9
3. Hooke, *Diary*, 170, 171
4. *Wren Soc.*, IV, 19
5. Ibid.
6. E. Croft-Murray, *Decorative Painting in England 1537–1837*, I, 45, 216
7. *Wren Soc.*, V, 21
8. See above p. 73
9. *Wren Soc.*, XI, 72
10. D. Green, *Sarah, Duchess of Marlborough*, 214
11. Walpole, *Anecdotes*, III, 250
12. D. Green, *Sarah, Duchess of Marlborough*, 105
13. Tipping and Hussey, *English Homes*, IV, ii, 66
14. D. Green, *Sarah, Duchess of Marlborough*, 146
15. Ibid., 204
16. J. Dryden, 'The Preface to an Evening's Love or the Mock Astrologer', in *Essays of John Dryden*, I, 136

17. Ibid., 137
18. Ibid.
19. J. Dryden, *The Art of Painting by C. A. du Fresnoy*, introduction
20. Pope, *Moral Essays*, IV, ll. 25–38

CHAPTER VII

1. Hooke, *Diary*, 185. See also p.352 for Wren's difficulties after the death of Joshua Marshall.
2. *The Complete Works of Sir John Vanbrugh*, IV, 23
3. Pratt, *Architecture*, 48; see also *Wren Soc.*, XVI, 49–50
4. H. J. Habbakuk, 'Daniel Finch, 2nd Earl of Nottingham: His House and Estate', in J. H. Plumb, ed., *Studies in Social History* (London 1955), 150–1
5. D. Green, *Blenheim Palace*, 60
6. *Wren Soc.*, V, 18
7. The comment of Sir John Moore in 1694, *Wren Soc.*, XI, 91
8. Pratt, *Architecture*, 87
9. *Wren Soc.*, XVI, 120
10. Pratt, *Architecture*, 147
11. *Wren Soc.*, IV, 60
12. Ibid., XVI, 149
13. I. Toesca, 'Alessandro Galilei in Inghilterra', *English Miscellany*, III (1952), 213
14. *Wren Soc.*, XVI, 63
15. Ibid., 55
16. Ibid., 69
17. Ibid., 103
18. Ibid., 129
19. Ibid., IV, 21
20. Tipping and Hussey, *English Homes*, IV, ii, 46

CHAPTER VIII

1. J. Duvignaud, *The Sociology of Art*, 38
2. L. Goldmann, ' "Genetic Structuralism" in the Sociology of Literature' in E. and T. Burns, eds., *Sociology of Literature and Drama*, 114
3. L. C. Martin, ed., *Religio Medici and Other Works of Sir Thomas Browne*, 9
4. Ibid., 33
5. Milton, *Paradise Lost*, IX, ll. 351–2
6. Ibid., XII, ll. 83–4
7. C. A. Patrides, ed., *The Cambridge Platonists*, 98–9

8. Ibid., 162
9. J. Donne, *The Progress of the Soul*, stanza xii
10. L. C. Martin, ed., *Religio Medici and Other Works of Sir Thomas Browne*, 13
11. Ibid., 7
12. Ibid., 10
13. Shaftesbury, *Characteristicks*, I, 35
14. Pope, *The Dunciad*, IV, 11, 471–5
15. M. Espinasse, 'The Decline and Fall of Restoration Science', *Past and Present*, 14 (1958), 83
16. R. Morris, *Lectures on Architecture*
17. T. Sprat, *History of the Royal Society*, 122–3
18. S. Wren, *Parentalia*
19. J. Dryden, *The Art of Painting by C. A. du Fresnoy*, preface
20. Ibid.
21. J. Donne, 'The First Anniversary'
22. J. Thomson, *The Seasons*, 'Summer', I, l. 1562
23. *The Spectator*, no.543
24. R. Morris, *An Essay in Defence of Ancient Architecture*, 4
25. Addison, *Remarks on Several Parts of Italy etc.*
26. C. Campbell, *Vitruvius Britannicus*, I, introduction
27. E. Gosse, *The Life and Letters of John Donne*, I, 219
28. J. Smith, 'The excellency and Nobleness of True Religion', in C. A. Patrides, ed., *The Cambridge Platonists*, 144
29. Ibid.
30. J. Dryden, *The Art of Painting by C. A. du Fresnoy*, preface
31. J. Dryden, 'Epistle Dedicatory', in *Essays of John Dryden*, I, 1
32. Ibid., 8
33. J. Dryden, 'Preface to an Evening's Love', in ibid., 146
34. K. Downes, *Hawksmoor*, 243–4
35. S. Wren, *Parentalia*, 289
36. J. Dryden, *Of Dramatick Poesie*, 9
37. S. Wren, *Parentalia*

CHAPTER IX

1. Quoted in P. Hazard, *The European Mind 1680–1715*, 6–7
2. S. Wren, *Parentalia*

3. Evelyn, *Diary*, II, 612
4. *The Tatler*, no.4, 18 April 1709
5. Quoted in P. H. Lang, *George Frideric Handel*, 196–7
6. C. Cibber, *An Apology for the Life*, 226
7. Ibid., 242–3
8. H. Walpole, 'On Modern Gardening', in *Works*, II, 520
9. Pratt, *Architecture*, 60–1
10. S. Wren, *Parentalia*
11. Ibid.
12. M. Whinney, *Wren*, 72
13. *Wren Soc.*, XI, 89

CHAPTER X

1. Quoted in V. Le-Tapiè, *The Age of Grandeur*, 77
2. Quoted in P. Palme's excellent *The Triumph of Peace*, 135–6
3. *The Tatler*, no.8, 28 April 1709
4. J. Dryden, 'Preface to Troilus and Cressida', in *Essays of John Dryden*, I, 209
5. *The Tatler*, no.12, 7 May 1709
6. Harris, Orgel and Strong, *The King's Arcadia*, II, 48
7. Walpole, *Anecdotes*, III, 77
8. Pope, 'Ninth Ode of Fourth Book of Horace', II, 9–16
9. C. Cibber, *The Careless Husband*, prologue
10. H. Walpole, 'On Modern Gardening', in *Works*, II, 524
11. H. J. Habbakuk, 'Daniel Finch, 2nd Earl of Nottingham: His House and Estate', in J. H. Plumb, ed., *Studies in Social History*, 141–78
12. H. Walpole, op.cit.
13. *The Complete Works of Sir John Vanbrugh*, IV, 56
14. Tipping and Hussey, *English Homes*, IV, ii, 86
15. Shaftesbury, *Characteristicks*, I, 223
16. *Wren Soc.*, XII, 26
17. Ibid., V, 45
18. Ibid., VI, 18
19. S. Wren, *Parentalia*
20. *Wren Soc.*, VI, 18
21. Ibid., 25
22. Ibid., XVI, 104–5
23. Ibid., VI, 15
24. Ibid., VII, 38

25. Ibid., 97
26. H. R. Trevor-Roper, *Archbishop Laud 1573–1645*, 124
27. See C. A. Patrides, ed., *The Cambridge Platonists*, 14
28. S. Wren, *Parentalia*
29. J. Gibbs, *A Book of Architecture*, VIII
30. Quoted in H. R. Trevor-Roper, *Archbishop Laud 1573–1645*, 48
31. Ibid.
32. *The Diary of Ralph Thoresby F.R.S.*, I, 60
33. *Wren Soc.*, X, 20, 47
34. Ibid., X, 39, 51
35. E. Croft-Murray, *Decorative Painting in England 1537–1837*, I, 44
36. *Wren Soc.*, XVI, 107–8
37. C. Dearnley, *English Church Music 1650–1750*, 69
38. Ibid., 16

CHAPTER XI

1. C. Cibber, *An Apology for the Life*, 317
2. Ibid.
3. *Wren Soc.*, IV, 56
4. A. Browning, ed., *English Historical Documents, 1660–1714*, 107–8
5. Ibid.
6. J. Evelyn, 'De Vita Propria', in *The Diary of John Evelyn*, I, 29, 110
7. D. Green, *Sarah, Duchess of Marlborough*, 277

8. L. Stone, *Family and Fortune*, 154
9. K. Downes, *Hawksmoor*, 99
10. S. Wren, *Parentalia*
11. *Wren Soc.*, XIII, 49
12. Ibid., 36
13. Ibid., 49
14. J. Lang, *The Rebuilding of St. Paul's*, 94
15. Ibid., 95
16. *Wren Soc.*, XVI, 62
17. Ibid.
18. Ibid., 76
19. Report of Bridgmen and Wise to George II explaining the high expenditure on the royal gardens (£60 an acre p.a.) quoted in C. Hussey's excellent *English Gardens and Landscapes 1700–1750*, 27–8
20. S. Wren, *Parentalia*
21. *Wren Soc.*, VI, 21
22. D. Green, *Blenheim Palace*, 50
23. J. Thomson, 'Spring', ll. 69–70 in *The Seasons*
24. *Wren Soc.*, XIII, 25
25. S. Wren, *Parentalia*
26. *Wren Soc.*, XVI, 96
27. Ibid., 97

CHAPTER XII

1. K. Downes, *Hawksmoor*, 244
2. J. Dryden, 'Defence of the Epilogue', in *Essays of John Dryden*, I, 163

Bibliography

This bibliography must be selective. It is restricted, therefore, to works which are either mentioned in the text or the footnotes, or those which I have found particularly useful. It is further divided into two sections: works by contemporaries and works by secondary authorities. On the whole, major works of English literature have not been included in the bibliography since many satisfactory editions exist and are readily available.

1. Contemporary writings

J. ADDISON *Remarks on Several Parts of Italy etc.* (London 1718)

SIR THOMAS BROWNE *Religio Medici and Other Works of Sir Thomas Browne*, ed. L. C. Martin (Oxford 1964)

A. BROWNING, ed. *English Historical Documents 1660–1714* (London 1953)

Calendar of State Papers Domestic

Calendar of Treasury Papers

C. CAMPBELL *Vitruvius Britannicus* (London 1715–25)

C. CIBBER *An Apology for the Life with an Historical View of the Stage during his Own Time* (London 1740)

O. E. DEUTSCH *Handel, A Documentary Biography* (London 1955)

J. DRYDEN *Essays of John Dryden*, selected and ed. W. P. Ker (Oxford 1900)

Of Dramatick Poesie an Essay (London 1668)

The Art of Painting by C. A. du Fresnoy, with Remarks (London 1695)

J. EVELYN *Diary*, ed. E. S. Beer (Oxford 1955)

J. GIBBS *A Book of Architecture* (London 1728)

R. HOOKE *The Diary 1672–1680*, eds. H. W. Robinson and W. Adams (London 1935)

N. LUTTRELL *A Brief Historical Relation of State Affairs 1678–1714* (Oxford 1857)

R. MORRIS *An Essay in Defence of Ancient Architecture: or a Parallel of the Ancient Buildings with the Modern showing the Beauty and Harmony of the Former and the Irregularity of the Latter* (London 1728)

An Essay upon Harmony (London 1739)

Lectures on Architecture, Consisting of Rules, Founded upon Harmonick and Arithmetical Proportions in Building, Designed as an Agreeable Entertainment for Gentlemen (London 1759)

R. NORTH *The Lives of the Norths* (London 1826)

C. A. PATRIDES, ed. *The Cambridge Platonists* (London 1969)

S. PEPYS *The Diary*, ed. H. B. Wheatley (London 1920)

SIR R. PRATT *The Architecture of Sir Roger Pratt*, ed. R. T. Gunther (Oxford 1928)

J. RICHARDSON *Works* (London 1792)

ANTHONY ASHLEY-COOPER, THIRD EARL OF SHAFTESBURY *Characteristicks of Men, Manners, Opinions, Times in Three Volumes* (6th edn., London 1737)

T. SPRAT *The History of the Royal Society* (London 1667)

R. STEELE *The Tatler* (1709–1710), *The Guardian* (1713)

W. TEMPLE *Complete Works* (London 1814)

R. THORESBY *The Diary of Ralph Thoresby, F.R.S. Author of the Topography of Leeds 1677–1724*, ed. J. Hunter (London 1830)

SIR J. VANBRUGH *The Complete Works of Sir John Vanbrugh*, eds. B. Dobrée and G. Webb (London 1927–8)

J. WEBB *A Vindication of Stone-heng Restored* (London 1664)

H. WALPOLE *Anecdotes of Painting in England with some account of the Principal Artists and Incidental Notes on Other Arts; collected by the late Mr. George Vertue . . . with considerable additions by the Rev. James Dalloway* (London 1828)

Works (London 1798)

S. WREN *Parentalia or Memoirs of the Family of Wrens* (London 1750)

Wren Society Publications, vols I–XX (London 1924–43)

2. Secondary Authorities

J. ASHTON *Social Life in the Reign of Queen Anne* (London 1882)

H. M. BAILLIE 'Etiquette and the Planning of State Apartments in Baroque Palaces', *Archaeologia*, vol. 101 (1967), 168–99

M. I. BATTEN 'The Architecture of Dr. Robert Hooke, F.R.S.', *Walpole Society*, XXV, 83–113

L. R. BETCHERMAN 'Balthazar Gerbier in seventeenth-century Italy', *History Today*, May 1961, 325–31

L. I. BREDVOLD *The Intellectual Milieu of John Dryden* (Michigan 1956)

R. L. BRETT *The Third Earl of Shaftesbury* (London 1951)

E. and T. BURNS, eds. *Sociology of Literature and Drama* (Harmondsworth 1973)

S. CHATMAN and S. R. LEVIN, eds. *Essays on the Language of Literature* (Boston 1967)

P. CHARPENTRAT *Le Mirage Baroque* (Paris 1967)

H. COLVIN *A biographical dictionary of English architects 1660–1840* (London 1954)

E. CROFT-MURRAY *Decorative Painting in England 1537–1837* (2 vols, London 1962–70)

R. DANNIELLS *Milton, Mannerism and Baroque* (Toronto 1963)

C. DEARNLEY *English Church Music 1650–1750* (London 1970)

H. T. DICKINSON *Bolingbroke* (London 1970)

Walpole and the Whig Supremacy (London 1973)

K. DOWNES *English Baroque Architecture* (London 1966)

Hawksmoor (London 1959)

R. DUTTON *The Age of Wren* (London 1951)

J. DUVIGNAUD *The Sociology of Art*, trans. T. Wilson (London 1972)

M. ESPINASSE 'The Decline and Fall of Restoration Science', *Past and Present*, 14 (1958), 71–88

M. P. FRANCASTEL 'Baroque et classique: une civilisation', *Annales E.S.C.* (1957), 207–22

C. J. FRIEDRICH *The Age of the Baroque 1610–1660* (New York 1952)

E. H. GOMBRICH *In Search of Cultural History* (Oxford 1969)

E. GOSSE *The Life and Letters of John Donne* (London 1899)

D. GREEN *Blenheim Palace* (London 1951)

Sarah, Duchess of Marlborough (London 1967)

H. J. HABBAKUK 'Daniel Finch, 2nd Earl of Nottingham: His House and Estate', in J. H. Plumb, ed., *Studies in Social History* (London 1955)

'English Landownership 1680–1740', *Economic History Review*, X (1939–40), 2–17

J. HARLEY *Music in Purcell's London* (London 1968)

J. HARRIS, S. ORGEL and R. STRONG *The King's Arcadia: Inigo Jones and the Stuart Court Catalogue of a Quartercentenary Exhibition* (Arts Council of Great Britain 1973)

SIR H. HARTLEY, ed. *The Royal Society, its origins and Founders* (London 1960)

F. HASKELL *Patrons and Painters* (London 1963)

P. HAZARD *The European Mind 1680–1715* (London 1953)

C. HUSSEY *English Gardens and Landscapes 1700–1750* (London 1967)

R. F. JONES *Ancients and Moderns* (St Louis 1961)

J. LANG *The Rebuilding of St. Paul's after the Great Fire of London* (Oxford 1956)

P. H. LANG *George Frideric Handel* (New York 1966)

J. LEES-MILNE *The Age of Inigo Jones* (London 1953)

Earls of Creation (London 1962)

English Country Houses: Baroque (1685–1715) (London 1970)

V. LE-TAPIÈ *The Age of Grandeur*, trans. A. Ross Williamson (London 1960)

Le Baroque (Paris 1968)

L. LIPKING *The Ordering of the Arts in Eighteenth Century England* (Princeton 1970)

B. LITTLE *Catholic Churches since 1623* (London 1966)

M. MACK *The Garden and the City* (Oxford 1969)

P. MATHIAS 'The Social Structure in the Eighteenth Century', *Economic History Review*, 2nd series, vol. 10 (1958), 30–45

C. OMAN *Henrietta Maria* (London 1936)

S. ORGEL and R. STRONG *Inigo Jones: The Theatre of the Stuart Court* (London 1973)

P. PALME *The Triumph of Peace* (London 1957)

N. PEVSNER *The Buildings of England*, Penguin Books (Harmondsworth 1958–74)

J. PYE *Patronage of British Art, An Historical Sketch* (London 1845)

E. F. SEKLER *Wren and his Place in European Architecture* (London 1956)

B. SPRAGUE ALLEN *Tides in English Taste (1619–1800)* (New York 1969)

L. STONE *Family and Fortune* (Oxford 1973)

'Social Mobility in England, 1500–1700', *Past and Present* 33 (April 1966)

R. STRONG *Splendour at Court* (London 1973)

J. SUMMERSON *Sir Christopher Wren* (London 1953)

J. THIRSK 'The restoration land settlement', *Journal of Modern History*, vol. 26 (1954), 314–29

'The sales of Royalist land during the Interregnum', *Economic History Review*, 2nd series, vol. 5 (1952–53), 188–207

H. A. TIPPING and C. HUSSEY *English Homes; Periods 1–4, 1066–1736* (6 vols, London 1929–37)

I. TOESCA 'Alessandro Galilei in Inghilterra', *English Miscellany*, III (1952)

H. R. TREVOR-ROPER *Archbishop Laud 1573–1645* (London 1940)

E. WALKER *A History of Music in England* (3rd edn, London 1952)

E. WATERHOUSE *Painting in Britain 1530–1790* (London 1953)

M. WHINNEY *Sculpture in Britain 1530–1830* (London 1964)

Wren (London 1971)

M. WHINNEY and O. MILLAR *English Art 1625–1714* (Oxford 1957)

List of Illustrations

Index

C4